BUILD
YOUR OWN
SPORT PLANE

BUILD YOUR OWN SPORT PLANE

with
Homebuilt Aircraft Directory

DON DWIGGINS

Foreword by
Paul H. Poberezny, President,
Experimental Aircraft Association, Inc.

HAWTHORN BOOKS, INC.
Publishers/NEW YORK

Library of Congress Catalog Card Number: 74-2575

ISBN: 0-8015-0970-X

2 3 4 5 6 7 8 9 10

All photographs by the author unless otherwise noted.

All aircraft plans and photographs reproduced herein are used with permission of the designers. However, such use implies no endorsement by the author or the publisher of this book. Consult your nearest FAA General Aviation District Office or the United States Hang Gliding Association for pertinent airworthiness directives prior to flight.

CONTENTS

FOREWORD   vii

1   BORN FREE   1
    The Homebuilt Aircraft Movement

2   THE FIRST HOMEBUILTS   9
    Where It All Began

3   WHICH PLANE SHOULD YOU BUILD?   21
    There's a Wide Choice of Types

4   GIVE IMAGINATION TO YOUR WINGS!   32
    The Wing Is the Heart of an Airplane

5   GETTING IT ALL TOGETHER   42
    Tips on Aircraft Construction

6   PAUL REVERE'S HORSE   57
    Selecting the Right Engine

7   TEST FLIGHT   67
    The Proof Is in the Flying

8   THOSE MARVELOUS MONOPLANES   76
    Single-Wingers Have Lots to Offer

9   FASTER, HIGHER, FARTHER   91
    How to Improve Your Performance

10   DOUBLE-DECKERS ARE A DELIGHT   115
      The Biplanes Have It!

11   BUILD YOUR OWN RACING PLANE!   131
      How to Join the Homebuilt Hot Rods

12   THE WATER BIRDS   142
      Amphibians and Seaplanes Are More Fun

13   PROJECT SCHOOLFLIGHT   151
      Homebuilts Are a Young Person's Game

14   RESTORATIONS AND REPLICAS   166
      Wonderful Wings from Yesteryear

15   SAILPLANES AND GROUND-SKIMMERS   178
      Riders of the Winds

HOMEBUILT AIRCRAFT DIRECTORY   193

DIRECTORY OF LARGER EAA CHAPTERS   219

SCHOOLFLIGHT TECHNICAL REPRESENTATIVES
(Operating under EAA's *Project Schoolflight*)   233

FEDERAL AVIATION ADMINISTRATION
      GENERAL AVIATION DISTRICT OFFICES   236
      FLIGHT STANDARDS DISTRICT OFFICES   239
      ENGINEERING AND MANUFACTURING DISTRICT OFFICES   239

GLOSSARY   241

BIBLIOGRAPHY   247

INDEX   249

FOREWORD

Over the past twenty-three years, we have seen the Experimental Air-craft Association grow from a handful of aviation enthusiasts to a worldwide organization with members in fifty-three countries and nearly 500 active chapters. Over 90,000 memberships have been issued over the years. In a relatively short time, EAA has become an influential voice in aviation around the world.

What has been the cause of this rapid expansion and of the tremendous enthusiasm of EAA members? Why has the sport aviation movement caught on so well?

It really narrows down to a very simple and basic factor: man's desire to get into the air and experience the freedom and joy of flight. To many, the construction of one's own aircraft is the only way that this may come about. With the cheapest production aircraft available today costing nearly $10,000, thousands have discovered that the constructing of their own airplanes allows them the opportunity of aircraft ownership that would not otherwise be financially possible.

From another view, many build their own aircraft simply because of the educational value and the personal satisfaction that can be derived. Many have built their own just for the sake of building; that is, to see the work of one's own hands and efforts take shape and become a living machine when it first takes to the air.

Then there are others who believe that the joy of flight can best be experienced at the controls of a custom-built aircraft. Indeed, whether it be high performance or economy that one is looking for, many times a custom-built aircraft is the only one that can meet the requirements.

What of the future? We can expect continued growth, of that I am sure. Our annual Fly-In Convention at Oshkosh, Wisconsin, is truly a measure of that growth and has continued to set new records every year. More and more people are discovering the truly unique good fellowship, spirit of cooperation, and feeling of accomplishment that mark the ranks of EAA.

It is also our hope that more efforts will be directed and more solutions found in making the aircraft a more practical, useful mode of recreation. Indeed, it is interesting to note that the vast majority of aircraft owned in the United States is used for recreational purposes.

My thanks go to Don Dwiggins, who has put into words what so many of us in EAA feel about this fine movement and the many people involved. We owe him a debt of gratitude.

PAUL H. POBEREZNY
President
Experimental Aircraft Association, Inc.

BUILD
YOUR OWN
SPORT PLANE

1
BORN FREE
The Homebuilt Aircraft Movement

Every summer, for the past twenty years or so, a strange event has taken place in the sky above the green countryside of Oshkosh, a pleasant little midwestern college town in Wisconsin. Hundreds of largely unidentified flying objects darken the sky, flying in from all parts of the nation and from distant lands.

These objects are the creations of men, women, and youngsters, and they are called homebuilt aircraft, or homebuilts for short. Their builder-pilots are, for the most part, members of the unique Experimental Aircraft Association (EAA), whose 450 chapters throughout the world boast approximately 85,000 dedicated enthusiasts of the active pursuit of freedom of the sky, in a world growing more and more complex. They are, in short, a breed of folks who were born free.

You'll find all sorts of EAA people at Oshkosh in the summertime —airline captains on their days off, doctors, lawyers, dentists, housewives, schoolboys and girls, and a few stray dogs that dash about, wagging their tails and having as much fun as the EAA members.

Many people arrive by air in their own store-bought airplanes or come in comfortable campers. However, what everybody is there to see are the homebuilt aircraft—and it is interesting to note that more than 1,100 showed up at the 1973 EAA Fly-In. Some planes are so new that their paint isn't dry, and a good number arrive in trailers, their graceful wings still uncovered, and perhaps minus an engine.

But the majority of the homebuilts arrive through the air, from Alaska, Canada, Mexico, and virtually every one of the forty-eight contiguous states. You'll even see the latest flying contraptions from Europe, South America, and wherever EAA members have been spending their winter months busily sawing, hammering, welding, and gluing their dream ships together in time for the big meeting.

Then, parked wingtip to wingtip, they present a thrilling array of original designs, telling you the spirit of fun is still a major attraction in aviation today—the interest is not simply transportation. Never before had so many experimental aircraft gathered in a single place as at the 1973 meeting held in Wittman Field, named for a noted race pilot and pioneer homebuilt designer, Steve Wittman.

Some years ago Wittman designed a squarish two-place airplane that seemed to lack all the fancy streamlining that spells speed today. And when Steve sat down to fly, everybody gasped. He'd included a number of unorthodox design features learned from his years as a racing pilot, and his homebuilt—the *Tailwind*—has been one of the fastest and most popular designs over the past two decades.

Today Wittman is leading the way in another homebuilt design breakthrough, in a new class of racing planes called the Formula Vees, unusual in that they must be powered with converted automotive Volkswagen engines. Wittman's own design, called the *Witt's Vee,* is capable of speeds of three miles a minute.

Another lovely green Formula Vee racer turned up at Oshkosh '73 —John Monnett's sleek *Sonerai I,* along with a new and bigger stablemate, the two-place *Sonerai II.*

The static aircraft displays are only part of the fun at the big EAA Fly-In; like a three-ring circus, the show rushes along with many things happening at once. In the sky, homebuilt aircraft designers circle past the grandstands waggling their wings, and behind the display areas you can attend numerous workshops where the latest techniques in welding, woodworking, tin-bending, and other aircraft construction ideas are demonstrated.

EAA's president is a veteran ex-military pilot, Paul Poberezny, who brought together a number of sport flying enthusiasts in 1951 to form what later became the world's largest organization of its kind. It had a grass-roots beginning at a small flying field called Hales Corners Airport on the outskirts of Milwaukee, Wisconsin, where today the EAA Air Museum exhibits more than 120 unusual aircraft of historical or technical interest.

Some of the 1,100 homebuilt planes that showed up for the Oshkosh, Wisconsin, 1973 Experimental Aircraft Association Fly-In.

John Monnett's *Sonerai I* (left) and *Sonerai II* (right) stand wingtip to wingtip.

At the EAA Air Museum you'll find a 1912 Curtiss *Pusher;* authentic World War I and II British, German, and American fighter aircraft; a replica of Charles Lindbergh's *Spirit of St. Louis;* the world's tiniest aircraft; and an array of homebuilt, aerobatic, and racing planes.

From its inception EAA has dedicated its efforts to saving sport aviation in the United States from being crowded out of the sky by too many governmental restrictions, which have continuously threatened to gobble up the last bit of blue left to the freedom of what is called uncontrolled airspace.

As the national aviation system has grown to include roughly 300,000 miles of radar-monitored airways, more and more restrictions have had to be imposed for safe separation of all air traffic. The biggest aircraft fleet is that of general aviation, whose 140,000 ships—including some 5,000 homebuilts—far surpass both the airline and the military fleets combined. To operate along the federal airways, and into and out of controlled airports, all these ships must, of course, carry expensive radio equipment.

More and more homebuilt aircraft now use these controlled airspaces, and so must comply with the growing number of avionics requirements. They must carry special radar signal-reply devices called transponders, automatic altitude-reporting devices called encoding altimeters, distance-measuring equipment (DME), standard VOR (Very High Frequency Omnidirectional Radio Range) navigation and communication radios, emergency locator transmitters, and so on.

Yet there still remain vast reaches of sky, mostly at low level, where you can fly your own airplane as you please, carrying only minimal avionics equipment, so long as you meet basic safety requirements set forth in what are called the federal air regulations.

In Frankfort, New York, a designer-builder named Bob Barrows built a lovely little flying machine he calls *Grasshopper,* in which he flies from one hayfield to another to visit friends in peaceful rural areas of the Mohawk Valley.

In Tallahassee, Florida, Lester Durden wanted an amphibian flying boat in which he could fly into the wilderness of the bayou country to go after the bass, perch, grouper, red snapper, gar, and catfish that lurk there. He called his flying machine the *Catfish Special.*

In Ramona, California, Ron Wier got to tinkering around his garage, installed a VW engine up front in an open-framework con-

Bob Barrows's *Grasshopper* from New York's Mohawk Valley.

Lester Durden's *Catfish Special.*

traption that looks like a flying bathtub. Today he enjoys sailing over hayfields in his *Draggin' Fly*. In fact Wier was inspired by a homebuilt design from out of the dim past—the Ramsey *Flying Bathtub,* one of a number of historic originals that many homebuilders are turning to again today, seeking out the nostalgia of a simpler world where you could find peace and quiet in the sky.

Speaking of peace and quiet, perhaps the greatest feeling of solitude in the sky comes when you're flying a motorless sailplane or a recently resurrected type of aircraft called the hang glider. Such ultralight flying machines offer the quiet thrill of soaring in a manner akin

5

to true bird flight. And hang glider pilots have stayed aloft for more than ten hours nonstop.

At Oshkosh you'll also see many replica planes. These are homemade copies of early classics, like the Bleriot *XI Channel-Hopper,* in which the Frenchman Louis Bleriot became the first person to fly across the English Channel in 1909. Still more popular are replicas— real and imagined—of World War I and II fighter aircraft.

Two Allegheny Airlines pilots, Don Stewart and Tom Raybourn, got to arguing one day about which was the best of the combat ships that flew over the trenches in 1918. They spent a rainy afternoon at an Adirondack State Park fishing camp looking through a history book, studying the funny old British, French, and German fighters that were manned by the world's first flying aces.

What resulted was a thing they called the *Foo Fighter* or the *JD-1* (the first Jim Dandy airplane). It included the best lines of the Bristol F2B, the Spad, Pfalz, Albatros, and whatever else caught their imagination. At Oshkosh '73 the author was offered a chance to fly this hot little single-seater, and couldn't turn it down. The flight was an unforgettable experience, one in which the green Wisconsin fields down below were suddenly transformed as if by magic into the battle-fields of Verdun.

One of the most copied fighter planes is the North American *P-51 Mustang* of World War II vintage, whose lines identify it as one of the aerodynamically cleanest planes ever to fly. Today you'll see two-third-scale *Mustangs,* three-quarter-scale *Mustangs, Baby Mustangs,* and *Mini-Mustangs,* powered with a wide variety of engines but all unmistakably copies of "the fighter that won the war," as the *P-51* was often called.

A persistent dream of the homebuilder is to design and build an airplane that fears no weather—if a storm looms ahead, the pilot simply lands, folds back his wings, and transforms his airplane into an automobile. He then drives happily along the highway until a rainbow graces the sky, marking the passing of the storm. Then out go the wings and up goes the pilot, to leap over the mundane, grounded highway traffic and make like a bird once more.

Dewey Bryan, a General Motors engineer, translated such a dream into a series of test craft, the third of which flew very nicely—the *Bryan III Roadable Aircraft.* The folding-wing wonder became a familiar sight on the highways in Michigan as well as the skyways above it, and only once was Bryan stopped by a perplexed traffic cop,

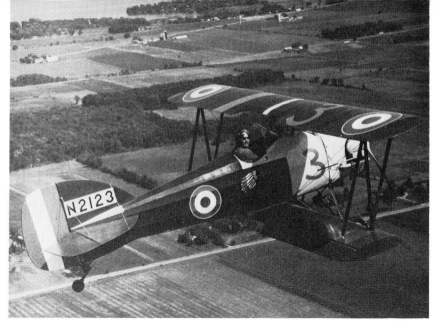

The *Foo Fighter* or *JD-1* with Don Stewart at the controls during EAA Fly-In at Oshkosh.

who finally tore up the ticket he started to write, unsure what the darned thing was.

One of the more exciting homebuilts to appear at Oshkosh '73 was the *BD-5J*, a remarkable little bullet-shaped jet aircraft that streaks across the sky at 350 mph. Yet the *BD-5J* is not the ultimate in homebuilt speedsters, for still faster ones are on the drawing boards in a number of garages and kitchens, designed to compete in a proposed new air racing category—the Unlimited Homebuilts.

Just as in the past, the homebuilt movement today remains one of the most vital forces in aviation, one in which new breakthroughs point the way to higher performance in speed, range, altitude, and load-carrying capacity.

The *Bryan III Roadable Aircraft.*

But for the average do-it-yourself aircraft builder the goal is personal freedom, the thrill and excitement of seeing a real airplane take shape in the backyard workshop, a plane that someday will give new wings to the builder's imagination.

There are an estimated 10,000 homebuilt aircraft projects currently under way, with half as many already flying, according to the EAA. Encouraged by both the EAA and the Federal Aviation Administration, the movement promises to expand still further.

Significantly, not only veteran pilots but also the youth of America are now involved in the mushrooming homebuilt movement, largely through efforts of such groups as the EAA and its active Project Schoolflight. In a later chapter you will read of activities now going on in countless school workshops where students are learning a trade while participating in an air age education program that is already national is scope.

2
THE FIRST HOMEBUILTS
Where It All Began

Long before the Wright brothers first flew a heavier-than-air flying machine in 1903, skimming the sand dunes of Kill Devil Hill in a frail biplane powered with a 12-horsepower engine, homebuilt aircraft were already pioneering the coming air age with faltering flights.

Forgotten and unsung, these backyard heroes didn't make the history books for a simple reason—they didn't know how to fly. It was one thing to wrest the secret of flight from the birds, but quite another to put it to practical use.

Since man first went aloft in a hot-air balloon in the late eighteenth century, inventors in countless backyard workshops have struggled to put together mechanical contraptions that could maneuver in the sky like birds instead of bubbles. Back in the sixteenth century Leonardo da Vinci was one of the first to learn that there was no future in a wing-flapper, or ornithopter, design.

Until lightweight, internal combustion engines came along toward the end of the nineteenth century, homebuilt enthusiasts achieved only partial success with steam power. Notable was a flight on May 6, 1896, of a prototype steam-powered tandem monoplane designed by Samuel P. Langley, director of the Smithsonian Institution in Washington, D.C.

9

Otto Lilienthal flew homebuilt gliders in the 1890s. (*National Air and Space Museum, Smithsonian Institution*)

Langley's model, named *Aerodrome Number 5,* rose from a launch rail atop a houseboat on the Potomac River, reached an altitude of more than a hundred feet, and finally landed, 1 minute 49 seconds later, more than 4,000 feet distant. Efforts to duplicate this success with a man-sized machine failed—for the simple reason that the pilot, Charles Manley, simply did not know how to fly.

Another prominent inventor, Octave Chanute, had better luck at about the same time Langley was trying to perfect a powered bomber for use in the Spanish-American War of 1898. Chanute, a bridge builder by profession, designed a biplane glider braced with inter-plane trusses that looked something like a flying bridge. The canvas wings, curved like those of a bird, totaled 135 square feet in area, and the 23-pound machine could lift a 180-pound man in gliding flight. More than 2,000 successful glides were made with the Chanute machines at Dune Park, near Gary, Indiana.

Even before Chanute, others were sliding down the sky in home-built gliders—Otto Lilienthal in Germany, Jean-Marie le Bris in France, Melville M. Murrell in Panther Springs, Tennessee, back in 1877, and—if we can believe local legend—an old prospector named Lyman Gilmore in Grass Valley, California, in the 1890s.

It took the brothers Orville and Wilbur Wright to put it all together. After learning the secret of gliding flight, riding their Chanute-type

Wilbur Wright in 1903 Wright biplane. Wilbur flew this ship on December 14, 1903, three days before Orville made his famous "first" flight. Wilbur's trip ended in a crash and was disallowed, but he flew 105 feet just the same.

December 17, 1903—Kitty Hawk—the first "successful" Wright flight.

biplanes tethered like kites and then in true soaring flight, they stuck in their homebuilt engine and on December 17, 1903, launched the age of controllable, powered manflight.

It didn't take long for word to get around the country that man had "conquered the sky." By 1910 three exhibition teams of daring "birdmen" were touring the United States and abroad—the Wright Exhibition Company, the Curtiss Exhibition Company, and the Moisant International Flyers.

Spurred by such exhibition flights, homebuilt enthusiasts now had a tangible target, and flying machine inventors at last gained a measure of respectability in the eyes of their curious neighbors.

The first popularized set of homebuilt plans—for a rudimentary Chanute-type hang glider with a 20-foot wingspan—was made available in a 1907 issue of *Popular Mechanics.* According to the directions, you started out with a 20-foot plank of straight-grained spruce, free from knots, and sawed four wing spars of cross section measuring three-quarters of an inch by an inch and a quarter. To the spars were nailed curved ribs; and the wings, covered with muslin, were spaced 4 feet apart. Vertical and horizontal tail surfaces were added, and the whole thing was braced with piano wire. Readers were advised about the gliding procedure in this fashion:

> To make a glide, take the glider to the top of a hill, get in between the arm sticks and lift the machine up, run a few steps against the wind and leap from the ground. If the weight of your body is in the right place, you will go shooting down the hillside in free flight. The landing is made by pushing the weight of the body backwards. This will cause the glider to tip up in front, slacken speed and settle. The operator can then land gently and safely on his feet.

How many future aviators were born of such glides in Chanute-type double-deckers is not recorded, nor is it known how many eager homebuilders landed in the hospital with broken legs, but the call of sky adventure was loud and clear and thousands responded.

Many pilots of today's giant jet liners made their first flights in such homebuilt contraptions, and in recent years a resurgence of interest in hang gliding is attracting new thousands to the sport that first got America off the ground.

Not only hang gliders but also powered aircraft joined the ranks of homebuilts in 1910 when *Popular Mechanics* offered, for two dollars, working drawings of the *Demoiselle,* a dragonfly-shaped machine designed by a Brazilian sportsman, Alberto Santos-Dumont. Placed on exhibition in Paris the year before, *Le Santos No. 20,* as it also was called, attracted widespread interest as the world's smallest flying machine.

Demoiselle measured only 18 feet from wingtip to wingtip, half the wingspan of a modern Piper Cub. Its empty weight was a mere 242 pounds, as it was made of bamboo and light muslin. Its 2-cylinder engine produced 30 horsepower, yet it swung a fat-bladed propeller that measured 6 feet 6 inches in diameter and was so heavy it acted as a flywheel, producing enormous gyroscopic loads. Santos-Dumont steered *Demoiselle* with an elevator lever and a control wheel linked to the rudder.

That such a tiny machine could actually fly amazed everyone who saw it, and Santos-Dumont was immediately flooded with requests for plans from homebuilders. In announcing their sale, *Popular Mechanics* explained:

> The machine is unencumbered by patent rights, the famous aviator preferring to place his invention at the disposal of the world in the interest of the art to which he has devoted his life.

By contrast, Orville and Wilbur Wright jealously guarded the patent rights to their Kitty Hawk biplane, and by the time World War I exploded they were deeply involved in litigation, trying to prevent their design from being copied. By 1916 Congress, confronted with the threat of involvement in the war, arranged a patent truce with the Wrights and others and appropriated $640 million to construct a skyful of warplanes.

But by then it was virtually too late and most of the active World War I combat planes were of foreign make. At the time of the armistice on November 11, 1918, the United States had at the war front only 757 pilots and 481 observers, with 740 planes and 77 balloons.

Again, *Popular Mechanics* saw a great potential market for homebuilt aircraft when returning pilots came marching home. In fact more than 11,000 officers and 120,000 enlisted men were in flight training when the shooting stopped.

Despite a glut of thousands of brand-new crated Standards and JN4D training biplanes that flooded the postwar market as war surplus ships, there was a strong appeal in sport plane flying. Among the most popular ready-built offerings were two biplanes that appeared in 1919—Aircraft Engineering Corporation's $2,500 *Ace* and Cantilever Aero Company's *Christmas Bullet*, a 200-mph biplane with flexible wings, designed by Dr. William Whitney Christmas and powered by a Liberty Six engine generating 185 horsepower. Another firm, Gallaudet Aircraft Corporation, sought to cash in with a monoplane design, the *Chummy Flyabout*, billed as their "peacetime offering to the world of outdoor sport."

The tremendous supply of war surplus aircraft did indeed create a postwar slump in sales of such sporty factory models, and again the swing went toward the do-it-yourself homebuilt, such as the *White Monoplane* offered in 1917 by a Los Angeles designer, George D. White. For two dollars you could get plans for a peculiar machine that had the tail positioned up front.

"Think of flying with an ordinary twin cylinder motorcycle engine!" White exclaimed in his advertising. "This is the only aeroplane that will do it. It is the smallest and most efficient of all aircraft. No longer is flying the sport of acrobats or millionaires. If you can use a hammer, saw, and a pair of pliers and have a shed, barn, a basement or a back yard, you can build one of these remarkable flyers for a few dollars and in spare time if necessary."

Perhaps still the world's cheapest homebuilt, excluding hang gliders, was the 1919 *Penguin,* complete plans for which ran in *Popular Mechanics* in September 1919. Developed from a military ground trainer that wasn't really supposed to fly, the *Penguin,* powered with a motorcycle engine, could be constructed today for $49.95. In fact, a replica was built for that amount and flown by Tom

The 1919 *Penguin.*

Gunderson, a retired crop duster in Twin Valley, Minnesota. It now reposes in the EAA museum.

"I tell you," Gunderson said recently, "for a young person to start flying now is as hard as when I was young, back before World War II. The way I figure it, there are a million small fishing boats around, but what we need is a small, cheap sport plane for fun and training."

In 1916 *Penguins* were used to train pilots for the Lafayette Escadrille in France. *Aviation* magazine reported at the time:

> First of all, the student is put on what is called a roller, It is a low-powered machine with very small wings. It is strongly built to withstand the rough wear it gets, and it cannot leave the ground. The apparatus is known as the *Penguin,* both because of its humorous resemblance to the quaint Antarctic birds and its inability, in common with them, to do any flying.
>
> A student makes a few trips up and down the field in a double-control *Penguin* and learns to steer with his feet. Then he gets into a single-seater and tries to keep the *Penguin* in a straight line. The slightest mistake will send the machine skidding off to the right or left, and sometimes, if the motor isn't stopped in time, over on its back. Something is always broken on a *Penguin,* so a reserve flock is kept on hand.

The postwar years of flying belonged to the barnstormers—gypsy flyers who sank $600 into a war surplus Jenny or Standard and hit the backcountry trail trying to make a living hopping passengers for a penny a pound. They buzzed small towns and landed in nearby hay-fields and hawked tickets, pleading: "Anybody else wanna take a chance?"

Little by little, as the barnstorming crates eventually eliminated themselves in flaming crashes, the homebuilt movement got back in gear, with an assist from the government. Passage of the Air Commerce Act of 1926 brought to an end the era of the wild men of the sky. No longer could you fly without a pilot's license, in an airplane that carried no airworthiness certificate. From then on, government regulation would make the fly-boys toe the line and watch safety factors.

One year later private flying was booming more energetically than ever. America suddenly had a flying hero, Charles A. Lindbergh, an unknown airmail pilot who hopped the Atlantic solo in a ship he himself helped to design—a Ryan monoplane, the *Spirit of St. Louis.*

15

A replica of Charles A. Lindbergh's famous *Spirit of St. Louis.*

A leader finally emerged in the homebuilt arena—Edward B. Heath, a New York State pilot who first soloed in 1909, at the age of twenty-one, in a ship of his own design. During World War I Heath built airplane parts by the thousands in Chicago, and in 1926 he came up with the first of a famous series of small sport planes, the Heath *Parasol.* This plane used a 27-horsepower Henderson motorcycle engine, and its lower wing panels were borrowed from a junked Thomas Morse Scout military ship.

At the 1927 National Air Races in Spokane, Washington, Heath won all the light plane and sport plane events with this ship, which gained fame as the Spokane *Super Parasol.* Heath began turning them out in his Chicago factory and arranged for them to be purchased complete or in kits. Plans cost five dollars.

On August 23, 1928, Heath unveiled a hot little homebuilt racing plane, the *Baby Bullet,* and shipped it to Los Angeles for the National Air Races at Mines Field. There Heath easily whipped the field to win a $1,500 purse in a 50-mile closed-course race, averaging 112 mph. In the trials Heath's *Baby Bullet* easily lapped an Army plane with an official top speed of 145 mph. In the race, however, he had to carry a handicap weight of 75 pounds of scrap iron. Nevertheless, the little mid-wing monoplane racer, equipped with a 32-horsepower English Bristol Cherub engine, was the fastest ship in the world for its power.

By 1931 Heath had gone on to design, build, and fly a *Model V*, with V-shaped wing struts. It flew quite well, but Heath was killed on February 1 of that year, test flying a new low-wing ship, before any of his designs could win the approval of a government-type certificate.

A parasol aircraft is one with a high wing that sits above the fuselage, and the design proved very popular in the 1930s. Another noteworthy parasol ship of that period was the Corben *Baby Ace,* which appeared in 1931. In 1955 it was extensively redesigned as the *Baby Ace Model D,* and today close to 350 amateur-built *Baby Aces* are flying, most of them built from kits or plans supplied by the Ace Aircraft Manufacturing Company, 106 Arthur Road, Asheville, North Carolina 28806.

The *Baby Ace Model D* has a cruise speed above 100 mph and stalls at 34 mph, a speed range that allows the pilot to fly cross-country and land in small fields with ease. It is powered by a 65-horsepower Continental engine. Plans for the *Model D* sell for $28.50, and the whole airplane shouldn't cost more than $2,000.

Another favorite parasol plane from the 1930s is the Pietenpol *B.4A Air Camper,* a tandem two-seater designed in 1950 by a midwesterner, Ben M. Pietenpol, of Spring Valley, Minnesota, who found an old Model T Ford engine in his barn and decided to build a flying machine around it. The *Air Camper* was an instant success with amateur builders in the prewar years.

The Heath *Parasol* sport plane. (*Stouffer's Photo Service, Lake Zurich, Ill.*)

Built largely of wood with fabric covering, the *Air Camper* remains a popular homebuilt, although many today carry different engines, such as the 65-horsepower Continental A65 and Lycoming 0–145, and the 60-horsepower Franklin. Its performance is similar to that of the *Baby Ace.*

As a depression-era sport plane the *Air Camper* made an ideal economy flyabout; it became popular with a four-cylinder, water-cooled Model A Ford engine producing 40 horsepower on cheap gas that sold for only seventeen cents a gallon. *Modern Mechanix* featured the *Air Camper* as an aerial machine that could go fast, fly 200 miles to town, and land in a ball park.

Pilots liked the automotive engines—they could land their ships on a country road, taxi into a garage, and find a mechanic who could fix a blown head gasket or screw in a new porcelain plug if one had blown up in a rainstorm.

In 1930 the do-it-yourself craze was sweeping the nation as a depression-born phenomenon, and the Pietenpol *Air Camper* quickly replaced the primary glider as aviation's favorite backyard building project. It was destined to become the first widely accepted American homebuilt, safe and easy to fly, cheap to build. You could even buy a completed *Air Camper* from the Pietenpol factory for $750, flyaway.

Today there are eight *Air Campers* still flying behind Model B Ford engines of 60 horsepower. One of these was built by Doug and

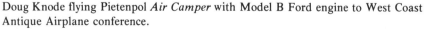

Doug Knode flying Pietenpol *Air Camper* with Model B Ford engine to West Coast Antique Airplane conference.

Top: Landing wheel assembly. *Bottom:* Detail of tail assembly and wheel.

Maryann Knode, of Santa Clara, California, who consistently win prizes for excellence in workmanship at West Coast fly-ins. Their *Air Camper* fuselage is built up around one-by-one-inch Sitka spruce longerons covered with plywood to the cockpit and aluminum up front. The graceful curve of the wing is similar to the Eiffel 36 aerofoil, which worked so well in the Curtiss Jenny wings.

Flying one of these oldies today is like flying back across time into yesterday's golden age of homebuilts, a time when any mechanically minded farm boy could nail and glue together a flying machine and go chase butterflies when his day's work was done. There were many other homemade contraptions flying in the 1930s, most of them long forgotten—the *Flying Flea, Harlequin Longster, Irwin Meteorplane, Flying Mercury, Storms Flying Flivver,* and the Ramsey *Flying Bathtub.*

Fortunately, we *can* go home again, to those happier times, by building a replica from plans easily available, using far better materials and engines that are now on the market. The big question is, of course: Where do we start? The next chapter deals with that important subject.

3
WHICH PLANE SHOULD YOU BUILD?
There's a Wide Choice of Types

The time comes when every amateur aircraft builder gets to thinking about his dream ship and its precise nature and form. Maybe he's on an ego trip and wants a big, flashy, noisy job that flies with the thunder of the gods. Maybe he's a fresh-air fiend who loves to fly in an open cockpit, or even without a cockpit. Perhaps he's a low-and-slow ground-skimmer type who enjoys sailing low across the countryside in a high-wing parasol plane, watching the Fords roll by.

There are two ways to go—either buy a set of plans or a kit and assemble a tried-and-true design that has government approval, or start from scratch and create something entirely original. The Home-built Aircraft Directory in the back of this book lists most of the popular amateur aircraft now flying. Selecting the one you find most interesting is purely a subjective matter that only you can decide.

The serious homebuilder wants safety, first of all, then performance, utility, and style—though not necessarily in that order. He may begin the project simply by doodling a design on the back of a menu while munching hot pizza and letting his mind take wings.

Speaking of wings, what shall it be—a high-, mid-, or low-wing type? For cross-country cruising, a high wing offers the best view of the landscape down below. If you prefer looking up at the clouds or flying around an airport traffic pattern, the low-wing design will offer better visibility. A mid-wing aircraft is sturdy, with thrust and drag forces well balanced, but it may be awkward to climb into.

Stolp *Starlet* on runway ready for takeoff.

A biplane lover likes the symmetry of wings spaced above and below the thrust line, an arrangement that simplifies trim changes under various power settings and normally gives good visibility. But there are more areas between the wings where interference drag can set in, and working out the biplane design balance is more complex.

Whether you favor one, two, or three wings, the choice is yours— you're not out to please other customers, as commercial aircraft designers must. However, designing an aircraft is an art as well as a science, and while the art of self-expression is one thing to an abstract painter, it's quite another to the homebuilder.

You have to start somewhere, and perhaps the most logical starting point would be your nearest FAA/GADO (general aviation district office), where you can pick up a copy of Advisory Circular AC 20-27A, issued by the FAA in 1968: *Certification and Operation of Amateur-Built Aircraft.*

In this document you'll find information and guidance for building everything from conventional airplanes to gliders, free balloons, helicopters, and gyroplanes, with appropriate references to federal air regulations that must be observed. It tells you, for instance, that an experimental certificate for an amateur-built aircraft may be issued if the major portion of the aircraft has been fabricated and assembled by "persons who undertook the construction project solely for their own education or recreation," which protects your amateur standing.

So long as you build at least 51 percent of your dream ship, you can still qualify for an "X" license as an amateur homebuilt, even though

OR-71, Owl Racer, is typical mid-wing homebuilt.

you go to the corner airplane store, or nearest mail-order catalog, to order your engine, propeller, wheels, brakes, and standard aircraft materials such as tubing, fabric, pulleys, fasteners, extrusions, and so on. Aircraft that are merely assembled from prefab kits, all precut and predrilled, won't get by as amateur-built aircraft.

This advisory circular has some good advice to consider before you start building, including the following points:

• The design should avoid dangerously sharp corners, edges, knobs, or protuberances, unless they're adequately padded.

• Where possible, use FAA-approved components and established aircraft quality materials, especially when building such important parts as the wing spars, critical attachment fittings, and fuselage structural members.

• The FAA suggests you install at least the minimum flight and engine instruments required under the federal air regulations (FAR 91.33) for visual flight rules (VFR) flying—an airspeed indicator, altimeter, magnetic compass, tachometer, oil pressure gauge, temperature gauge for water-cooled engines, oil temperature gauge for air-cooled engines, manifold pressure gauge for altitude engines, fuel gauges, landing gear position indicator if retractable, and safety belts. (Special requirements for instrumentation for night and instrument flight will also be found in FAR 91.33.)

• Prior to first flight the engine should be run up for at least one hour, from idling to full power, and a flow check made to insure an adequate fuel supply.

• A firewall should be provided between the engine compartment and fuselage to reduce fire hazard, and a means of providing carburetor heat should be added to prevent icing.

If you contact the nearest FAA flight standards service before starting your project, you'll also get government assistance in planning periodic inspection during construction, before wings and fuselage are covered and other areas permanently closed.

In conclusion, AC 20-27A also advises on such other necessary details as final inspection, proper registration, flight testing, and operating limitations, all in the interest of safety—yours and everybody else's.

While there's really no end to the possibilities in planning to build your own aircraft, a lot depends on your personal inclinations and your pocketbook, as well as your skill at handicraft. Though there are plenty of successful designs available, you still may want to try for something entirely original. If you lack technical knowledge of aeronautical engineering principles, you'd do well to enlist the aid of a qualified designer, but for starters, let's look more deeply into the various factors that will influence your design choice.

We've already briefly discussed wings—whether your ship will be a monoplane, biplane, or whatever, and whether it will be a low-, mid-, or high-wing design. In another chapter we'll give further consideration to wing design choices. But, for the moment, let's attend to such matters as the power plant, landing gear, fuselage structure, cockpit arrangement—all factors that have a bearing on the overall design. First, we'll list the major points of interest to be included.

Performance

If we are looking for high speed, the aircraft must, basically, be aerodynamically clean, with a minimum of struts and wire braces. Hence the choice would be a monoplane.

For a fast-climber we'll want our craft to have a low wing loading, a high power loading, and—for reasons we'll came to later—the longest possible wing trailing edge.

For a high ceiling we'd consider an aircraft with low wing loading and high aspect ratio (the ratio of wingspan to wing chord), plus, of course, a supercharged engine.

Low landing speeds require relatively low wing loading, or relatively high lift coefficient, or both. The lift coefficient can be increased by using flaps or other lift-increasing devices.

Landing Gear

To cut down aerodynamic drag, we may want to go to retractable landing gear, which can increase the complexity of design while adding extra weight. A low-wing design is most suitable, to provide wheel wells into which the gear can retract.

Structure

You'll find that a tubular steel fuselage construction is more efficient for a small aircraft than for a large one, and fabric wing covering may be desirable because of cost, ease of application, and lower weight than metal covering. However, for flight speeds in excess of 150 mph aluminum skin may be preferable.

Many other considerations come to mind in laying out the initial design. Will your aircraft have a nosewheel (tricycle gear) or tail wheel (taildragger type)? Should the engine be cowled or uncowled? Should the cockpit be open or enclosed?

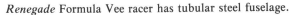

Renegade Formula Vee racer has tubular steel fuselage.

The moment now comes when you'll pull out an old love letter and start doodling on the back. The proper place to begin is with the estimated gross weight. You'll need this figure early, because on it depends the amount of wing area required to meet a specific landing speed.

The importance of wing loading was not fully recognized until after World War I, when passenger and airmail transport appeared on the aviation scene. Engineers learned that, other things being equal, the landing speed of an aircraft varies as the square root of its wing loading. Other things being equal, cruising speed varies, on the average, about as the fourth root of the wing loading. Other things being equal, the absolute ceiling is reduced by about 1,000 feet for every 10 percent increase in wing loading. A similar increase in wing loading also cuts down the rate of climb by roughly 40 feet per minute.

As late as 1938 the old Bureau of Air Commerce was sufficiently concerned about high wing loadings to limit the design landing speeds for small aircraft to 65 mph. The quest for higher performance through higher wing loadings led to design loadings of about 24 pounds per square foot in the early 1930s.

Wing loadings today are less than half that figure, for both modern aerobatic biplanes and other sturdily built amateur aircraft—and, of course, far lighter for high-performance soaring craft. Where the importance of wing loading formerly was dictated by landing speeds and strength of available materials, today other considerations are more important to the homebuilt designer. Improved materials of lighter weight and greater strength are available, but most important is the area of flight performance.

Pilots know that the stalling speed of a wing increases in direct proportion to any increase in wing loading, which affects not only the landing speed but the stalling speed in a turn. Measured in terms of Gs (forces of gravity), the wing's load factor will double in a 60-degree bank and increase by a factor of five in an 80-degree bank. A typical light aircraft that stalls at 85.5 mph in level flight will stall at 102 mph in a 45-degree banked turn.

Homebuilt aircraft, like other aircraft, must be designed to absorb certain maximum stresses, which is why a thorough stress analysis is necessary prior to construction of a new design. The FAA has definite limits for maximum safe load factors for aircraft in various categories. In aircraft under 4,000 pounds gross weight, the load limit is 3.8 Gs for normal category aircraft (no aerobatics or spins); 4.4 Gs for utility category aircraft (mild aerobatics, spins permitted); and 6.0 Gs for aerobatic category aircraft.

Thus an aircraft licensed in the utility category (4.4 Gs) could not be legally flown in an 80-degree banked turn, which would impose 5.0 Gs. Which is why your homebuilt must be designed to withstand stresses far beyond those imposed in level flight—to so-called ultimate load factors.

This is all to show why it's essential to begin your homebuilt project with a good idea of what your craft's gross weight will be, prior to deciding on wing shape, wing area, and other design details. If you study proven designs of other aircraft of the same type you have in mind, you'll find that weight estimates are not too complicated. An experienced aircraft designer can tell at a glance roughly what the final gross weight will be, based on specifications set forth on desired payload and performance.

One rule-of-thumb method of estimating gross weight is to approach it on the basis of power loading, or the amount of horsepower available in a certain engine, divided into the gross weight. Empirical data tell you that you may want a power loading of about 16 pounds per square foot, roughly that of a modern commercial trainer like a Cessna 150, which has a 100-horsepower Continental 0-200-A power plant.

$$\text{If power loading} = \frac{\text{gross weight}}{\text{total engine power}} = \frac{W}{P},$$

then $16.0 = \dfrac{X}{100}$, and $X = 16 \times 100$ or 1,600 pounds, which is the gross weight of a Cessna 150.

Another way to go at it is to estimate as closely as possible the individual weights of power plant, pilot and payload, fuel load, and miscellaneous equipment, which normally total about 65 to 70 percent of the gross weight. If these items total 450 pounds, then design gross weight $= \dfrac{450}{0.7} = 642$ pounds.

Once you know approximately how much your aircraft is going to weigh, and how much power is available, you can begin the fun of roughing out what is called the "three-view"—a sketch of what your aircraft will look like from top, side, and front. You have a choice of hanging the engine and propeller up front (tractor) or behind (pusher), or maybe even on top, on an engine mount called a pylon.

When you've decided on the wing area necessary to support a certain gross weight in a desired number of pounds per square feet, you'll want to think up a sound aspect ratio (ratio of wingspan to wing chord), because the span of the wing not only is a convenient reference dimension but also helps to determine such functions as stability and ease of control.

A wing with a 20-foot span and 2-foot chord would have the same wing area (20 x 2 = 40 square feet) as one of 10-foot span and 4-foot chord (10 x 4 = 40 square feet), but the former would have more roll control (leverage) than the latter, being longer. The first wing would have an aspect ratio of 20:2 or 10:1, the latter an aspect ratio of 10:4 or 2.5:1.

The average homebuilt will have an aspect ratio of not less than 6:1 (its span six times its width), while sailplane wings may have thinner aspect ratios, as high as 14:1. Here it's important to locate on your three-view a dimension called the mean aerodynamic chord (MAC), which is roughly the average distance from the wing's front (leading) edge to its rear (trailing) edge, whether the wing is curved like a bird's or straight. The reason for its importance is that the final center of gravity of the homebuilt will usually fall at a point about 25 percent back along the MAC, a station often called the quarter-chord position.

Once you've got that figured out, you can locate the tail post of the aircraft quickly—it's normally 2.5 to 3 times the length of the MAC behind the quarter-chord point. The landing gear also is located with reference to the quarter-chord, or center of gravity, position, whether of the tricycle or taildragger variety. In the former the main gear is located behind the center of gravity, and in the latter ahead of it, for landing stability.

If all this seems complicated—and it is—then the best thing is to select an already proven homebuilt design and stick with it faithfully, knowing that all the engineering problems have already been worked out for you. Some homebuilts are the result of long hours of careful wind-tunnel study, while others were simply "eyeballed" and refined by trial-and-error fixes until the final configuration flew properly in all modes of flight.

One such "eyeball" design is a pretty little green monoplane named *Moon Maid*, designed by Richard Doyle of Franklin Park, Illinois. Doyle started out to build a gyrocopter but, when things didn't work out as he'd planned, he lengthened the fuselage by 4 feet and added a pair of wings with a span of 23 feet 6 inches and a 50-inch chord. It

Richard Doyle's *Moon Maid.*

now flies just fine, behind a 1,523-cc Volkswagen engine of about 50 horsepower, the first VW-engined aircraft ever to fly to the EAA Oshkosh convention under its own power. *Moon Maid* cruises along at 80 mph and climbs at 600 feet per minute. Doyle knows that for sure because he made a tape recording while climbing to the craft's service ceiling, then played it back with a stopwatch.

Ron Wier's *Draggin' Fly,* down in Ramona, California, was another eyeballed homebuilt, patterned largely after the Ramsey *Flying Bathtub* of the 1930s. The only mechanical drawing Wier made was for the rib jig, and the result was fine. Wier let the author fly his creation, which was super fun. It climbed at 60, cruised at 60, glided at 60, all behind a little VW engine, and landed on a dime on its little go-kart wheels.

While we're on the subject of eyeball designs, let's not overlook *Skeeter,* a snazzy little low-wing single-seater that started life as a fanciful charcoal sketch of a flying machine executed by Dennis Kyrk for a friend, LeRoy Huff, to hang in his office in Oklahoma City. Another friend, Leonard Eaves, recruited two more pals, Lloyd Pearson and Bob Stout, to join him in seeing what they could come up with that looked like Kyrk's sketch.

Among the ideas that went into the project were a curved cockpit roof, to add extra lift to that of the wing. Up front is a Lycoming 0-290-G engine, tightly cowled to preserve the unusual profile dreamed up by the three inventors. *Skeeter,* which carries the registration number N1111V, uses a graceful NACA 64-412 airfoil that gives fine performance—a cruise of 150 mph true airspeed (TAS), a maximum speed of 170 mph, a glide at 80 mph, and a touchdown velocity of 60 mph.

Ron Wier's *Draggin' Fly*.

Skeeter, an unusual "eyeball" design homebuilt.

It may not be exactly orthodox to go about constructing an aircraft this way, but more and more homebuilt enthusiasts are doing it. Some new radical homebuilts with truly amazing performance are described in later chapters, but the majority of the 5,000 or so flying today are just fun machines, with safety and enjoyment the main goals.

For the novice homebuilder this is the best and safest way to go—to follow closely a set of plans created by experienced aeronautical engineers, like the Thorp *T-18* low-wing, all-metal two-seater designed by John Thorp, originator of a whole line of popular sport aircraft. The complete plans for the *T-18* were finished and run off the press long before the first one was built, by the noted racing pilot Bill Warwick. You can't go wrong in a ship like that!

4
GIVE IMAGINATION
TO YOUR WINGS!
The Wing Is the Heart of an Airplane

Of all the challenging design features of a homebuilt airplane, the most fascinating, most important, and least understood is the wing. By the simple act of slicing through dead air, the wing transforms it into a precisely generated and controlled windstorm, which produces the sustaining force called lift.

There are all sorts of wings flying today—the long, thin, tapering wings of slender sailplanes . . . the short, stubby wings of racing planes, like flashing scimitars . . . the elliptical wings of World War II fighters like the legendary British Spitfire . . . the swept wings of subsonic aircraft . . . the deltas of the Machbusters. Why the differences?

In selecting one kind of wing over another, your first consideration should be the kind of performance you expect—high speed, high lift, fast climb, low stall, or a combination of these factors. Strength is equally important. How much wing loading do you have in mind? A sailplane with high aspect ratio need not have the built-in design strength of a racer that may pull six Gs in a tight pylon turn, or an aerobatic ship that will be subjected to punishing snap maneuvers.

A wing with beautifully rounded tips may look pretty, but you may be paying a penalty in poor climb performance by not squaring them off to increase the length of the trailing edge. John Thorp, designer of the Thorp *T-18* homebuilt, once turned a stock Piper *PA-14 Family*

Elliptical wing on *Stinger* (Formula One racer).

Semielliptical wing on *Starduster Too*.

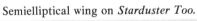

Cruiser into a virtual STOL (short takeoff and landing) type simply by extending the trailing edge of the wing out to a squared instead of a rounded tip. This achieved two things. It improved lateral control considerably, by moving the tip vortex away from the aileron. Also, squaring off the *PA-14*'s wingtips produced a greatly improved aspect ratio, the span squared divided by the wing area, resulting in a greatly improved climb performance.

According to the noted German aerodynamicist Sighard F. Hoerner, the effective span of a wing is the span of its trailing edge. The concept isn't new. It goes back to the 1920s when designers referred to it as the momentum theory of lift—all a wing really does is deflect air downward to produce the reactive force called lift.

Herein lies a matter of concern if you're trying to design a short-field aircraft that can climb fast out of a mountain meadow surrounded by high trees to get to your favorite hideaway fishing spot. Flying at a speed aerodynamicists call V_y (best rate of climb velocity), says Thorp, half your thrust horsepower is producing lift while the other half is producing propulsion that gives forward velocity. As you settle down into cruise flight and go faster, this effect becomes minimal, and at high speeds only some 6 to 7 percent of your total engine power is producing lift while the balance is propulsion or thrust.

If it's speed you're after, rather than a fast climb, you'll be more interested in ways to reduce drag, which works opposite to thrust. Drag comes in two varieties—parasitic and induced. Induced drag is that produced by the movement of air that creates lift, while parasitic drag is due to skin friction and everything else that doesn't contribute to lift.

Thus, in considering wing design, it's essential to know how much induced drag to expect, and what can be done to minimize it. Roughly half the wing's induced drag occurs at the wingtips, in the form of twisting eddies called vortexes. The other half occurs along the wing's trailing edge, in the form of bound vortexes.

Both wingtip and trailing edge vortexes are produced by a rotary motion of air flowing over a wing, called vorticity. Pilots once assumed that lift came from a negative pressure on top of the wing that virtually lifted the airplane from the ground; others claimed the lift came from positive pressure underneath the wing that pushed it up. Both were partly right and partly wrong—the total lift comes from the downward flow field *behind the wing,* which serves as a sort of wind deflector.

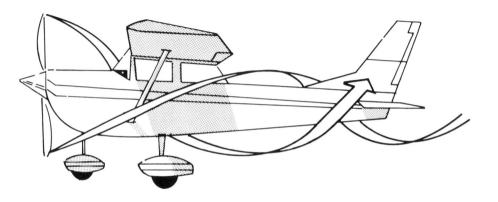

Top: Propwash is produced by propeller's rotation, and assumes a corkscrew flow most noticeable at low airspeeds. *Bottom:* A wing generates lift by producing pressure differences over its surface that result in downstream swirling air masses called vortices, which form at the wingtips. These tiny tornadoes also cause severe wake turbulence (an energy flow created by wingtip vortices when a wing produces lift), which pilots once thought was due to "propwash." (*Diagrams from FAA manuals*)

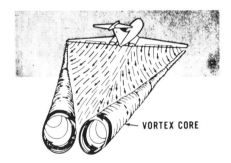

VORTEX CORE

Theoretically, if we had a wing of infinite span we'd have no wingtip vortex to worry about—only the bound vortex along the trailing edge. That is why sailplanes have long skinny wings whose extended downwash produces a lower velocity (and lower drag) than a wing of shorter span, and so provide a higher ratio of lift to drag (L/D).

But do you really want a high L/D? In soaring you do, because you simply want to float around inside a rising air bubble that lifts your glider faster than its sink rate. In air racing you don't necessarily want a high L/D because you're working with high power loadings and short-span wings that can take more punishment.

There's little you can do about wingtip vortex, which is a phenomenon whose strength is pretty much attributable to span loading (the weight of the aircraft divided by the wingspan squared). Aerodynamicist Hoerner suggested one remedy—redesigning the wingtips into a curved shape, called a conical camber, similar to that assumed by some birds in slow flight.

A high L/D in your wing design will give your aircraft greater range through greater aerodynamic efficiency, which means less fuel burned per mile. To achieve an optimum L/D, you must consider a phenomenon called lift distribution. Wind-tunnel research reveals that spanwise lift distribution varies with the strength of the air circulation over the wing, decreasing from a maximum at midspan to zero at the wingtips. Thus spanwise lift distribution assumes the shape of half an ellipse, and it follows that minimum induced drag occurs when the spanwise distribution is elliptical. The result is a constant downwash along the trailing edge, and the higher the aspect ratio, the smaller the downwash velocity—and hence the better the wing's L/D.

Designers of some homebuilt racing planes have gone to elliptical wing shapes in the belief that this is the best way to capitalize on elliptical spanwise distribution of lift for minimum drag. Examples are the Formula One racers: *Stinger,* designed by Art Williams, a Lockheed aerodynamicist, and *Shark,* the creative design of a crop duster, Harvey Mace.

Actually there are other ways to achieve nearly elliptical pressure distribution with wings of low and medium aspect ratio than simply using an elliptical planform. One way is to twist the wing, decreasing the angle of attack toward the tip. Another is to square off the tip and so extend the trailing edge, as Thorp did with the *PA-14.*

One of the most surprising planforms to come along was a stubby, squared-off wing arrangement used on *Bonzo,* Steve Wittman's famous *D-12* racer that added thrills to the Thompson Trophy Races of the 1930s. Wittman, after several modifications, settled on a square wing with a span of 17 feet 2 inches and a chord of 5 feet 6 inches, producing an aspect ratio of roughly 3:1. The experts appeared dubious when Wittman unveiled *Bonzo* for the first time, but they gasped when he ran away from the pack, with a wing that held a perfect elliptical distribution of lift.

For years designers wondered why it was that seabirds could skim along over the waves in calm air for long periods of time with nary a flap of their long, curved wings. Today we have learned part of their secret—they're flying in what we call *ground effect.* This also explains why some low-powered aircraft can get off the ground but won't climb more than a few feet.

Top: Cessna 170 flying in ground effect. *Bottom:* Leaving ground effect.

At the moment of takeoff, for example, an aircraft flies at a high angle of attack that produces high induced drag, yet the induced drag effect is reduced by as much as 50 percent by ground interference with the vortex pattern *behind the wing.* Ground effect diminishes rapidly with height—at half the wingspan dropping to about 8 percent. Years ago pilots were aware of ground effect, though vague about what it really was. They simply believed the wing settled on some kind of an air cushion underneath it.

Pelicans possess another secret of flight we're beginning to understand better—they can change the curve of their wings in flight to suit their needs. Skimming the waves in ground effect in search of a meal, our pelican spots a fish. He immediately pulls upward, arches his wings, hovers, and then dives for his prey.

Mechanically operated, variable-cambered airfoils aren't new to aviation. In the 1900s several patents appeared covering such devices, which could change the wing shape to whatever flight characteristic the pilot wanted—a fat camber for slow flight, a thin camber for higher speed. Today we have an assortment of designs for flaps and leading edge slots and similar means of altering wing shape in flight.

In choosing the wing you want for your homebuilt project, you must first select a planform that will give you the required wing area, after gross weight and span have been settled on. Remember that increasing the span by 10 percent can reduce the induced drag by 20 percent; hence the greater the span, the greater the efficiency. There's a limit to span, however—weight. Too much span means the total weight of the aircraft is supported too far out from the wing root, requiring heavier spars to reduce the bending moment. However, a greater span loading means better climb performance with the same total gross weight.

We've discussed elliptical wing planforms, which offer minimum induced drag; now what about tapered wings? Noel Becar, a well-known designer and member of the EAA, points out that a tapered wing is easier to build than an elliptical wing, and offers only about 1 percent more drag.

In selecting the airfoil you intend to use, there's a wealth of data available in engineering libraries—NACA (National Advisory Committee for Aeronautics) Technical Reports 93, 124, 182, 244, 315, and 824. From these reports a wing's flight characteristics can be predicted with some certainty, as the result of thorough wind-tunnel testing by NACA, the forerunner of NASA (National Aeronautics and Space Administration).

Many such flight characteristics, Becar points out, are in conflict with one another. A good high-speed airfoil seldom provides the lowest possible landing speed, for example; hence compromises are in order. Becar suggests five points to consider in choosing an airfoil section:

• A high coefficient of maximum lift, for lowest landing speed.

• A rounded peak to the lift curve, to give a gradual rather than an abrupt loss of lift at wing stall.

• A reasonably low center of pressure travel, to minimize stability and trim problems with changes in speed and angle of attack.

• The highest possible L/D ratio to allow cruising on lowest horsepower, and for best glide angle.

• Adequate airfoil thickness to house spars of required depth (shallower spars must be wider to achieve equal strength, so they become heavier).

Best average airfoil thickness for a conventional wing design runs around 12 percent of the chord, the NACA reports reveal; wings for fast aircraft are limited to a thickness ratio of about 9 percent, while tapered cantilevered wings need a depth up to 15 percent.

Standard airfoil sections in use in the United States today number only about a dozen, according to Becar. These include the well-known Clark airfoils developed by Colonel Virginius E. Clark; the USA series developed by the U.S. Army; the N series developed at the Philadelphia Navy Yard; the M series developed by Dr. Max M. Munk at NACA; and others developed exclusively at NACA during the 1920s and 1930s.

Occasionally you'll find a homebuilt sporting an airfoil of British RAF, French Eiffel, or German Gottingen shape, adapted for special requirements. However, generally speaking, well-proven, orthodox airfoils are the best. You may want to go to a sharp-nosed wing for speed, but this way you also get a wing that stalls quickly, with little warning. A blunter nose section will fly at lower velocities, but it won't go as fast.

Dr. A. A. Blackstrom, of the Mississippi State College Aerospace Department, seems to feel that basic airfoil selection is of little consequence unless the homebuilder does a professionally clean job of building his wing. High performance, according to Dr. Blackstrom, depends as much on attention to details in fabrication as on your choice of an airfoil or wing planform.

Thus any reasonable airfoil will give good performance if well constructed—and as Dr. Blackstrom points out, there's really no need to go to fancy flaps and slots and conical cambered tips for safe, slow flight characteristics. "The best low speed device ever invented," he concludes, "is a low wing loading."

There are other considerations in wing design beyond selection of the airfoil and planform, span, and wing area, of course. Wing dihedral—upsweep—usually runs from 3 to 6 degrees, and may extend along the full span or only at the outer portions. Ultimately, wind-tunnel or flight testing must be used to determine the amount of dihedral required.

The angle of incidence of the wing—the angle between the wing chord line and the thrust line of the fuselage—must be considered in relation to a number of factors: flap clearance, three-point landing attitude in a taildragger, interference drag, and whether the aircraft is

Wool tufts show effect of a "root stall"—it begins at wing root and spread outward.

meant to fly at high speed, when the angle of incidence should be close to the anticipated angle of attack at high-speed flight for least drag.

Ailerons—the controls that move the aircraft about its longitudinal (fore-and-aft) axis—come in a variety of shapes, forms, and sizes. Their function is to induce a roll by creating a higher relative angle of attack when depressed into the slipstream. The Wright brothers' biplane at Kitty Hawk used wing-warping instead of ailerons, with the operator deflecting the wingtips into the relative airflow by moving a shoulder yoke connected by wires to the wingtips. (This idea was originated in 1884 by the Frenchman Alexander Goupil.)

Modern ailerons are patterned after the movable wingtip plates conceived by Alexander Graham Bell and built into the historic 1911 biplane *White Wing* by members of the Aerial Experiment Association, the basis of a bitter patent fight between the AEA and the Wright brothers. As in the wing-warping method, the movable flaps (ailerons) simply create a positive pressure when deflected by moving the stick or wheel sideways, inducing a roll.

Incidentally, a drawback of poorly designed ailerons is their tendency to induce drag when deflected, causing the airplane to yaw about its vertical axis. A major function of the aircraft's rudder is to neutralize aileron drag and so offset this yaw tendency.

Some ailerons are balanced aerodynamically, to make them easier to move, while others are mass balanced. One clever designer, Richard VanGrunsven of Forest Grove, Oregon, designed an exceptional monoplane, the *RV-3*, with ailerons mass balanced with lengths of half-inch galvanized water pipe inside the ailerons' leading edges— simple to install, and even rustproof!

A major consideration in aileron placement is the ailerons' position in relation to the rear spar. Construction is far simpler if they can be hinged directly to the spar; if this can't be done, a false spar must be installed to carry them. If the spar is too far forward from the trailing edge, the chord width of the aileron may be excessive, resulting in "barn-door" sluggishness of operation.

Care should be taken to avoid flutter either in the ailerons or in the wing itself, for flutter can become quickly destructive. Flutter can be avoided in ailerons with proper mass or aerodynamic balancing. Wing flutter can be controlled by careful attention to structural rigidity, by making sure all hinges and control links are tight, and by proper streamlining to avoid buffeting.

Numerous other details of wing design come to mind, such as providing space for retraction of landing gear, flap arrangement, fuel tank installation, rib design and construction, and ease of removing the wings for roadability. This last point can be an important consideration because it's nice to be able to fold back the wings, or remove them, and tow your homebuilt home for storage in the garage when you're not out flying.

The EAA, in fact, has held competitions for best roadability design, in an effort to spur interest in the homebuilt movement among pilots who want to avoid the cost of tiedown and storage at the local airport. Besides, it's fun to be able to go out into the garage and tinker with your homebuilt after dinner, instead of watching television.

5

GETTING IT
ALL TOGETHER
Tips on Aircraft Construction

You don't have to be a graduate aeronautical engineer to design a homebuilt aircraft, though it might help. There's nothing like having a nice cooperative wind tunnel available, and maybe a Univac computer, to run your stress analysis through, along with knotty problems in flight dynamics, weight, and balance.

Few homebuilders are blessed with such luxuries. Rather, they are ordinary people with varying degrees of mechanical aptitude and flying background. They come in all ages, sizes, and shapes, and in both sexes, yet they all have one thing in common—a passionate urge toward creativity, a desire to build something that will fly. Example:

Once upon a time a little boy sat on the bank of the Viliya River in a country called Lithuania and watched a very beautiful airplane that flew overhead each day. It was a very special airplane with swept wings, and the pilot used to chase hawks and go wheeling off across the fields, sometimes upside down.

The war came and Communist troops invaded the country and the little boy moved away forever, but he never forgot the airplane. After the war his family brought him to America, where he grew up and went to college at the University of California, Los Angeles, and learned to fly. In the back of his mind he tried to remember what that first airplane looked like, but as a boy he hadn't been trained to look for details—he just saw the whole exciting thing at once.

Rimbydas Kaminskas's *Jungster I.*

Jungster II.

Then one day he picked up a magazine and saw a photograph of *his* airplane—a Bucker Jungmeister! He tried in vain to find one to buy, in France or Spain or Switzerland, and finally decided to build a small, four-fifth-scale version on his own. He read up on aircraft design and stress analysis, and finally threw the books aside. Designing an airplane, he decided, was more art than science.

This young man, whose name was Rimbydas Kaminskas, called his ship the *Jungster I,* a shortening of Jungmeister. Wisely, he built it to his own size, starting with a cockpit just big enough to seat him comfortably. It finally flew, a lovely little biplane powered with a Lycoming 0-235 engine of 108 horsepower, in October 1962. It had been simple to build, mostly of wood, and it was sensitive and responsive, but Rim wanted something a little bigger and faster. He sold *Jungster I* and turned to his next homebuilt design, which he called *Jungster II.*

Jungster II turned out to be an exciting parasol monoplane with a swept wing. It weighed only 750 pounds, and with a Lycoming 0-360 engine of 180 horsepower it climbed so fast people called it "The Elevator." It could climb to 10,000 feet from a standstill in three minutes flat.

Bitten by the homebuilt bug, Rim couldn't stop now. He sold the rights to *Jungster I* and *Jungster II* to a Canadian firm, which has since marketed hundreds of sets of plans, and got busy on *Jungster III,* a fanciful concept with the top wing shaped like a seagull's. An airline pilot named Jim Hall bought *Jungster III* and began racing it in the sport biplane class, under the name *Jonathan Livingston Seagull.*

At last report Rim was busy on two other homebuilts—*Jungster IV,* a two-place biplane, and *Jungster V,* a single-place version of the *Jungster IV,* stressed for competition aerobatic flying. Rim Kaminskas's story is a good example of how homebuilt designs come about, and there are others.

Take the case of three brothers, John, Mark, and Tim Sorrell, who own their own antique aircraft restoration shop in Tenino, Washington.

Over the past several years the Sorrell brothers have gotten to fooling around with ways to improve on the basic design of the old ships they rebuild. They constructed half a dozen ships, each with a negative stagger biplane wing arrangement, the lower wing ahead of the upper wing, like the classic Beech Model 17 Staggerwing.

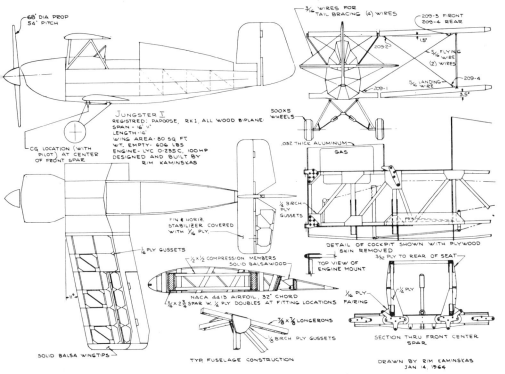

68" DIA PROP
54" PITCH

3/16 WIRES FOR
TAIL BRACING (4) WIRES

209-3 FRONT
209-4 REAR

1.5"

5/16 FLYING
WIRE
(2) WIRES

209-2

209-1

5/16 LANDING
WIRE

209-4

3.5"

JUNGSTER I
REGISTRED: PAPOOSE, RK1, ALL WOOD BIPLANE.
SPAN - 16' 11"
LENGTH - 16'
WING AREA - 80 SQ FT
WT. EMPTY - 606 LBS
ENGINE - LYC 0-235 C, 100 HP
DESIGNED AND BUILT BY
RIM KAMINSKAS

CG LOCATION (WITH
PILOT) AT CENTER
OF FRONT SPAR

500 X 5
WHEELS

.032 THICK ALUMINUM

GAS

1/8 BIRCH
PLY
GUSSETS

DETAIL OF COCKPIT SHOWN WITH PLYWOOD
SKIN REMOVED

FIN & HORIZ.
STABILIZER COVERED
WITH 1/16 PLY.

1/16 PLY GUSSETS

1/2 x 1/2 COMPRESSION MEMBERS
SOLID BALSAWOOD

11"

3/32 PLY TO REAR OF SEAT

TOP VIEW OF
ENGINE MOUNT

1/4 PLY

NACA 4413 AIRFOIL, 32" CHORD
3/4 x 2 3/4 SPAR W. 1/4 PLY DOUBLES AT FITTING LOCATIONS

1/16 PLY
FAIRING

7/8 x 7/8 LONGERONS

1/8 BIRCH PLY GUSSETS

SOLID BALSA WINGTIPS

SECTION THRU FRONT CENTER
SPAR

TYP. FUSELAGE CONSTRUCTION

DRAWN BY RIM KAMINSKAS
JAN 14, 1964

Jungster I building plans. (*Courtesy of K and S Aircraft Supply*)

Jungster III.

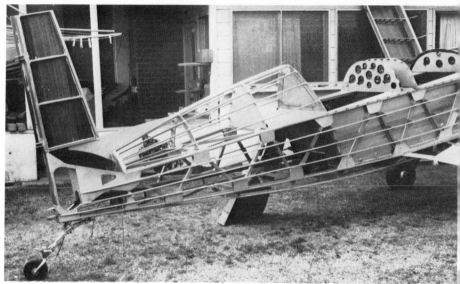

Fuselage of the *Jungster IV.*

The sixth Sorrell homebuilt, which they called the *HiperBipe,* was flown to the 1973 Oshkosh EAA convention and amazed everybody with its unusual shape, roominess, and performance. Equipped with a 180-horsepower engine, the *HiperBipe* cruised at 160 mph, stalled at about 50 mph, and had a range of nearly 600 miles. The *HiperBipe*'s fuselage, viewed from the top, appears squarish, with both sides parallel instead of tapering. The result is that the top of the fuselage produces lift, as does a wing section. An unusual feature is that the *HiperBipe* is stressed for aerobatic flight and its performance, according to the Sorrells, is comparable to the two-place Pitts. The name, incidentally, is a sort of contraction of "high-performance biplane."

Another homebuilt that attracted interest at Oshkosh was a curious little biplane that hadn't yet flown—the creation of Roger F. Petersen of Brownton, Minnesota. Peterson's dream ship had a wingspan of only 7 feet and weighed 410 pounds gross, yet it had an acceptable wing loading of 9 pounds per square foot. Petersen had plans to run taxi trials during the winter, when Buffalo Creek (Minnesota) ices over.

"It's difficult to make accurate predictions on such a radical and unusual design," he admitted.

The Sorrell and Petersen biplane designs have one thing in common —both show a freedom of spirit and imaginative searching for something new and different, which is the real hub of the homebuilt move-

The Sorrell brothers' *HiperBipe.*

ment. Either the builder conforms to proven designs or tries out a radical concept, which is how it all began in the first place.

A good example of simplicity in unorthodox design thinking is an unusual "fresh air" contraption called the *PDQ-2,* somewhat resembling a motorized Northrop-type primary glider of the 1930s. *PDQ-2* was exhibited at Oshkosh by its imaginative builder, Wayne Ison of Elkhart, Indiana, and caused plenty of comment. Powered with a 600-cc JLO German snowmobile engine, this tiny monoplane, with a wingspan of only 16 feet 6 inches, weighs 210 pounds empty.

Wayne Ison's *PDQ-2.*

According to Lowell Farrand, who flew *PDQ-2,* the ship handles beautifully and is quite stable. It reportedly climbs at 60 mph, which would seem fast enough with the pilot sitting out in the open air, snuggled back against the engine pylon with wings sprouting from his shoulders. The wings are foam-filled, with spruce spars, and the whole thing is coated with marine resin. The pilot perches on a tiny seat supported by a springy metal T-shaped landing gear.

Before launching your own homebuilt project, you should ask yourself a few basic questions and try for some valid answers. How much money do you want to spend? How good a craftsman are you? How good a pilot are you? How much time do you intend to devote to constructing it?

A weekend do-it-yourself builder can easily put in five or six years on a homebuilt project, while others with ample shop facilities can turn out a ship in a matter of a few weeks or months. A large number of homebuilders have had little experience with metalwork and so prefer to use wood construction with fabric covering, a tried and true technique that goes back to the beginning of aviation.

Many other homebuilders have a solid background of metalworking in aircraft plants, body shops, or maybe even guttering and spouting plants, if you'll pardon the reference. The use of metals in aircraft construction is so common today it's hard to remember there was a time when most flying machines were fabricated from spruce, wire, and doped fabric.

The earliest effort to develop quality steels for aircraft construction goes back to a time before World War I, to work done by the governmental Engineering Standard Committee at a period when aluminum alloys were virtually unattainable.

Most aircraft metals are subject to corrosion, which may take place over an entire metal surface or may be penetrating in nature, forming pits. Corrosion may be increased by contact with materials that absorb water, such as wood, felt, dirt, and surface film. Various processes are available to protect metals against corrosion. Aluminum alloy structural surfaces usually are treated before fabrication by electrically anodizing them in chromic-sulfuric acid tanks. Magnesium sheet gets the cold nitric-chromic acid treatment. Steel surfaces are oxidized or plated during the manufacture.

The typical amateur-built aircraft is neither all metal nor all wood but will consist of a steel tubing fuselage, solid spruce spar wings, and fabric skin. Such contruction fits more easily into the average budget than an all-metal homebuilt, yet the latter—in such models as the Thorp *T-18* and the Pazmany *PL-4A*—ideally meets the special requirements of light weight and durability.

The switch from wood to metal aircraft construction came about in 1932, following the crash of a wooden Fokker trimotor that took the life of Knute Rockne, the great Notre Dame football coach. Investi-

Jim Bede's *BD-5 Micro* shown in component form as it is received by the customer, and as a finished product. (*Courtesy of Bede Aircraft, Inc.*)

The Pazmany *PL-4A.*

gation of sister ships showed an alarming loss of strength due to internal rot. Metal wings were used as early as the 1920s, however, when the Ford and Junkers transports appeared.

Today the use of metals in homebuilt aircraft has resulted in greater performance, simply because metal aircraft can actually be made lighter than wooden aircraft by a factor of two. Higher power loadings, made possible by more powerful and lighter engines, combine with the light strength of metal construction to open an exciting area of design for those who have basic metalworking skills.

Ladislao Pazmany, designer of such successful homebuilts as the T-tailed, metal *PL-4A,* recommends a minimum of three major power tools for the garage metalworker—a band saw, a drill press, and a belt or disc sander, along with the usual tin snips and other hand tools, and an inexpensive "tin-bender."

Pazmany, incidentally, did such a fine job in designing an earlier model, the side-by-side, all-metal *PL-1* sport plane, that in 1970 it was accepted as the basic trainer for the Chinese Air Force in Taiwan. The choice was dictated by several considerations. First, the Chinese Air Force wanted the cadet trainer to be safe and easy to fly. Second, it sought a craft that would be inexpensive and easy to construct, in factories on Taiwan. Third, an all-metal craft was wanted.

It took exactly 100 days to assemble the first *PL-1* for the Chinese "Homebuilt Air Force," and the prototype was first flown on Generalissimo Chiang Kai-shek's birthday—October 30, 1968. Two

Top: Pazmany's metal bender. *Bottom:* Pazmany's drill press.

more prototypes were completed in June 1969, and finally a production run of thirty-five improved versions of the *PL-1B* and *PL-2* got rolling. Today a number of other Asian countries use Pazmany "homebuilt" trainers to start their cadets toward military careers in flying, a fine tribute to the booming homebuilt movement in the United States.

Designers of metal homebuilts normally prefer to stay away from complicated compound curves, and as a result such "tin" craft as John Thorp's exceptional *T-18* frequently have a squarish look. Thorp glued tufts of wool all over his *T-18* and rigorously test flew it while a second plane flew alongside carrying a photographer. The pictures showed no drag interference caused by the squared-off corners.

Riveting has come a long way since the early 1930s when big tin birds like the Ford trimotor took to the air. In 1933 the NACA launched a wind-tunnel study and concluded that rivets should be countersunk flush with the surface of the skin, at least over the first 40 percent of the wing chord, and along the fuselage sides back to its maximum diameter, to reduce parasitic drag.

Today inexpensive and easy-to-install "pop rivets" are widely used, and according to Thorp there's "no justification for arbitrarily banning their use." Often the holes in the middle of pop rivets are filled with epoxy automobile putty for a smoother finish. Certified 4130 chrome-molybdenum steel tubing is in almost universal use today in fuselage structures, because of ease of assembly and superior strength when formed into geodesic patterns that resist collapse under high impact, as in a crash landing.

And what about wood construction?

Maybe only God can make a tree, if you believe Joyce Kilmer, but it's simply amazing what beginning homebuilders can create from a plank of Sitka spruce and other aviation-grade timber that comes free from knots, with growth rings closely spaced. The excellence of Sitka spruce is attributable to the long, cold winters and brief summers along the Oregon–Washington coast. Quarter-sawn and carefully selected Sitka spruce has a tensile strength of 6,000 pounds per square inch, weighs only 45 pounds per square foot, and has a strength-to-weight ratio of 153—higher than steel.

Modern resins, glues, and preservatives can give wood an indefinite life, and the ease with which it can be worked makes it ideal for the amateur craftsman. Laminated woods with cross-plies aren't new, though modern resins are. The ancient Pharaohs made mummy cases

Preliminary woodwork in the preparation of easy-to-build *Fly Baby*.

of plywood, and some are still in good condition. Casein glue, in wide use some years ago, has largely been replaced by synthetics. Casein, made from powdered milk and lime, is exceptionally strong, but fungus thrives on it.

The first airplanes were wooden, and even during World War II wood was widely used to alleviate a metal shortage. The famed wooden de Havilland Mosquito bomber was hurriedly designed and went into action just twenty-seven months after its conception. The

Mosquito was built with a three-fourth-inch skin of Port Orford plywood sandwiched over a balsa core, covered with fabric, and painted. This lightweight warplane easily outran enemy fighters with top speeds above 400 mph. Many USAF trainers were built largely of wood, including the Fairchild PT-19, the Cessna UC-78 twin-engined "Bamboo Bomber," and the wood-winged Vultee BT-13 basic trainer.

A pioneer in the use of wood in aircraft construction was the legendary Howard Hughes, who developed a special process for plastic-bonding laminated veneer sheets together. His record-breaking racer, the *H-1*, had wooden wings, and his monster *HK-1* flying boat, in many respects the largest aircraft ever built, was nicknamed the "Wooden Wonder" or the "Spruce Goose."

Hughes adapted a synthetic bonding process called Duramold and initially employed it in a long-forgotten, twin-engined fighter, the *D-2*, with which he sought a production contract from the Army Air Force (Lockheed won the contract with the P-38 Lightning). The *D-2* was built of birch veneer, laminated with Duramold into a tough, lightweight skin stronger than steel, years ahead of its time.

For the homebuilder, wood offers maximum ease of workability. If you got a passing grade in woodshop in school, you qualify as an expert aircrafter. You need only basic woodworking tools such as a circle saw, band or jigsaw, drill, plane, chisel, C-clamps, and a glue pot.

Unfinished fuselage and tail assembly of wood-framed *Fly Baby*.

Peter Bowers, designer of the popular, all-wooden *Fly Baby,* says: "Wood was chosen in consideration of its relatively low cost, general availability, and the shop facilities, tooling, and skill possessed by a person undertaking construction of a full-scale airplane for the first time."

You can usually order such items as wing spars, fuselage longerons, and rib cap strips from the corner lumberyard, all precut to proper dimensions, but to qualify your aircraft as amateur-built you'll have to saw the ends off to proper length yourself.

Bowers adds: "Building a wooden airplane is a whole collection of little jobs whose degree of difficulty or simplicity, independent of the builder's skill, is influenced in a large degree by available work area and conditions. A standard one-car garage with a workbench across one end is suitable for the entire job."

For twenty dollars you can learn all you want to know about woodworking, but never got around to asking, by ordering a manual entitled *Bowers Fly Baby Model 1A* from Peter M. Bowers, 13826 Des Moines Way, Seattle, Washington 98168. In it Bowers gives these typical tips:

> All wood-to-wood joints are by glue in shear or by bolting. Bolt heads and nuts bearing against bare wood opposite a metal fitting should be backed up by large-diameter wood washers. Wood screws are never used for joining; small nails are used to hold glue joints under pressure while drying, and then become completely redundant. Wood surfaces are protected from damage during clamping by use of clamping backup blocks to distribute the load.

Other Bowers tips:

• Cut as many pieces of the same size as possible at one time.
• Mix glue with specific jobs in mind—the "pot life" of Weldwood glue, for example, is four hours, so it can't be saved for tomorrow.
• The best applicator for Weldwood glue is a half-inch or three-fourth-inch paintbrush. Wash it out in hot water before the glue sets.
• Plan your varnishing so as not to block other work, and remember that dust from saws and grinders can settle on your job from across the room.

Bowers's *Fly Baby,* incidentally, remains one of the easiest-to-build and finest-flying homebuilt designs in the sky today. It first flew in 1960 as a low-wing monoplane, and in 1962, powered with an 86-horsepower engine and a redesigned fuselage, it won the 1962 EAA competition for simple homebuilts and was so inspirational that hundreds of homebuilders asked Bowers to write a book about it—so he did.

More than a hundred *Fly Baby*s are in action today, and more are coming all the time, in a variety of shapes—monoplanes, biplanes, open- or closed-cockpit funsters, racers, float planes. In conclusion, Pete Bowers offers this advice to novice homebuilders:

"Try to plan your work ahead for several days and have all the necessary materials on hand; much time can be lost wondering what to do next."

Above all, he says, avoid the eager buddy who is anxious to be helpful but doesn't know an aileron from a hacksaw.

Bowers adds: "Then there's the curious, friendly type who drops around from time to time to see how you're doing, and brings along a friend who has to have the whole project explained to him in detail. You end up with an added expense to the overall job of paying for groceries, coffee, and beer that they consume sitting around keeping you from working!"

"You yourself can be your own worst enemy," Bowers says pointedly, "when you get to sitting around in the half-finished cockpit perched on a pair of sawhorses, shooting down imaginary Red Barons. Just try to make *some* tangible progress each work period."

The only problem is, when you get your homebuilt done, what will you do with your spare time? The answer is easy—go fly it!

6
PAUL REVERE'S HORSE
Selecting the Right Engine

Aficionados of hangar flying love to sit around flying field hideaways on a Sunday afternoon, rattling off impressive-sounding specifications of any unusual-looking aircraft that happens to land and taxi up to the gas pump, yet many of them falter when it comes to identifying the power plant that makes the thing go.

Today, as never before, the homebuilder can select from a huge variety of engines in a wide range of horsepower categories, makes, shapes, and sizes, in addition to the all-important matters of price, reliability, and maintenance cost.

More and more amateur aircraft owners are turning to converted automotive engines, motorcycle engines, snowmobile engines, and even small jets that lately have challenged a market once dominated by the "big three" aircraft engine makers—Continental, Lycoming, and Franklin, the latter firm having returned to active production in 1974 in an effort to recapture the enthusiastic following it once held.

Over the years many engine makers have come and gone. Hence, when an unknown airmail pilot named Charles A. Lindbergh hopped the Atlantic nonstop in 1927 in a Ryan M-1 long-range conversion, wiseacres could quickly tell you it was the one and only *Model NYP* (New York–to–Paris), called the *Spirit of St. Louis,* but few could recollect which engine powered it.

The talented engine designer, Charles L. Lawrance, when asked why it was that few people remembered that Lindy's life depended on his reliable Model J-5 Wright Whirlwind, replied, "Who remembers the name of Paul Revere's horse?"

The situation was quickly righted for Lawrance, with poetic justice —the coveted Collier Trophy for 1927 did *not* go to Lindbergh for his great flight, but instead to the engine designer. Said the National Aeronautic Association:

> Mr. Lawrance was the pioneer in the development of the air-cooled engine in America. The original model of the Wright Whirlwind was designed by Mr. Lawrance in 1921 . . . . The outstanding performance of the Wright Whirlwind engine during 1927 embraces many records of national and international interest. The transoceanic and other flights made with the engine have resulted in widespread public confidence and interest in aeronautics.

Public confidence in aviation had been a dubious matter prior to 1927. Following the end of World War I the entire aviation industry geared itself to war surplus, water-cooled power plants like the Curtiss OX-5, the Hispano-Suiza, and the Liberty engine.

However, when Monsieur Louis Bleriot flew across the English Channel in 1909, his *Model XI* monoplane carried a three-cylinder radial engine of 24 horsepower, the creation of Alessandro Anzani, a maker of motorcycle engines. Its three cast iron cylinders, bolted to an aluminum crankcase, carried rudimentary fins for air cooling, a daring departure from contemporary practice.

After an unsuccessful, turn-of-the-century fling at steam-engine power, most pioneer aircraft carried power plants adapted from motorcycle and racing car engines of the internal combustion type, and the majority—the Antoinette, the Duthiel-Chalmers, the E.N.V., the R.E.P., the Clement-Bayard, and even the Wright brothers' 12-horsepower engine—demanded elaborate systems of copper tubing for water cooling.

One might liken the state of the art of engine design in the early 1900s to that of nuclear power reactor design today—both depended on cumbersome, bulky, and inefficient liquid heat-exchange systems to operate. When World War I exploded, there was no time to develop air-cooled radials. Production emphasis went to water-cooled V-8s produced by a maker of motorcycle engines named Glenn Curtiss, who had designed a strong little 80-horsepower job called the Model O to power his early flying boats. Modified to produce 105 horsepower, it became known as the O+, and when someone inadvertently tilted the plus sign, it was forever mislabeled the OX.

Competing with Curtiss's OX-5 engines, the Wright-Martin Company manufactured a Yankee version of the Hispano-Suiza, designed by a Swiss engineer, Marc Birkigt, and at the war's end Detroit had geared to mass production of the 400-horsepower, 12-cylinder, water-cooled Liberty engine. A thousand a week were coming off the lines when the armistice was signed.

Ted Hohman rebuilt this OXX-6 engine.

Doolittle's *Gee Bee* racer used a radial engine. (*U.S. Air Force photo*)

The U.S. Army stuck faithfully with water-cooled airplane engines through the 1920s, while the Navy switched to air-cooled radials, encouraging Lawrance, a Navy line officer, to lead the way. By 1927 the Navy was completely involved in air-cooled aircraft engines, but the Army would continue flying water-cooled, in-line engines through another world war.

Today you'll find both air-cooled radials and water-cooled, in-line engines adapted to power homebuilts, in relatively small numbers. The basic controversy over their relative merits is based on two different philosophies on power plants. The radial provides more cubic inches of swept cylinder volume per pound of metal, whereas the automobile-type, in-line engine produces twice the horsepower per cubic inch to equal the radial's power-to-weight ratio, with the result that the latter type has higher compression, hotter valves, and other characteristic problems.

Early aircraft engines were so completely unreliable that Orville Wright once recommended to Congress that the federal government build airports spaced not less than twelve miles apart across the country, so pilots would always have a place to land in the event of engine failure.

In the 1930s homebuilts like the Pietenpol *Air Camper* flew well behind Henry Ford's Model A and Model B engines, which amounted to a cost breakthrough—secondhand automobile engines were easy to find, but they had drawbacks. Anyone who ever drove a Model A or Model B Ford car will remember that the rear main bearings often leaked oil badly. With the engine installed backward in an airplane, so that the propeller could be attached directly to the flywheel flange, the main bearing cap had a tendency to split. (Conventional aircraft engines carry long front sleeve bearings, or widely spaced ball bearings, to carry the higher torque loads.)

In converting an automotive engine to aircraft use, consideration must be given to the rpm (revolutions per minute) on which its rated horsepower is based. A good feature of the Ford Model A is its relatively low rpm, delivering full power at from 2,000 to 2,200 rpm, something you don't find in a Ford V-8, Plymouth, or Chevrolet engine. In converting the latter to aircraft use, reduction gear drives are required so they can run at 3,000 to 3,500 rpm crankshaft speed without overrevving the propeller.

Because the efficiency of a propeller falls off rapidly above 2,500 to 3,000 rpm, motorcycle engines and similar high-speed power plants

Chain gear of 1:3.86 ratio used on *Whing-Ding*.

Whing-Ding with pusher engine.

are fitted with reduction gears in conventional installations. A typical example is the McCullough 101-A two-cycle, 15-horsepower, go-kart engine installed in the tiny homebuilt *Whing-Ding* by its designer, Bob Hovey. The 101-A weighs 11 pounds, turns up at a whining 9,500 rpm, and swings a 48-inch propeller blade at 2,460 rpm through a 1:3.86 ratio chain drive.

Many homebuilt aircraft designers and constructors prefer to stick with highly reliable, standard aircraft power plants that offer a wide range of available power, from the Continental A40 (40 horsepower) to the popular Lycoming I0-360 (200 horsepower).

One newly developed production power plant is Teledyne Continental's 285-B2 Tiara (285 horsepower) of the flat-opposed type, which greatly increased the performance of the exciting Spencer amphibian *Air Car,* described more fully in Chapter 12.

Builders of ultralight homebuilts are constantly on the lookout for small, lightweight, reliable engines of low horsepower, such as the 55-horsepower, 2-cylinder German Hirth engine, with which Jim Bede's *BD-5* "pocket-pursuit" homebuilt can top 200 mph. Successor to the *BD-5,* the jet-powered *BD-5J* attains a top speed of 6 miles a minute with the French-designed and U.S.-built TRS Turbine, a reaction engine that weighs only 66 pounds and delivers 200 pounds of thrust. New on the market is the tiny Gluhareff G8-2 jet engine, whose makers, EMG Engineering Company of Gardena, California, claim 75 pounds thrust delivery from 12 pounds weight.

In 1974 considerable research was being done in an effort to adapt to aircraft use the controversial rotary engine developed in Germany in 1956 by Felix Wankel, and currently in widespread use under the hoods of the German NSU Spider and the Japanese Mazda automobiles.

The basic Wankel is pistonless. Its two moving parts are an eccentric rotor and a drive shaft; its three-lobed rotor rotates in a single direction inside a trochoid chamber that conforms to the rotor's shape.

A pioneer researcher in the field of rotary engines, Harold Gallatin, an EAA member living in Wauwatosa, Wisconsin, has developed a Wankel conversion that weighs 135 pounds and delivers 130 horsepower. He built up his experimental engine from a pair of Wankels scrounged from NSU Spiders, stacking them in a way to eliminate extra cast iron side covers, flywheels, and geared accessories. During the conversion process Gallatin developed a unique automatic ignition system that dispenses with spark plugs, achieving ignition from the glow-plug principle.

One other revolutionary aircraft engine deserves mention—the Rotary-V power plant designed by Frank Turner of Graham, Texas, which reportedly produces 400 horsepower from 325 pounds weight. Turner's engine has two revolving cylinder blocks, each with four cylinders and four angled pistons. There is no crankshaft.

Now we come to the converted Volkswagen engine, the hottest thing in homebuilt power plants flying today. VWs are relatively inexpensive, widely available new or secondhand, and highly reliable, with an acceptable power-to-weight ratio thrown in. But because VW engines produce their rated power at high crankshaft rpm, most aircraft conversions employ reduction units of one kind or another, to match them to slower-turning propellers.

Reduction drives have been highly controversial ever since the Wright brothers installed one with a 3:3.1 ratio, to swing the propeller on history's first successful heavier-than-air flying machine in 1903. The reliability of the Bug engine is such that some people get the idea all you have to do is bolt one up front and go fly, but that simply is not so. Since the first VW engines were used in homebuilts some two decades ago in Europe, in *Jodels* and *Turbulents* and similar craft, debugging the Bug engine has become something of a national pastime in America.

As a first step, consideration must be given to propeller characteristics, and whether you want to install a large-diameter, slow-turning propeller or a smaller-diameter propeller that turns faster to deliver the same thrust. The limit of a propeller's efficiency is related directly to its tip speed, which in small Formula One racers can approach sonic velocities and set up destructive shock waves.

Examples of direct-drive and reduction-drive installations are easy to find. There are several hundred homebuilts now flying behind direct-drive VW engines, wherein the engine crankshaft and propeller turn at the same rpm and hundreds more behind reduction-geared VWs, in which the propellers turn slower than the crankshaft. You don't get something for nothing, however. With a reduction gear you pay a weight penalty, yet in many cases reduction gear does offer increased performance.

Don Stewart, an Allegheny Airlines captain, designed the popular little homebuilt *Headwind* and a reduction unit he calls the Maximizer when he found his 36-horsepower VW engine turned up only 2,700 rpm under static thrust. Stewart figured he'd get better efficiency if the engine ran faster and the propeller turned slower, so he designed the Maximizer with 1.6:1 ratio. The horsepower at the propeller jumped from 18 to 32, with the engine revving up at 3,600 rpm and the larger, slower prop turning only 2,200 rpm.

Over the years, the Volkswagen engine has increased in size and power from 1,100 cc and 26 horsepower to 1,800-cc versions of 85 horsepower, fuel injected. Installed in Formula Vee class racing planes, these little engines produce speeds up to 3 miles a minute.

Hot rodding VWs has become a major challenge among homebuilt enthusiasts, and a growing number of firms are engaged solely in turning out VW conversions for airplanes. To name a few, there's Ted Barker in Carlsbad, California; John Monnett in Elgin, Illinois; Gyrodynamic Systems in Redlands, California; and Bob Huggins in Tulsa, Oklahoma. Huggins's original developmental work was taken

Engine conversion: This is the simplest and most straightforward approach by C. A. Ackerman. It has been flown on the *VP-1* prototype from the beginning without any problems, and is still being flown. It does, however, require dependence on the VW fuel pump, which is not required on carburetors mounted below. (*Courtesy of C. A. Ackerman*)

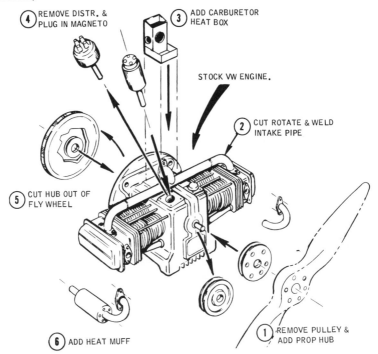

4 REMOVE DISTR. & PLUG IN MAGNETO

3 ADD CARBURETOR HEAT BOX

STOCK VW ENGINE.

2 CUT ROTATE & WELD INTAKE PIPE

5 CUT HUB OUT OF FLY WHEEL

6 ADD HEAT MUFF

1 REMOVE PULLEY & ADD PROP HUB

Ladislao Pazmany of *PL-4A* fame inspects A. Lloyd Paynter's dual-ignition VW conversion engine.

over by Revmaster in Chino, California, while Huggins continues to sell conversion manuals.

One controversy over VW conversions is whether you should go to dual ignition. Barker's position is that dual ignition is not only unnecessary but involves a possibly hazardous service problem, due to the difficulty of fitting a second spark plug into the small cylinder head. Dual ignition also involves installation of a more complex magneto drive system, or possibly the use of special magnetos that, in effect, are two magnetos in one. The requirement for dual ignition, according to Barker, is a hangover from pre–World War II days when magnetos weren't as reliable as they are today.

Revmaster offers both single- and dual-ignition conversions of standard VW automotive engines which, it points out, have established a good reputation for reliability and durability through mass production of more than 12 million units.

Another advocate of dual ignition is Lloyd Paynter of San Diego, California, whose experimental conversion is called the Hummingbird. Paynter has attracted the interest of such homebuilt designers as Ladislao Pazmany, who would like to uprate the power of a standard 1,600-cc VW engine in his *PL-4A* to somewhere near its rated maximum output of 65 horsepower.

65

Recently, at Oshkosh, veteran homebuilt designer Steve Wittman displayed an experimental installation of a stock Oldsmobile engine in the airframe of a Wittman *Tailwind,* with the idea of encouraging other homebuilders to find a practical way to convert inexpensive automotive power plants for aircraft use.

Automotive junkyards are full of old cars with cheap engines that can be rebuilt and modified for duty in the sky, a challenge to inspire any aircraft homebuilder with mechanical ingenuity. Ken Rand, designer of the popular little styrofoam *KR-1,* powered his prototype with a 1957 VW 1,200-cc engine rated at 36 horsepower, which he bought from a junkyard for thirty dollars and overhauled.

Who says flying has to be expensive?

7
TEST FLIGHT
The Proof Is in the Flying

You've just spent two of the happiest years of your life putting together your backyard bomber. A homebuilder's dream. A carport contraption that takes your breath away, just to look at it. Silver wings . . . sleek fuselage . . . a throaty engine that really purrs.

But now your wife is tapping her foot and saying, "Honey, when are you gonna get that thing out of here and into the air? I need this space for our new clothes dryer!"

It suddenly dawns on you that the past months have been spent on a project that was so much fun you've almost lost sight of your big goal —actually flying it! Now it's time to put away your hammer and saw, sweep the sawdust into a corner, and trail your beauty to the airfield.

If you're like the majority of homebuilders, you can't afford to put money into a construction project and still own a viable airplane on the side, so you're probably a little rusty on the controls. So, before that first glorious flight, you've got to make a decision—either go out and buy some refresher flight time or call up a qualified and current pilot you can trust to take your aircraft up for a maiden flight while you stand on the sidelines, biting your nails.

No matter who makes the first test hop, it cannot happen until the FAA has completed all the required inspections, even though your bird carries the big word Experimental painted on her sides. Nothing flies today without FAA approval. This is the FAA's guarantee that

Author Don Dwiggins test hops *Draggin' Fly.*

you have done a reasonably good construction job and have put together something that won't fall apart.

The paper work you'll have completed will include a careful weight-and-balance check. First, you drain out all the fuel and oil. Then perch your ship on three scales—one under each wheel. Let's say the nosewheel scale reads 800 pounds and each main wheel scale reads 1,000 pounds—total empty weight is 2,800 pounds.

Now you want to find the empty-weight center of gravity, which normally you'd want to fall at about the quarter-chord point, or one-fourth the distance of the chord back from the wing's leading edge, plus or minus a few degrees (fully loaded to gross weight, the center of gravity must fall close to the empty-weight center of gravity).

All weight-and-balance problems are really simple when you get down to basics and use the following equation:

moment = weight x arm

or

$$\text{arm} = \frac{\text{moment}}{\text{weight}}$$

The arm is the horizontal distance to the center of gravity being considered, measured from any convenient reference point (called a datum), usually the firewall, or maybe the leading edge of the wing, or perhaps the propeller spinner.

The moment is the product of the weight multiplied by the arm. Thus, in our 2,800-pound baby, our figures are:

Item	Weight	Arm	Moment
Nosewheel	800	10 inches	8,000
Main wheels	2,000	130 inches	260,000
Total	2,800		268,000

In this case the nosewheel was found to be 10 inches rearward of the datum, and the main wheels 130 inches rearward of the datum.

The center of gravity is found from the moment equation:

$$\text{arm} = \frac{\text{moment}}{\text{weight}} = \frac{268,000}{2,800} = 95.75 \text{ inches.}$$

Thus we can accurately locate the center of gravity as being just 95.75 inches aft of our datum reference point.

To find the gross-weight center of gravity, we follow the same procedure. We locate the center of gravity of each item—fuel, oil, passengers, baggage—then multiply all weights times arms to get the total moment, then divide the total moment by the total weight to arrive at the gross center of gravity.

Through flight testing, certificated aircraft are carefully evaluated to locate the permissible shift of center of gravity fore and aft, a complex procedure that establishes what is called the load-limit envelope. If the center of gravity is located ahead of its design position, the aircraft will be more stable but will be nose-heavy. If the center of gravity is located rearward of its design position, the airplane will be less stable, tail-heavy, and possibly dangerous in a spin.

Weight-and-balance data also are important in regard to maximum loading because if you exceed the maximum allowable gross weight, you may never get off the ground, at least at a high-density-altitude airport, where hot, thin air can be a real hazard to safe flight.

Once your paper work is in order, your flight test program can get under way, but it should be done cautiously, step by step, not all at once. However, more than one homebuilder has suddenly found himself in a situation where the best thing he could do was to charge ahead. Consider the case of USAF Colonel Earl Payne (Ret.), who built a perfectly lovely flying machine from 1,500 pounds of wrecked L-19 junk he bought at a salvage sale, fashioned after the plans for a *Teenie Two,* a homebuilt designed by Cal Parker.

Colonel Earl Payne's *Teenie Two* taxiing through base house project to airport.

Teenie Two is a classic homebuilt with very good flying habits, but Colonel Payne had made some changes and wasn't too sure how things would turn out when he taxied his machine down the streets of the housing area of Mountain Home AFB, Idaho, with kids yelling, women screaming, dogs barking.

He completed the taxi tests cautiously on the ramp. Then came the big day, May 26, 1972. He hadn't installed a wind screen yet, but he got his craft rolling down the runway and lifted off into ground effect, for what he had planned to be just a short hop before going back on the deck.

Suddenly his left wing dropped, and full right aileron brought no response. He remembers: "After a few seconds I was able to maintain wings level with full aileron, a lot of rudder, maximum leaning, and will power. And by the time I coaxed enough turn in to get back over the runway, the end was too near so I was obliged to keep going.

"My long red scarf was dragging at my neck, threatening me with strangulation," he shudders. "So I throttled back to 80 mph and began a 180-degree turn to the left. To my amazement I was able to get it lined up with the runway, and when I started to descend on final a wonderful feeling came over me. It was the first time since takeoff that I felt I had a chance of getting back on the ground in one piece.

"At last—over the concrete . . . wings level . . . about to touch down . . . then ahead . . . Oh, no! The jet barrier cable! If I hit that, it would rip all three landing gears off my little bird! I finally made it over the cable and chopped the throttle. I was back on the ground. What a relief! What a thrill! I did it—I built an airplane and flew it!"

For Colonel Payne, 201 combat missions over Korea and Vietnam in thundering jets held no more thrills than that first hop in his little homebuilt, powered with a Ted Barker 1,600-cc VW engine.

Before you make your first test flight, be sure at the outset that you sit comfortably in the cockpit, have adequate vision forward, up, down, left, and right, and can easily reach all controls. Close your eyes and run a blindfold check over and over, until you can automatically tell where everything is.

Prior to takeoff, there's a simple way to get the feel of control response, a method recommended by Herman (Fish) Salmon, a veteran Lockheed test pilot who has made first flights in a good

Lockheed test pilot Herman (Fish) Salmon inspects wing of Dwight Brooks's *Lysander* restoration prior to test hop.

number of homebuilts, such as his own Cosmic Wind, the *Minnow*. Fish has this advice to offer:

"A high-speed taxi run is fine on a large runway," he says, "but you can't get away with it on a short grass strip. With a taildragger you can fly standing still in a brisk breeze. Just point your craft into the wind and see how it tends to weathercock, holding the tail up in the air.

"Find out if you have adequate response with pitch control, moving the stick forward to raise the tail. Do this with the brakes on, but definitely not with the wheels chocked. If it gets away from you, you can always ease off on the brakes and roll forward a couple of feet to regain control. But if your wheels are chocked, you might accidentally tip over on your nose."

Guard against overcontrolling on the first takeoff, Salmon advises, and take it real easy until you get to a safe altitude, away from populous areas. After a few turns, return and land as smoothly as possible, and check your center of gravity. "In the Cosmic Winds," says Salmon, "we started out with what we thought was a real good center of gravity, about 22 percent MAC, but after the first flight we found we had to move it forward to nearly 16 percent MAC."

Take all the advice you can get from anybody who has seen a similar homebuilt fly, even a kid with a model plane who asks, "Hey Mister, is this thing supposed to be this way?"

"Disassemble all the information input you can get, both from experts and nonexperts, and be open-minded about what you hear," Salmon continues.

If you plan to perform approved aerobatics in your homebuilt, you'll have to demonstrate to the FAA which specific maneuvers you want your ship certificated to do.

As in aerobatics and spin testing, flight-flutter testing should be done only at the highest feasible altitude, advises veteran homebuilt designer John Thorp. He recommends testing one set of controls at a time, up to V_d —a speed 10 percent greater than the maximum indicated airspeed the aircraft need ever be flown. This speed is called the V_{ne} (never-exceed velocity) and is marked with a red line on the airspeed indicator.

Approach the V_d flutter test speeds incrementally, not all at once, and remember that while the aircraft may not flutter at 110 percent of V_{ne} at sea level, it *may* flutter at the same indicated airspeed at altitude, because flutter susceptibility is a function of true airspeed, not indicated airspeed.

P. H. Spencer (*left*) and Colonel Dale Anderson run high-altitude takeoff tests at 6,200-foot altitude at South Lake Tahoe Airport on Spencer amphibian *Air Car*.

Elevator flutter tests should be run in level flight at normal cruising power, trimming the ship to fly hands off. Then slap the stick or wheel (control column) back sharply, in the aft direction, to raise the elevators on the tail and make the nose go up. Repeat the test over and over until you reach a speed 10 percent above redline speed (V_{ne}, or never-exceed velocity for safe flight), making at least three attempts at each increment.

Aileron flutter testing comes next, starting at cruising speed with the airplane trimmed for level flight. Pull back slightly on the stick, then bat the ailerons a sharp sideways blow with the open hand, displacing them by at least 3 degrees (a larger displacement is not necessary and can be structurally dangerous at high speeds).

By approaching the V_{ne} speed gradually, you can ascertain any incipient flutter condition that may develop. "Evidence," says Thorp, "that you have tickled the dragon's tail!" Corrective design steps may then be taken, before proceeding with further flight-flutter testing.

Lastly, the rudder is flutter tested the same way as the other control surfaces, by pulling the stick back a little to induce deceleration, before booting the rudder. To check each surface at V_{ne} with a transient instead of a constant speed, it will be necessary, of course, to initiate the checks at velocities slightly above V_{ne}.

Flutter may be destructive. Hence the homebuilder must demonstrate through flight testing that his bird won't flutter at any airspeed normally flown, and up to 10 percent above the redline speed.

A similar, and frequently more tedious, flight test chore is running airspeed calibrations, which involves flying over a measured distance through the normal speed range, in opposite directions to eliminate wind effect. You can use a stopwatch and fly over section lines of known distance separation, normally a quarter-mile apart, or use a more precise speed trap if one is available.

USAF Colonel Dale Anderson (Ret.), codeveloper of the Spencer amphibian *Air Car* homebuilt with designer P. H. Spencer, checks his airspeed to critical values by flying over a carefully measured one-mile course along the outer breakwater in Long Beach, California.

You can do the same thing between two VOR stations, for example, providing you know the precise distance in either statute or nautical miles. Using statute miles, Colonel Anderson computed one cruise-power airspeed by flying the 19.7 statute miles between Van Nuys and Los Angeles VORs, in both directions, timing each run with a stopwatch. The southward run took 575 seconds, the northward run 484 seconds. The average speed was computed at 134.94 mph, using the formula:

$$\frac{5,280 \times 19.7 \times 3,600 \text{ (seconds)}}{5,280 \times 575} = 123.34 \text{ mph (south)}$$

and

$$\frac{5,280 \times 19.7 \times 3,600 \text{ (seconds)}}{5,280 \times 484} = 146.53 \text{ mph (north)}.$$

In the above formulas the speeds in miles per hour are computed by converting statute miles to feet (5,280) and one hour to seconds (60 minutes x 60 seconds).

The test flight, of course, isn't finished until after you've landed, rolled out, and taxied back to the barn for congratulations or tales of woe. Prior to landing, run through a series of landing stalls at altitude to determine your best approach speed. If you're flying into a rather short field, use the formula 1.3 x V_{so} (1.3 x stall speed) = approach speed on final approach. Thus, if your bird stalls at an indicated 50 mph, multiply 50 x 1.3 = 65 mph indicated airspeed on final. That provides a safe margin above the stall, though not enough to cause an overshoot. On final approach, incidentally, "eyeball" your glide terminus and hold to an imaginary glide slope with throttle changes, being careful not to change to nose attitude, and you'll find you can make a perfect short-field landing every time.

There's a good reason for this. In an airplane, unlike an automobile, the throttle is not your basic speed control—it's your altitude control, whether in level flight or in climbing or descending. Your proper speed control is your elevator, which regulates the airplane's pitch attitude. Thus holding the pitch steady on final guarantees a steady airspeed, and minor throttle changes will overcome glide-path variations due to updrafts and downdrafts.

There's much, much more to flight testing a homebuilt and, as in any new machine, caution is the byword until you are thoroughly familiar with your aircraft's habits. The day will finally come when you've flown off the hours required by the FAA before you can leave your test flight area, and the sky is yours. Then go enjoy it!

8
THOSE MARVELOUS MONOPLANES
*Single-Wingers Have
Lots to Offer*

A persistent argument among homebuilders is whether an aircraft designed for pleasure flying should have one set of wings or two. If God had intended his aerial critters to have two sets of wings, he'd have given them two sets of wings, say the monoplane lovers, who sometimes are referred to as mono*maniacs*. Instead, they point out to the bipe types, God designed the soaring hawks, the fighting eagles, the hurrying hummingbirds with single wings, and when man challenged the sky he naturally imitated the God-given design of his feathered friends.

Admittedly, the Wright brothers' *Kitty Hawk* was a biplane, patterned after Octave Chanute's trussed-wing hang glider, but six decades before that William Henson and John Stringfellow were successfully flying graceful model monoplanes powered with steam engines in England.

The influence of the Wrights lasted nearly a quarter of a century—despite a few monos like the Bleriot *Model XI* and Santos-Dumont's delightful *Demoiselle*—with the result that the skies over Verdun belonged to the bipes. Between the two world wars, sport planes, by and large, carried two sets of wings if they were intended for aerobatic flight; you could build an airplane stronger that way.

Today modern construction techniques, materials, and design refinements have brought back the monoplane as the favored shape for the greatest percentage of homebuilts, as well as commercial aircraft. In another chapter we'll examine what has happened to the biplanes, but for now, rather than trying to figure out a brand-new monoplane design, let's look at a number of successful single-wing amateur-built aircraft and see what they have to offer.

Aside from carryovers from the prewar years, like the Corben *Baby Ace* and the Pietenpol *Parasol* monos, the homebuilt mono with greatest historical interest is probably Peter M. Bowers's wooden *Fly Baby,* which took to the skies in 1960 and two years later won the EAA design contest as the best homebuilt then flying.

Although you can hang extra wings on *Fly Baby* and turn it into a biplane, it really set its fine track record as an easy-to-build, easy-to-fly, and inexpensive folding-wing mono bird that can be trailed home from the airport when the day's flying is done. Well over a hundred *Fly Baby*s are airborne today, and Bowers himself has flown a third of these.

Fly Baby uses push-rod aileron controls because each wing system is separate, and they are therefore easier to disconnect for folding back preparatory to trailering. You can use standard aircraft components in construction, such as engine mounts, cowlings, fuel tanks, and even complete undercarriages, so long as you build 51 percent of the

Fly Baby in 1962. Right wing is folded, with the tip resting on the stabilizer. The wing hinge is entirely separate from the wing spar fittings, eliminating the need for critical machining of complicated fittings. One person can fold the wings in about 15 minutes.

aircraft yourself, as already noted, to retain your standing as an amateur aircraft builder.

One of the few homebuilts that can haul a pair of floats through the sky, *Fly Baby* makes a nice seaplane. This single-seat ultralight job may look a bit old-fashioned, but it performs well, with a 120-mph maximum speed behind an 85-horsepower engine. It'll cruise at 105 to 110 mph, climb at 1,100 feet per minute, and range 320 miles—not bad for a wooden wonder that weighs only 605 pounds empty!

Among the simpler-to-build monos is Bud Evans's single-seater, wooden homebuilt, the *VP-1,* and its two-place sister, the *VP-2,* the result of a designer's efforts to come up with the ultimate in simplicity and safety. A former Convair design engineer, Evans avoided compound curves and other tricky problem areas. The *VP*'s wings are built around two spruce spars that are simply straight boards with no tapering, beveling, or box construction involved, being only 12 feet long and easy to handle.

The *VP*'s fuselage is essentially built up of three simple bulkheads, four longerons, flat plywood skin, and some vertical stiffeners, and it can be put together on a flat table, like a model plane. The ailerons hinge directly to the rear spar with simple eyebolts, and while the wide chord of the controls makes them a little heavy, in flight they're solid. Wingtips are simply the outboard ribs, and the only wing fittings are four flat plates at the roots and some drag-wire straps and aluminum bushings pressed into the spars for flying strut attachment. The engine, of course, is the simplest available—the ubiquitous Volkswagen, and you can operate the 2,100-cc version for only two dollars an hour.

Two-place *VP-2.*

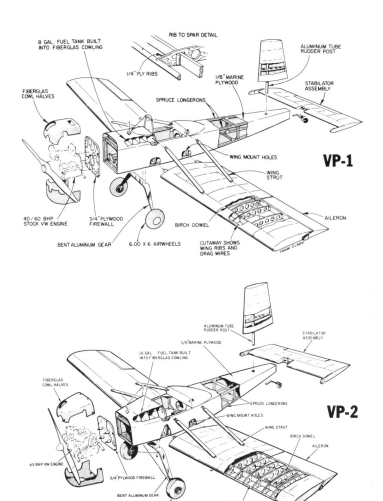

Construction detail for *VP-1* and *VP-2*. (*Courtesy of W. S. Evans*)

Among other interesting homebuilts powered with Volkswagen engines, perhaps the most unusual I've had the pleasure of flying was the *Draggin' Fly,* which Ron Wier of Ramona, California, "eyeballed" after the Ramsey *Flying Bathtub.* A real funster.

Perhaps one of the simplest VW-powered homebuilts is Don Stewart's *Headwind,* which first flew on March 28, 1961—the birthday of Elizabeth Stewart, his patient wife.

Dick and Dona Stimson assemble their *Teenie Two* in 15 minutes.

Top: Teenie Two is almost assembled. *Bottom:* Dick Stimson wings aloft.

Similar to the old Aeronca *C-2 Bathtub,* the *Headwind* has been modified as the *Headwind B,* with wooden instead of aluminum ribs for easier construction, a higher-lift airfoil (NACA 4412 instead of NACA 2412), a wider span (24 feet 6 inches), rubber doughnut–type shocks, and a 36-horsepower VW engine with a reduction gear of his own design. Called the Maximizer, it permits the engine to turn at an efficient 3,600 rpm to the propeller's 2,200 rpm.

On its first flight, incidentally, the *Headwind* "felt so good I just took off and kept right on flying," says Stewart.

One of the most exciting all-metal, VW-powered, ultralight home-builts (310 pounds empty weight) is Cal Parker's *Teenie Two,* which Navy Lieutenant James E. Fausz, who test flew it, called "a joy to fly" as an aerobatic aircraft. "Hammerhead stalls were invented for the *Teenie Two,*" he says.

Teenie Two is not to be confused with an earlier model, *Jeanie's Teenie,* introduced on the cover of *Popular Mechanics* magazine in 1969 as a VW-powered, all-metal plane a beginner could build—with over-the-counter parts and hand tools—for under $1,000.

More than 7,000 sets of plans were sold for the earlier model, but, unfortunately, says designer Cal Parker, many incorporated modifications that hurt performance and added unnecessary weight.

Ken Rand makes a fast takeoff in his *KR-1.*

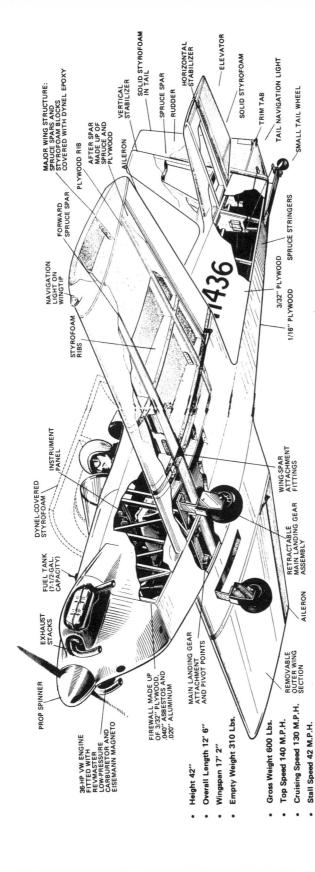

PROP SPINNER

EXHAUST
STACKS

36-HP VW ENGINE
FITTED WITH
REVMASTER
LOW-PRESSURE
CARBURETOR AND
EISEMANN MAGNETO

FUEL TANK
(7-1/2-GAL.
CAPACITY)

FIREWALL MADE UP
OF 3/32" PLYWOOD,
.040" ASBESTOS AND
.020" ALUMINUM

INSTRUMENT
PANEL

DYNEL-COVERED
STYROFOAM

NAVIGATION
LIGHT ON
WINGTIP

STYROFOAM
RIBS

MAIN LANDING GEAR
ATTACHMENT
AND PIVOT POINTS

REMOVABLE
OUTER WING
SECTION

AILERON

RETRACTABLE
MAIN LANDING GEAR
ASSEMBLY

WING-SPAR
ATTACHMENT
FITTINGS

1/16" PLYWOOD

3/32" PLYWOOD

SPRUCE STRINGERS

FORWARD
SPRUCE SPAR

PLYWOOD RIB

MAJOR WING STRUCTURE:
SPRUCE SPARS AND
STYROFOAM BLOCKS
COVERED WITH DYNEL EPOXY

AFTER SPAR
MADE UP OF
SPRUCE AND
PLYWOOD

AILERON

VERTICAL
STABILIZER

SOLID STYROFOAM
IN TAIL

SPRUCE SPAR

RUDDER

HORIZONTAL
STABILIZER

ELEVATOR

SOLID STYROFOAM

TRIM TAB

TAIL NAVIGATION LIGHT

SMALL TAIL WHEEL

- Height 42''
- Overall Length 12' 6''
- Wingspan 17' 2''
- Empty Weight 310 Lbs.

- Gross Weight 600 Lbs.
- Top Speed 140 M.P.H.
- Cruising Speed 130 M.P.H.
- Stall Speed 42 M.P.H.
- Range 750 Miles

Detailed specifications and plan of the *KR-1*. (*Courtesy of Ken Rand*)

"The only thing in common with the *Jeanie's Teenie* and the *Teenie Two* is the method of construction," says Parker, who has a two-place version of the latter on the drawing boards.

Flying behind a 1,500-cc VW engine of 53 horsepower, *Teenie Two* can cruise at 110 mph, burning only two and a half gallons an hour—44 miles to the gallon. One *JT-2,* built by Richard Stimson, Jr., of Los Angeles, carries a bigger VW engine of 1,600 cc and 65 horsepower, a direct-drive Ted Barker conversion that cruises at 115 mph.

Another VW-powered homebuilt design of note is Ken Rand's *KR-1,* which I found a delight to fly, very responsive on the controls, with a fast roll rate, a high cruise, and good short-field performance characteristics. Ken has sold more than 3,000 sets of plans, and so far at least two dozen are flying, from Alaska to California and Florida. I recently saw four *KR-1*s under construction in one shop, at the Northrop Institute of Technology in California.

You get the feeling that Ken Rand is just a boy airplane modeler who never grew up—the *KR-1* is tiny, with a 17-foot wingspan, and weighs only 340 pounds empty. It is built largely of wood and styrofoam, which makes compound curves easy to fashion. In 1973 the

The *RV-3* in flight.

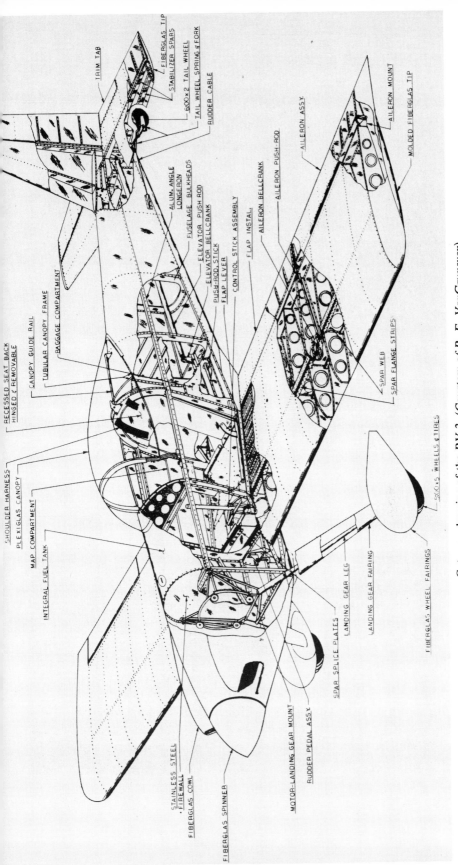

Cutaway drawing of the *RV-3*. (*Courtesy of R. E. VanGrunsven*)

TRIM TAB

FIBERGLAS TIP

STABILIZER SPARS

500×2 TAIL WHEEL

TAIL WHEEL SPRING & FORK

RUDDER CABLE

AILERON MOUNT

AILERON ASS'Y.

MOLDED FIBERGLAS TIP

ALUM. ANGLE LONGERON

FUSELAGE BULKHEADS

ELEVATOR PUSH ROD

ELEVATOR BELLCRANK

PUSH-ROD, STICK

FLAP LEVER

CONTROL STICK ASSEMBLY

FLAP INSTAL.

AILERON BELLCRANK

AILERON PUSH-ROD

RECESSED SEAT BACK HINGED & REMOVABLE

CANOPY GUIDE RAIL

TUBULAR CANOPY FRAME

BAGGAGE COMPARTMENT

SPAR WEB

SPAR FLANGE STRIPS

SHOULDER HARNESS

PLEXIGLAS CANOPY

MAP COMPARTMENT

INTEGRAL FUEL TANK

500×5 WHEELS & TIRES

LANDING GEAR LEG

LANDING GEAR FAIRING

FIBERGLAS WHEEL FAIRINGS

STAINLESS STEEL FIREWALL

FIBERGLAS COWL

FIBERGLAS SPINNER

MOTOR-LANDING GEAR MOUNT

RUDDER PEDAL ASS'Y.

SPAR SPLICE PLATES

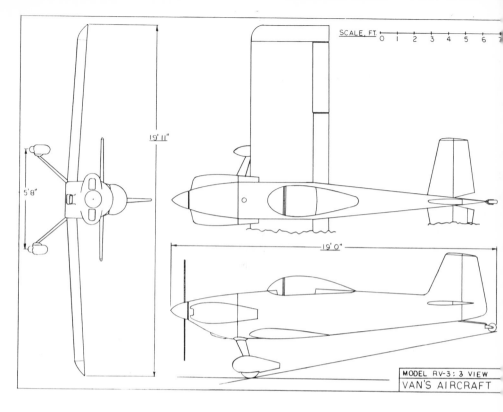

SCALE, FT.
0 1 2 3 4 5 6

19' 11"

5' 8"

19' 0"

MODEL RV-3: 3 VIEW
VAN'S AIRCRAFT

Cutaway drawing of the *RV-3*. (*Courtesy of R. E. Van Grunsven*)

KR-1 won second place in the EAA's Pazmany efficiency contest, with a fantastic speed range, from a slow-flight speed of 46.8 mph to a high-speed run at 140.8 mph, a tribute to its clean design. The gear is retractable and a two-place *KR-2* is now flying.

If the *KR-1* is outstanding, the homebuilt that won first place in the 1973 EAA Pazmany efficiency contest was in many ways still better— Richard VanGrunsven's *RV-3,* an all-metal, high-speed, aerobatic, single-placer that offers just about everything you could want—excellent range (600 miles) and fuel economy (26 miles per gallon), a good payload (355 pounds), and fine short-field capability. VanGrunsven flies from a 670-foot private airstrip in Forest Grove, Oregon, and uses only half the runway.

The *RV-3*'s engine is a Lycoming 0-290G of 125 horsepower, and her lines are so clean she'll cruise at 170 mph, with a top speed of 195 mph. I found her easy to handle, with a fast roll rate (170 degrees per second), yet stable and easy to land for a taildragger, her length (19 feet) being almost equal to her span (19 feet 11 inches). Square wingtips allow maximum trailing edge span for fast climb (1,900 feet per minute), and the bubble canopy offers excellent all-around vision.

If wide-angle vision is what you want, why not eliminate the fuselage altogether and ride out in the open, on the front spar of a *RLU-1 Breezy?* It consists of a wing, an engine, a tail, and a funny framework to sit on.

Kids yell, "Hey, Mister, where's the rest of your plane?" Others gasp, "Gosh, was anybody hurt?" It does sort of resemble a basket case, but it's fun to fly.

Breezy was born of a back-of-an-envelope design by three corporate pilots whose initials form RLU—Charley Roloff, Bob Liposky, and Carl Unger, of Chicago. Tired of being jet jocks, they wanted a funny puddle-jumper in which to blow off steam. They scrounged the wing from a wrecked Piper *PA-12 Super Cruiser,* got out their welding equipment, and built what has become an increasingly popular home-built design. Using a 90-horsepower engine, the *RLU-1* cruises at 75 mph and stalls at 30 mph, and the greatest fun is to fly low and slow over the countryside, chasing hawks and waving at pretty girls, who will sometimes jump aboard for a ride, if you land in a convenient hayfield.

There are other fun, low-and-slow homebuilts to consider. Take Robert Barrows's little parasol monoplane, the *Grasshopper,* which

For a ride out in the open you can't beat the *RLU-1 Breezy.*

Robert Barrows's parasol monoplane, the *Grasshopper.*

he uses exclusively to visit farmer friends up and down the Mohawk Valley near his home in Frankfort, New York. Or Bob Hovey's *Whing-Ding,* an open-air bipe that weighs only 118 pounds and actually gets off the ground with a 15-horsepower McCullough chainsaw engine.

USN Commander John C. Powell of Middletown, Rhode Island, worked up a design for a two-holer parasol monoplane, *Acey Deucy,* that first flew in June 1970 and attracted so much attention that he worked up a set of plans and has sold more than 60 sets. *Acey Deucy* is of standard construction with steel tubing fuselage and tail, and a fabric-covered, spruce spar wing. It carries a Continental A-65, weighs 750 pounds empty, and cruises at 87 mph on 75 percent power. It lands at 27 mph with two on board, 25 mph solo. Commander Powell had flown *Acey Deucy* more than 300 hours at this writing.

Another intriguing little taildragger is *Woody's Pusher,* the design of Harris L. Woods of Aerosport, Inc., Holly Springs, North Carolina. A tandem two-holer, *Woody's Pusher* is meant to be a fun airplane that can cruise along at 85 mph behind a 65- or 75-horsepower engine, mounted on a pylon behind the parasol wing. Aerosport offers two other little homebuilts, called the *Rail* and the *Quail,* both of which weigh under 500 pounds.

Ace Aircraft Company in Asheville, North Carolina, sells plans for both the Corben *Baby Ace* and another ultralight homebuilt, the *Ace Scooter,* which it says can be built for under $600 (plus engine and instruments) in about 450 hours. Designed by Ken Flaglor, *Scooter* carries a 1,500-cc VW engine, tractor-mounted with the thrust line

From Forest Grove in the rolling hills of Oregon comes the *Mini-Coupe*. (Copyright © *1975 Mather Corporation*)

just above the wing. It gets off the ground in 250 feet, climbs 550 feet per minute, and flies like crazy at about 70 miles an hour, on a good day, which is every day for *Scooter* lovers.

From Forest Grove, Oregon, home port of the versatile *RV-3*, comes another noteworthy homebuilt, designed strictly as a beginner's airplane, both in ease of construction and ease of flying. The designer of the *Mini-Coupe* is Bill Johnson. His tough little bird has lines reminiscent of Fred E. Weick's supersafe *Ercoupe*, tricycle gear, twin rudders, and all.

Mini-Coupe's wing is a modified Cark Y, with good stall characteristics. Boasting a 1,600-cc VW engine, it has an excellent cross-country cruise speed of 90 mph, similar to a Cessna 140. *Mini-Coupe* construction kits come with most parts prebent, and all milling and machining already done. It takes about 350 hours to put one together, using mostly pop rivets. And it's a fine short-field ship.

At Charlottesville, Virginia, the old Mooney Mite Aircraft Company has been revived and is turning out plans for a modernized *M-18 Mite*, which Al Mooney designed back in 1947, and which topped out at 120 mph with a Continental A65-8, almost 2 miles per horsepower. The new *Mite* does even better—a redline speed

89

of 143 mph, 114-mph cruise speed, 43-mph stall, 600-mile range, with a Lycoming 0-145-B2 engine. Gear is manually retractable, and it takes off in 300 feet and gets 40 miles per gallon. What more could you ask?

Some homebuilders just like to be different. Richard Jameson, a West Coast aerospace engineer, is one of these folks—hence his pretty metal monoplane, the *Gypsy Hawk,* alias the *Red Brick,* is outstanding. His low-wing homebuilt has tricycle gear, an ample canopy over a roomy cockpit, a sleek look. *Gypsy Hawk* weighs 520 pounds empty, grosses 820 pounds, including 20 gallons of fuel in tip tanks. With a Continental A-65 engine, it cruises at 115 mph, but with a small wing area (63 square feet) it does not glide at all like a high-performance sailplane. "She sinks real fine," Jameson admits gallantly. "That's why I call her the *Red Brick.*"

A look-alike is Bill Warwick's fine little *Bantam W-3,* which carries a Lycoming 0-145 and will cruise at 115 mph with a bubble canopy. *Bantam* is all metal and riveted, except for the vertical fin, horizontal stabilizer, and the wingtips, which are fiberglass. The basic aircraft can be built for about $1,200, Warwick says.

Richard Jameson's metal monoplane, the *Gypsy Hawk.*

9
FASTER, HIGHER, FARTHER
How to Improve
Your Performance

As in the past, design breakthroughs, resulting from unfettered thinking and conceptual originality, are the hallmark of the backyard inventor who is not content to sit by and let the big commercial plane makers and the military decide which way he should go in aeronautical development.

Remember Benny Howard's funny-looking biplane, *Mister Mulligan,* which beat the best of the breed in the old Bendix Race days? And Matty Laird's *Super Solution,* which Jimmy Doolittle flew so well?

You'll find their counterparts today in modern minijets that scream around the sky at better than 300 mph, and a host of other homebuilt monoplanes that offer exciting new adventures in sport flying. Some are creations of qualified aeronautical engineers with considerable background and experience, while others are the product of hard work and creative thinking on the part of ordinary do-it-yourself enthusiasts.

The aircraft you hear about the most is, of course, Jim Bede's *BD-5J,* a bullet-shaped little homebuilt jet that has already nudged 385 mph in a dive, has a maximum sea level speed of 332 mph, can climb at 2,400 feet per minute, yet stalls down around 60 mph, with flaps down.

Bede first made aviation news when he designed what is now in production as the Grumman American Trainer, originally called the *BD-1.* For a while Bede played with the idea of a nonstop globe-

Jim Bede's *BD-2* powered sailplane.

The *BD-6* high-wing single-seater.

girdling flight in a powered sailplane, the *BD-2,* before he cracked the homebuilt market with the *BD-4,* a two- or four-place, high-wing, tricycle-gear metal aircraft that topped out at 183 mph with a 180-horsepower Lycoming. Later on he developed another small, orthodox, high-wing single-seater, the *BD-6,* a little fellow with a Hirth two-cycle engine of 55 to 70 horsepower that could cruise along at 140 mph.

But it was the *BD-5 Micro* that made the big news at Newton, Kansas. This little wonder ship, using the same Hirth snowmobile engine and a tiny pusher prop, could get its gear up and go at better than 200 mph full bore, or 190 mph on 65 percent power.

Switching power plants to a Microturbo TRS-18 single-spool turbo-jet of 200 pounds thrust and 66 pounds weight, the souped-up *BD-5J* (*J* for jet) seemed to be the ultimate small homebuilt, complete with automatic electrical fuel control system and miniaturized avionics that make it an all-weather ship—legally, that is. Stressed to ultimate load factors of $\pm$ 9 Gs, the *BD-5J* is highly aerobatic.

Still newer are two other fasties certain to gain a good following—the shrouded-propeller *JM-2* of Miller Aviation, Inc., Marble Falls, Texas, and the sophisticated *EOS/001* of Airmotive Engineers, Inc., Pontiac, Michigan.

Jim Bede's *BD-5 Micro. (Courtesy Bede Aircraft, Inc.)*

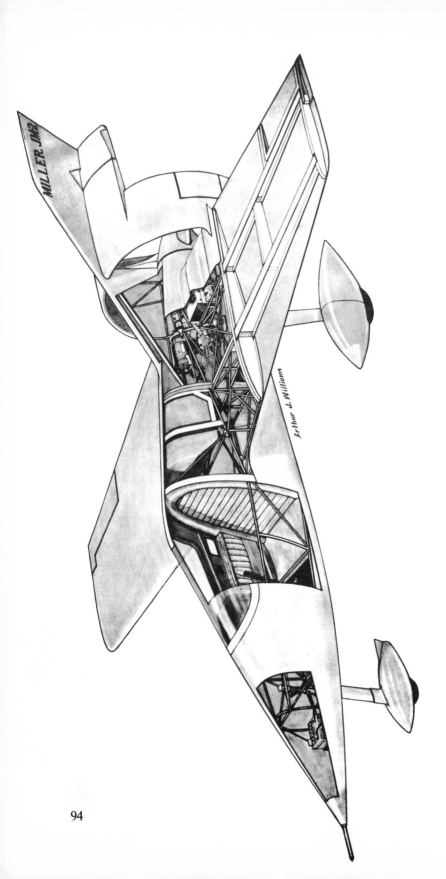

Cutout side view of Miller Aviation's *JM-2* sport plane racer. (*Courtesy of J. W. Miller Aviation, Inc.*)

MILLER JM2

Arthur J. Williams

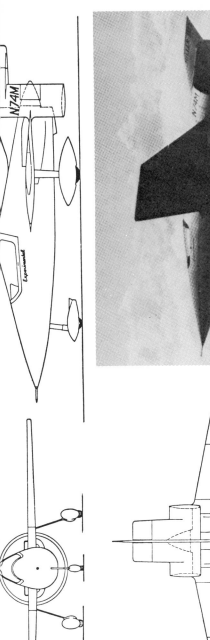

SPECIFICATIONS:
MANUFACTURER   J.W. MILLER AVIATION INC.
MODEL NO.   JM-2
LENGTH   19'-0"
SPAN   15'-0"
WING AREA   66 SQ. FT.
EMPTY WEIGHT   630 LBS.
ENGINE   CONTINENTAL O-200-B
PROP.   FIXED PITCH, 4 BLADE

J. W. Miller Aviation Inc.
Horseshoe Bay Airport
Route 3, Box 757
Marble Falls, Texas 78654
Tel. (512) 341-6101, (512) 598-2556

Detailed specifications and photo of
the JM-2. (Courtesy of J. W. Miller
Aviation, Inc.)

The *JM-2*, powered with the 100-horsepower Continental 0-200B engine, qualifies as a Formula One racer and in the future may revolutionize the action in close-course circuit events, for it has a top speed of 235 mph and a redline speed of 275 mph. A novel feature of the *JM-2* is its shrouded pusher propeller, with control surfaces actually a part of the duct, which blends into the tail of the airplane. The shroud doubles as a safety fence and noise suppressor, but its main purpose is to increase propeller efficiency by reducing tip vortex energy loss.

Weighing 600 pounds empty, the little single-seater, designed by J. M. Miller, has a wingspan of only 15 feet, wing area of 66 square feet, and wing loading of 15 pounds per square foot. Using a molded plastic skin over a metal framework for extra strength, the *JM-2* is a new-generation homebuilt that already has won its certificate of airworthiness and has flown off its 75-hour FAA restrictions. Kits and plans are available.

At the time this book went to press, the new *EOS/001* was completing taxi tests prior to launching a flight test program to place it alongside the *BD-5* and the *JM-2* as second-generation, high-speed homebuilts. In the *EOS/001* the pilot sits reclining to offer less frontal area. Says Rod Summers of Airmotive Engineers:

"*EOS/001* was conceived with the knowledge that sophistication and efficiency need not mean complication. *EOS/001* is not intended to be the simplest aircraft to construct; it is a balance of maximum design efficiency and minimum complication. Kits are available consisting of all extrusions and formed parts, and the use of custom wing spar extrusions provides the strength for one of the highest aspect ratios on a normally powered aircraft, offering superior L/D characteristics."

Weighing 420 pounds empty, *EOS/001* is expected to reach a maximum speed of 187 mph with an engine of only 55 horsepower, or 208 mph with a 70-horsepower engine. Cruising at 155 mph on 75 percent power, and burning 5.5 gallons per hour, its 20-gallon tank should give it a 3-hour range, or 465 miles, plus reserve.

One need not turn to such second-generation homebuilts for excellent performance, however. There are a good number of designs already flying with higher, farther, faster performance figures showing up all the time. This modern trend in high-performance homebuilts rightfully began with introduction of Steve Wittman's *Tailwind* in 1953.

Wittman, famous in air racing circles for the amazing performance of his square-winged little *Bonzo*, got the notion of putting all his racing ken into a homebuilt. He wanted to give pilots a simple, fast, economical cross-country plane, one that could carry two people and 60 pounds of baggage, but still perform like a lady at the low end of the speed spectrum.

"There we were, back in the 1950s, getting 220 and 230 miles an hour from the little Goodyear racers, which were limited to 190-cubic-inch engines," he explained. "I felt that with this kind of speed I could easily get excellent performance in a two-place job. An extra passenger would slow me down some, but not too much."

The best homebuilts were cruising around 110 mph at that time, and with that speed for a target he sketched the design for his *Tailwind*, which he felt could easily cruise at 150 mph.

"I was knocking 75 mph off *Bonzo*'s top speed, trading off 75 mph for a second seat," he said. "That was about as fast as most four-place ships were then flying."

What evolved was a two-place, side-by-side, light cabin aircraft with a high, squared-off wing, skinny little Wittman-patented landing legs (which Cessna Aircraft adopted for its 120/140 and 170 series), and room up front for an engine of anywhere from 85 to 160 horsepower. It was called the *W-8* (Steve's eighth design), and in more than two decades of flying it hasn't changed much.

For some years it stood absolutely alone in its class for high cruise speed (160 mph with 125 horsepower) and ease of aerobatic handling, although basically it was a utility aircraft. Not until John Thorp came along with his low-wing *T-18* could any two-place homebuilt match the *W-8*'s performance. "Thorp told me he'd simply designed a *Tailwind* upside down," Wittman says impishly.

John Thorp's fine *T-18*, one of the best homebuilt designs ever created, actually was the end result of many years of aeronautical engineering experience, and Thorp says it was a "sort of rebound from the Wing *Derringer*," much of which he designed.

"The *Derringer* simply had to be perfect," he explained. "I'd done design work on a number of other aircraft, like the Fletchers, the Piper Cherokee, the Lockheed *Big Dipper* and *Little Dipper*. After leaving Fletcher in 1955 I wanted to design something fine for general aviation. After all, I've spent most of my life dedicated to that goal."

In 1946 Thorp first flew his side-by-side *Sky Skooter*, which was more or less the prototype for the Piper Cherokee design. An all-metal bird with single-spar wings covered with corrugated metal skin, it was safe but slow. All it could do with a 200-horsepower engine was 120 mph in cruise mode. So back he went to the drawing board, and by 1961 Thorp knew he had what he wanted. A dream ship on paper, but he needed a prototype.

Along came Bill Warwick, an expert race pilot and constructor, who spent the next three years assembling the first *T-18,* which flew on May 23, 1964, with a huge tiger painted along the side.

"It looked like something right out of Disneyland," says Thorp.

Much of the magic of the *T-18*'s amazing performance lies in its laminar flow wing—the NASA 64_1-412 curve. Thorp's own *T-18,* which he spent nine years building, carries a 180-horsepower Lycoming engine and cruises at 168 mph indicated airspeed at 10,000 feet, on only 60 percent power. At full bore it will exceed 200 mph.

Flying with John Thorp, I found his *T-18* extremely agile, climbing skyward at 1,700 feet per minute on only 60 percent power at 130 mph IAS. It flew gracefully through wingovers, and in stalls it broke clean and sharp. Recovery was simple—just let go.

Ninety-four *T-18*s were already flying when I interviewed Thorp recently. Early in its history the *T-18* developed a flutter in its flying tail,

Prototype Thorp *T-18* built by Bill Warwick.

Designer John Thorp with a *Sky Skooter*. Piper Aircraft Company later assigned him to develop it into a four-place family plane, which became the Piper Cherokee.

but the problem was solved by a rigid, thorough, fully instrumented evaluation program that resulted in a complete tail redesign. Unlike the *Sky Skooter,* conceived as a foolproof sport plane, the *T-18* design offers maximum performance in speed, range, and maneuverability, plus comfort.

Another popular, high-performance homebuilt is the *Midget Mustang* and its two-seat sister ship, the *Mustang II,* which has an interesting history. The *Midget Mustang* was the creation of Dave Long, former chief engineer for Piper Aircraft, who designed it as a sort of scaled-down *P-51.* Both ships use the NACA 64212 airfoil, a laminar flow wing of the same family that gave the *P-51* its amazing speed advantage over enemy fighters in World War II aerial combat.

More than 1,100 sets of *Midget Mustang* plans have been sold, and perhaps a hundred finished versions are now flying. When Long was killed in a flight test accident in 1951, Bob Bushby of Glenview, Illinois, bought the rights to the plans from Long's widow. When he designed the *Mustang II*, it became a completely new airplane, with the wings the only interchangeable parts. The first *Mustang II* flew in 1966. Bushby favors using the 150-horsepower Lycoming 0-320 over the 160-horsepower 0-320-B because he considers that it is more reliable, uses lower octane fuel, and offers longer life between overhauls.

No jigs are required to build the *Mustang II*, which comes in two versions, the deluxe and the sport, the former stressed to 6 Gs and the latter to 9 Gs for aerobatic flying. All you need to build it, in addition to the usual hand tools, are a rivet gun and accessories, sheet metal cleco fasteners, tin snips, an air compressor, and the use of an 8-foot sheet metal bending brake.

Ed Nilson's *Mustang II*.

Ed Nilson of Vista, California, put his whole family to work building a *Mustang II* and they completed the job in exactly one year, one month, one day. His wife and daughter and two sons took turns bucking rivets and drilling holes and deburring things, and now they take turns joyriding with Ed. With a 150-horsepower Lycoming, their *Mustang II* cruises at 175 mph, and at gross weight (1,500 pounds) climbs at better than 1,500 feet per minute. The plane's range is in excess of 500 miles. Flying with Nilson, I found the visibility excellent—he'd installed a *T-18* canopy that offered extra headroom.

Insofar as wing style is concerned, low-wing designs predominate among the more recent homebuilt monoplanes. Three exceptions should be noted here, however—one mid-wing and two high-wing designs that are catching on in popularity because of excellent performance, low cost, and relative ease of construction.

The mid-wing *Stephens Akro*, designed by the late Ed Allenbaugh, is a highly aerobatic sport plane, an improved and one-third-larger-scale version of Art Scholl's former racer, *Miss San Bernardino,* with parts and plans available from Stephens Akro in Rubidoux, California. Scholl considers the design outstanding in aerodynamic efficiency, with the mid-wing configuration offering a sleek profile to both parasitic and induced drag. The *Stephens Akro* is of standard steel tube construction, with tapered wooden wings that use the NACA 2301 airfoil. A fine example seen frequently at air shows is one owned by Dean Englehardt.

An excellent, high-wing homebuilt is the *Daphne Model SD-1A*, designed by Art Szaraz of Bedford, Ohio, whose squarish fuselage and Wittman landing gear combine to closely resemble the Wittman *Tailwind* design. Powered with an 85-horsepower Continental, *Daphne* weighs 825 pounds empty, grosses 1,350 pounds, has a top speed of 149 mph, and cruises at 130 mph. Wings are conventional with spruce spars and plywood ribs, fabric covered. A two-place ship, *Daphne* is a good cross-country cruiser and won the 1970 Oshkosh flight efficiency contest with high and low speeds of 138.9 and 48.7 mph.

Where some amateur aircraft builders consider the ultimate homebuilt to be a single-place, highly aerobatic ship in which to get rid of hangups, there are other dedicated family types who enjoy loading up the airplane with the wife and/or kids to head for far horizons. Plane campers and other outdoorsmen have the same requirements in an airplane—something big and roomy, with a good range and cruise speed, plus a slow landing speed for short-field operation. In short, a bush plane, like the commercial *M-5 Maule Rocket*, which costs about $25,000.

The mid-wing *Stephens Akro*.

The *Daphne Model SD-1A.*

For one-third that amount you can build a six-place high-winger of 3,500-pound maximum gross weight that will cruise at 175 mph, range over 700 miles, and land at 63 mph—the new O'Neill *Aristocraft II*, with a remanufactured 350-horsepower Jacobs radial engine. An alternative is a slightly lighter (3,300 pounds) *Aristocraft II* with the 245-horsepower "Jake," which cruises at about 140 mph, lands at 60, and costs only $5,500 to build instead of $8,000.

A family plane has to be strong, reliable, and safe, says designer Terrence O'Neill of Carlyle, Illinois. "Building your own family airplane is a lifetime undertaking, something you'll probably only want to do once." Hence this ship is ruggedly designed around chrome-moly tubing and 2024-TS Alclad aluminum "skin and bones."

The history of the *Aristocraft II* dates back to December 1962 when O'Neill purchased rights to the Waco *Model W Aristocraft.* He began a type certification program for the *Model W Winner,* and subsequently offered plans for an amateur-built version, the *Aristocraft II,* very similar in design.

Initially the *Aristocraft II* appeared with a gross weight of 2,800 pounds for engines under 230 horsepower, then grew by 500 pounds when O'Neill discovered there were lots of old 245-horsepower Jakes around the country.

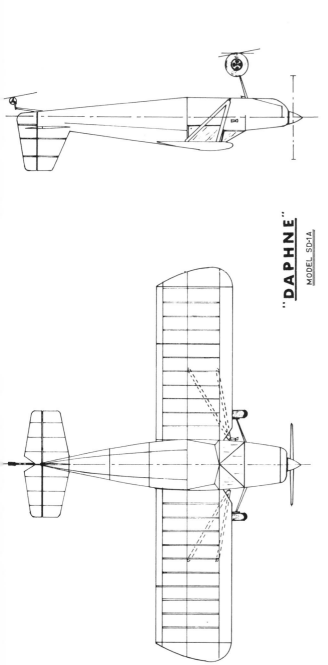

"DAPHNE"
MODEL SD-1A

DESIGNED BY:
ART SZARAZ   EAA 145
419 CENTER RD.
BEDFORD, OHIO
44146

SPECIFICATIONS:

WINGSPAN	26 ft. 3 in.
LENGTH	19 ft. 7 in.
HEIGHT	5 ft. 10 in.
WING AREA	130 sq. ft.
EMPTY WEIGHT	825 lbs.
GROSS WEIGHT	1350 lbs.
TOP SPEED	149 m.p.h.
CRUISE	130 m.p.h.
LANDING SPEED	45 m.p.h.
POWER	85 CONTINENTAL
PROPELLER	METAL 68/54

Detailed specifications of *Daphne Model SD-1A.* (*Courtesy of Art Szaraz*)

"The Jake turns slow," says O'Neill, "and it has lots of torque to twist a large-diameter prop, and this alone should result in a marked increase in takeoff and climb performance."

At press time the flight test program on this version was being completed. Remanufactured Jacobs engines of 245 horsepower are available for approximately $2,000, O'Neill says. The *Aristocraft II* has been provisionally type certificated by the FAA, and the plans include approved flight and maintenance manuals.

Four popular, conventional, low-wing monowing homebuilts of note are, alphabetically, the Cook Aircraft four-place *Challenger*, the single- and two-place Cvjetkovic *CA-61* and *CA-65*, the two-place Davis *DA-2A*, and the two-place tandem Wendt *Traveler*.

The Cook *JC-1 Challenger* has the thoroughly modern lines of a Piper Cherokee, the same engine (Lycoming's 150-horsepower 0-320) as the 1950 *PA-22 Tri-Pacer,* the large tail fin of the *Maule M-5.* Unique design elements include split Handley-Page type leading-edge slats that pop open automatically in a steep climbout. *Challenger* is expected to cost about $12,000 and offer the performance of a store-bought airplane twice as expensive.

This includes a speed range from a 145-mph cruise to a gentle 53-mph stall, which is enhanced by the leading-edge slats and single-slotted flaps. Horizontal tail surface is all-moving, with anti-

Cook Aircraft *JC-1 Challenger.* Note flaps and leading-edge slats.

Anton Cvjetkovic's VW-powered *CA-61 Mini-Ace.*

servo tab adjustable for trim. Gear is ultrawide (10 feet 10 inches) and the cabin is roomy enough for four passengers and 80 pounds of baggage.

Anton Cvjetkovic of Newbury Park, California, had a good thing going with his VW-powered *CA-61 Mini-Ace,* which began as a wooden single-seater with fixed gear and developed into a retractable two-place version of either wood or metal. The *CA-65,* all wood, has a ratchet device for manual gear retraction, and with gear up its tapered wing, streamlined canopy, and aerodynamically clean fairing provide a top speed of 167 mph with a 150-horsepower Lycoming up front. The double-spar wing consists of one piece. It incorporates side-by-side seats, controls, and landing gear mechanism as integral parts. The *CA-61* can be built in less than 1,000 hours, with either a VW or a Continental A-65 engine installed.

For reasons hard to fathom, a good many homebuilt aircraft outperform comparable stock production aircraft powered with identical engines. Part of the explanation for this phenomenon may be found in the lighter construction, but much of it results from careful handicraft and unhurried attention to detail. Consider Leon D. Davis's fine little *DA-2A* side-by-side two-seater, which cruises easily at 120 mph on 85 horsepower, the same engine that pulls the Cessna 140 along at only 100 mph.

Davis had ease of construction in mind when he designed the *DA-2A,* which first flew in 1966. This fine all-metal bird can be built for less than $2,000, and a jump seat can be installed behind the front seats for tiny passengers in place of baggage.

105

Harold Wendt's *Traveler.*

Picture-window view from Wendt *Traveler.*

It features tricycle gear, a butterfly V-tail, flat sides, and a curved top that adds extra lift. The useful load is 500 pounds. Some 200 sets of plans have been sold, and more than a score are flying. One, constructed by Herb Spilker of Ontario, Canada, is outstanding. He built it in seven months, from flat aluminum sheets, with no compound curves. It carries a Continental 0-200A engine of 100 horsepower and cruises at 130 mph.

"Ground handling is a delight," says Spilker. "It steers like a kiddy car!"

Harold Wendt, a professional aerodynamicist of La Mesa, California, started out to build a VW-powered, all-metal, side-by-side two-seater, but switched in midstream when he got an inspiration to cut down the frontal area by building a tandem two-seater. He then decided that wood construction would be much simpler. The result was the Wendt *Traveler*, powered with a Continental A-65 engine uprated to 75 horsepower.

Flying with Wendt, I found the visibility outstanding, with big "picture windows" along each side. The *Traveler* makes a good cross-country cruiser, comfortable and relatively fast—120 mph TAS at 2,450 rpm, with an honest 450-mile range.

It seems that everywhere you look there's a new, modern-looking airplane sliding down the sky on final approach, so it's hard to tell one from another without a program. A good example is the two-place *SA-102 Cavalier*, a sleek, low-wing, wooden homebuilt with Wittman-type spring gear, a gracefully swept tail, and even fuel tip tanks for extended range. *Cavalier* takes any four-cylinder Continental, Lycoming, or Franklin engine in the range of 85 to 135 horsepower and has sometimes appeared as a taildragger. It was designed by Stan McLeod of K & S Aircraft Supply in Calgary, Alberta, Canada. Hundreds of sets of plans have been sold, and more than 200 *Cavalier*s are flying or about to fly. This fine ship cruises at 145 mph, climbs at the rate of 1,000 feet per minute, and gets off the ground in 600 feet, using a 125-horsepower Lycoming.

Eugene Turner, an FAA expert on crash survival, naturally had safety first in mind when he designed a series of homebuilts, both single- and two-place, that use either tricycle or taildragger gear with the nosewheel in back. The wooden *T-40B*, which Turner designed for his personal use, retains the folding-wing concept that makes these craft special. In less than five minutes you can fold back the wings for trailing home.

WENDT "TRAVELER"

Fiberglass Tip

Trim and Anti-Balance Tab

Stabilator

Static Balance Weight

1/16" Mahogany Plywood

Fiberglass Battery Box

1/4" Marine Mahogany Plywood Formers

Longerons 7/8" x 7/8" Spruce

1/2" x 7/8" Frames

1/8" Mahogany Plywood Sides and Bottom

Spruce I-Beam

Ribs 1/4" Fir Marine Plywood

White Pine Leading and Trailing Edges

11 Gal. Fiberglass Fuel Tank-Both Tips

1/16" Mahogany Plywood Torque Box

1/8" Plywood Tension Ties

Steel Tube Turnover Quadrupod

Dural Carrythru Structure

Dual Stick Controls

Wing Attaches with 3 Bolts

Spring Steel Main Gear

3/4" 5-Ply Marine Plywood Firewall

3/32" Mahogany Plywood Back to 37% Chord

5 x 5.00 Wheels

Steerable Nosewheel

Cont. A65, A75, or C85 Engine

Fiberglass Cowl and Spinner

NASA 64₃A-418 Laminar Flow Airfoil

Wendt Aircraft Engineering
9900 Alto Dr.
La Mesa, Ca. 92041

Detailed construction plan for Wendt *WH-1 Traveler*. (*Courtesy of Harold O Wendt*)

108

WENDT WH-1 "TRAVELER"

Wing Span - 30 ft.

Wing Area - 118 sq. ft.

Wing Loading at Full Gross Weight - 11.8 lbs./ sq. ft.

Aspect Ratio - 7.63

Wing Airfoil NASA 64_{3A}-418

Weight Empty - 900 lbs. (incl. starter, alternator and radio)

Useful Load - 500 lbs.

Fuel - 22 gals.

Oil - 4 qts.

Baggage - 50 lbs.

Gross Weight - 1400 lbs.

Engine - Continental A65 to C85

Performance with Cont. A75 and wheel fairings

    Vmax (75 hp) - 131 mph
    Vcruise (2450 rpm) - 123 mph
    Vcruise (2350 rpm) - 115 mph
    Vstall - 65 mph (no flaps)
    Rate of Climb - 750 fpm (one person, S.L., std. day)
    Rate of Climb - 450 fpm (1400 lbs., S.L., std. day)
    Takeoff Distance - 800 ft. (1400 ft. alt., cruise prop)
    Landing Distance - 700 ft.
    Climb Speed - 80-85 mph
    Range - 400+ mi.
    Absolute Ceiling - 17,000 ft. dens. alt. (one person)

Specifications for Wendt *WH-1 Traveler.* (*Courtesy of Harold O. Wendt*)

The wooden Turner *T-40B*.

The original *T-40* cost only $850 to build and exceeded Turner's expectations by topping out at 145 mph on 65 horsepower, with a 128-mph cruise speed. With an 85-horsepower engine it cruised at 145 mph and topped at 170 mph. Grossing 1,050 pounds, the *T-40* won seventeen national awards for design and workmanship. However, Turner saw a need for a two-place version, so he sawed the *T-40* down the middle and widened it for side-by-side seating. Redesignated the *T-40A*, it cruises at 135 mph with two on board.

A redesign of the *T-40A*, after a landing mishap, resulted in a wider wing chord and double-slotted flaps, plus a slight reverse curve to the wing's leading edge that improved performance dramatically. Turner calls it his "droop snoot." These modifications to the *T-40A* resulted in the *T-40B*, an excellent performer.

Flying with Turner, we rotated at 60 mph, climbed initially at 1,400 feet per minute at 80 mph IAS, then settled into a cruise-climb at 800 feet per minute and 110 mph, to keep the 150-horsepower Lycoming from overheating. Flying on 65 percent power (2,450 rpm/20 inches), we indicated 145 mph at 3,000 feet on a standard day. The range is 520 miles at 155 mph, on 75 percent power.

The new *Sportaire*, a two-place, side-by-side, low-wing·homebuilt with tricycle gear and conventional welded steel tube fuselage, fabric and aluminum skinned, is the result of a dozen years of prior service and more than 1,000 prototype flying hours. The original design of Al

Trefethen of Lomita, California, it is now offered by David M. Rogers of Riverside, California.

Powered with a 125-horsepower Lycoming or Franklin, *Sportaire* is built from 260 square feet of detailed drawings that include full-size rib and fittings sketches that can be used as templates. This home-built will cruise at 132 mph, has a top speed of 145 mph, lands at 80 mph. Empty weight is 984 pounds and gross weight is 1,600 pounds. It can be outfitted for night or instrument flight, at the builder's option. Trefethen developed *Sportaire* from his earlier single-seater *Skyhopper* design.

To show there's no lack of imagination in homebuilt designs, consider two unusual designs with triangular-shaped wings—the Dyke *Delta* and Bert Rutan's *Vari-Viggen*. John Dyke of Fairborn, Ohio, developed the Dyke *JD-2 Delta* from remains of an earlier *JD-1* that was destroyed in a hangar fire. An exciting homebuilt that resembles a manta ray and is built largely of steel tubing covered with fiberglass, the *JD-2* flew in the summer of 1966.

Dyke developed the *JD-2* as a four-place ship with manually retractable landing gear and folding wings for towing home. Powered with a 180-horsepower Lycoming, it cruises at 175 mph TAS at 7,500 feet on 75 percent power. Dyke says the low aspect ratio (2.7:1) is the secret of its good performance, plus a light wing loading of 9.7 pounds per square foot.

Even more spectacular-looking is Bert Rutan's delta-shaped *Vari-Viggen*, a two-place tandem homebuilt with its elevator surface up front, as in the first Wright biplane. Rutan, a design engineer with Bede Aircraft in Newton, Kansas, was intrigued with the design of elevator up front (canard) as a student at California State Polytechnic University in 1963 and later as a design specialist at Edwards AFB Flight Test Center in California.

Rather than seeking high-cruise performance, Rutan was interested in perfecting the craft's low-speed handling characteristics. The *Vari-Viggen* is virtually stallproof and will take off, fly, and land with the control stick full back. He kept the homebuilder in mind by designing a flat-sided fuselage and flat-bottomed wing for simplicity of construction; the few compound-curve pieces are fashioned from fiberglass.

With a span of 19 feet and a wing area of 123 square feet, *Vari-Viggen* weighs 1,020 pounds empty. A 150-horsepower Lycoming is rear-mounted, and the elevator control surfaces are front-mounted on

John Dyke's Dyke *JD-2 Delta.*

Bert Rutan's *Vari-Viggen.*

the trailing edge of the canard. Flying with Rutan in *Vari-Viggen* is quite an experience in stallproof maneuvering.

"You can explore your instincts as a fighter pilot with complete safety," he says.

The overseas homebuilt movement has produced a number of fine performers, particularly in France, where the latest entry is Christophe Heintz's *Zenith*, designed to meet these specific requirements:

• An all-metal aircraft, safe, economical, efficient, and easy to build.

• Side-by-side seating with dual controls.

• Electrically operated flaps, powered with an inexpensive automotive power window motor.

• A wing area of 105 square feet, aspect ratio of 5:1, constant-chord wing of simple, cantilevered construction, with a single spar of aluminum alloy.

Zenith can carry engines from 85 to 160 horsepower, has all-moving tail surfaces, is stressed to 9 Gs for aerobatic flight, or 7.5 Gs at normal gross weight of 1,500 pounds. Powered with a stock Continental 0-200 of 100 horsepower, *Zenith* in 1971 won a handicap race at Iverdon, Switzerland, averaging 143 mph from block to block. Heintz recently moved to Ontario, Canada, and sells plans from there.

An earlier European do-it-yourself craft of considerable merit is Roger Druine's *D.31 Turbulent*, a single-place relative of Druine's popular *D.5*, a tandem two-seater. Both are wood. The *D.31* is an excellent performer, so good Rollason Aircraft in England and Flugzeugbau in West Germany put it into production.

Originally designed to be amateur-built, *Turbulent* weighs 342 pounds empty, has 80 square feet of wing area, and carries the smaller VW power plants. The wing uses a box spar with a built-up rear spar, conventional wooden ribs, and plywood-skinned leading edge. It has both leading-edge slats and Friese-type ailerons, which produce a laminar airflow over the wing, affording good control down to the stall at 29 mph.

One pretty *Turbulent* was built by Larry Weishaar of Springfield, Illinois, who won the 1972 Oshkosh EAA award for the most beautiful VW-powered homebuilt. Weishaar's *D.31* has the 1,200-cc VW engine of 33 horsepower, which gives him a cruise speed of 93 mph. *Turbulent* plans are available from Sturgeon Air Ltd. in Edmonton, Alberta, Canada.

Other foreign homebuilt plans are offered by E. Littner of Montreal, Quebec, Canada, including the *C.P. 60 Daimant* and *Super-Daimant, C.P. 80 Cougar, C.P. 328 Super-Emeraude, C.P. 750 Beryl, R.D. 012 Edelweiss* (2-seater), *R.D. 013 Edelweiss* (3-seater), and the *Y.C. 12 Tourbillon*. All have good track records.

10
DOUBLE-DECKERS
ARE A DELIGHT
The Biplanes Have It!

I think it may be because the first airplane I ever flew in was a biplane that double-deckers have a special meaning for me. I was a boy of seven, the ship was a lovely *JN4D Jenny*, and the pilot was a handsome gypsy flyer with a waxed moustache and shiny puttees and a leather helmet. He looked very much like some kind of god.

We took off from a bumpy little grassy meadow in Wheelerville, New York, and in a moment were soaring high over my home at Canada Lake, sweeping through graceful circles while I gazed in wonder at the familiar world I had known, one that never again would look the same from the ground. I saw it from a whole new perspective, one that would determine the course of my life. I had to be a flyer.

There was the sound of the wind through the wires to remember as we glided back to earth, the smell of hot castor oil from the OX-5 engine's smoking exhaust stacks, the giddy sense of being free. The landing was lousy and we almost groundlooped, but I forgave my hero that near mishap. We were back safe and sound, and my love affair with biplanes was forever sealed.

In World War II, I was lucky enough to become a Royal Air Force flight instructor on biplanes, this time rugged and beautiful PT-17A Stearmans, primary trainers that could do anything in the book but were tricky to land, with their narrow-tread gear. Nevertheless, a Stearman was sensitive, responsive, a fine aerobatic ship you could spin upside down or hurtle through outside snap rolls and know it would hold together. All in all, it was a trainer that made fine pilots of cadets who could master its whims.

Today, there are hundreds, maybe thousands of other airmen who feel as I do, and so their choice of a homebuilt design just naturally has to be a biplane. If one set of wings is fine, aren't two better?

The answer is obviously yes, if you rate an airplane's status on the basis of its ability to perform aerobatic maneuvers. In recent world aerobatic competition, biplanes have proved simply unbeatable, particularly when they happened to be designed by a southern gentleman named Curtis H. Pitts. His aerobatic bipes have been winning sky duels with such frequency that nobody questions their leadership as thoroughbreds of competition flying.

Thus there was good reason for Curtis Pitts to come up with the *S-1S*, a homebuilt version of the highly successful Pitts *S-1 Special*, which grew out of his personal dissatisfaction with the limited performance of an old Waco F he once owned as a fixed-base operator in Jacksonville, Florida, early in World War II. Pitts had installed a 90-horsepower Franklin engine with an inverted fuel system of his own design.

The Curtis Pitts *Specials* in flight.

116

Full inverted system allows Bud Hines to remain inverted indefinitely in his 4-aileron Pitts.

"It either worked perfectly or not at all," he remembers, "which eventually contributed to the loss of the aircraft."

A second Pitts *Special* was built in 1946 and was purchased by Betty Skelton, who flew it to fame in air shows all over the world as the famous *Little Stinker.* Over the years Pitts bipes have grown stronger wings, and in 1966 Curtis went to the four-aileron symmetrical airfoil, the extra two ailerons providing a faster roll rate, the symmetrical wing functioning the same way right side up or upside down. By 1972 he'd introduced the popular two-place *S-2A,* but he still had in mind the perfect competition aircraft, and unquestionably the Pitts *Special* was it.

In 1972 the winning U.S. Aerobatic Team that competed in France was all Pitts, and the sleek, low-wing foreign monplanes, like the Russian Yak and the Czechoslovakian Zlin, were hopelessly outclassed. Art Scholl, a team member, explains why the agile and rugged little Pitts bipe stole the show, and why he switched to a Pitts *Special* from his hot monoplane, the *Super Chipmunk*:

"If you can imagine, we fly in a 3,000-foot-long airspace, 3,200 feet high, with a 300-foot bumper underneath and approximately 800 feet wide. So long as we keep the aerobatic routines the way they are, we're going to see only small airplanes like the Pitts fly in competition."

The Pitts *S-1 Special* was so good, in fact, that he sold more than 2,500 sets of plans. Although a two-aileron ship, it can be retrofitted with the four-aileron symmetrical wings. For those who want to build the major portion of a Pitts *Special,* he offers a four-aileron version called the model *S-1C,* which has a modified M-6 airfoil with a wing area of 98.5 square feet. The entire airframe has been modified, with the 180-horsepower Lycoming and a fixed-pitch propeller recommended. Pitts doesn't actually sell plans for the *S-1C.* Instead, for technical and legal reasons, he sells you the right to build one, and after you sign an agreement not to fool around with design changes, you get your detailed drawings.

A Pitts *Special* weighs only 720 pounds empty, or 1,150 pounds gross, cruises at 143 mph, and has a top speed of 147 mph. Its roll rate is fantastic—180 degrees per second—and it travels uphill fully loaded at 2,600 feet per minute. But the real story of the Pitts isn't in statistics but in the sheer delight of flying a sturdy bipe so pretty it makes you want to cry.

There are other beautiful biplanes flying today besides the Pitts, some with the capability to outperform these champions, depending largely on the skill of the pilots flying them. Most, however, are considered "sport" biplanes rather than competition biplanes—weekend fun ships with varying degrees of responsiveness and complexity in construction.

In the fast-growing folklore of homebuilt aircraft, a few outstanding examples have appeared as biplanes that are reliable, exciting, easy to fly, and easy to build. Such a ship is the time-tested Stolp *Starduster Too SA-300,* one of a line of sport planes designed, until recently, by Lou Stolp, and subsequently by Stolp's successor, Jim Osborne, new president of Stolp Starduster Corporation at Flabob Airport in Riverside, California. Osborne's recent contributions have been the hot little *Acroduster Too* and *Acroduster One,* which appeared in that order.

Stolp began this fine procession of planes with *Starduster SA-100,* a little single-seater bipe that can be built for less than $1,800, followed

Pilot-homebuilder Roger Rourke immediately after takeoff in his *Starduster Too.*

Full view of the *Starduster Too.*

The *Acroduster One.*

by a monoplane—the parasol *Starlet*—and the Osborne-designed *V-Star SA-900,* a low-cost, low-power fun biplane. Next came the popular *Starduster Too,* which flies either as a highly aerobatic single-seater or as a two-place weekend funster.

Conceived in 1965, *Starduster Too* has been a runaway best seller on the homebuilt market; close to 200, built from kits or plans, are flying today. The *Starduster Too* was designed to fill a demand for a reasonably sized, two-place, open-cockpit sport plane, rugged enough for the wildest aerobatic flying and powered with either the 180- or 200-horsepower Lycoming 0-360 engine. Some have even bigger power plants.

The *Starduster Too*'s ruggedness comes from its simple and strong construction of 4130 steel tubing and sheet stock in the main structure, with no machined fittings or complicated bends required. The wings are built around spruce spars, the ribs consist of quarter-inch plywood, and the airfoil is a modified M-6 section. Rib plans and drawings of most fittings are full size, which saves much lofting time.

The *Starduster Too* has unique, Osborne-designed, semielliptical wings with four ailerons that give it a swift roll rate. The ailerons are controlled firmly by push-pull torque tubes rather than by control wires. The top ailerons are controlled by metal pushrods attached to the lower ailerons.

Powered with the Lycoming 0-360, the average *Starduster Too* weighs a bit over 1,000 pounds empty and grosses about 1,750 pounds. Its upper wingspan is 24 feet, its lower span 20 feet 6 inches, providing a total wing area of 162 square feet, lightly loaded for good short-field performance.

I have flown two *Starduster Too*s—Mahlon Ward's *N2MW* and Roger Rourke's *N2MR*—and found them to be virtually identical in performance. Both these West Coast gentlemen own their own metal shops, and naturally their craftsmanship in construction was impeccable. The average *Starduster Too* costs approximately $2,500 to build.

The next *'Duster* to come along was the *Acroduster Too SA750,* a scaled-down *Starduster Too* that is fully aerobatic either as a two-place or single-place ship, with the front cockpit sealed and the rear cockpit enclosed in a streamlined canopy. The *SA750* was the idea of a TWA pilot, Morgan Schrack, owner of the first one to fly.

In some ways the *SA750* was too hot to handle for novice pilots, so Osborne came up with a concept for the ultimate aircraft, *Acroduster One*—"the best aerobatic airplane in the world," he says proudly.

When Osborne invited me to fly this beauty, I readily accepted. There it was, the ship I'd always dreamed of flying, with the excitement of the Stearman PT-17A multiplied many times.

I found its roll rate fantastic—240 degrees a second, faster than a Pitts *S-1*. It cruises fast, too—185 mph TAS at 2,400 rpm, 24 inches manifold pressure, and tops out over 200 mph. Osborne retained the lovely elliptical wing shape and added even more maneuverability by designing the four ailerons to move with fore and aft movement of the control stick. With the ailerons in neutral, stick centered, the controls are in trail with the trailing edges of the wings, while pulling the stick back raises all four ailerons slightly, providing more roll control through a normal stall. Pushing the stick forward causes the ailerons to droop slightly, giving better control through an inverted stall maneuver.

Construction of *Acroduster One* is simple and straightforward. Fuselage and tail surfaces are of semimonocoque aluminum construction, the landing gear a single piece of bent-up aluminum, the wings spruce, plywood, and fabric. Osborne offers complete building kits,

The *Acro Sport* double-decker.

with everything included except the engine-propeller power train, and construction time is quite short—the fuselage can actually be assembled in one day by means of pop riveting.

Recognition of the popularity of biplanes is apparent in selection of the *Acro Sport* double-decker by the Experimental Aircraft Association for its Project Schoolflight, an ambitious program to introduce aeronautics in general, and homebuilding techniques in particular, to the youth of America. The *Acro Sport* and other fine school aircraft projects are discussed in another chapter.

Nostalgia for the "good old days" of prewar biplane flying, and a desire to build something small, inexpensive, yet easy to fly, prompted Barney Oldfield of Cleveland, Ohio, to design the *Baby Great Lakes* in the late 1950s. Since then the number of *Baby Great Lakes* builders has grown to more than 500.

Oldfield had for his inspiration a popular biplane that appeared in 1929, the *Great Lakes 2T-1*, which recently has returned to production in Wichita, Kansas. Although a 200-pound 6-footer, Oldfield had the small-boy urge to build a grown-up model airplane in which he could have some fun. He started doodling his design around a practical gross weight of 850 pounds, and figured two wings were better than one to carry the load.

What evolved was a little biplane with a 16-foot upper span and 14-foot lower span, both of a modified M-6 airfoil, the top wing mounted as a parasol. Oldfield admits to much excitement on his first hop, which started off inauspiciously with a groundloop, and ended with a perfect six-minute flight. When he entered it in his logbook, he says, "my hand was shaking so you can hardly recognize my signature. I still can't read it!"

A nice thing about the *Baby Great Lakes* is that you can do all sorts of aerobatic maneuvers with a low-powered engine, such as the Continental A-65, or even a 1,600-cc VW. At first Oldfield intended his bipe to be a one and only, but he got so many requests for plans that ten years later he made them available. One EAA chapter in Fulton, New York, became so intrigued with a *Baby Great Lakes* being built by one member, Dick Lane, that by 1970 a whole squadron of eleven was being built. Owners say the little bipe is quite easy to fly.

Hanging around small-town airports, listening to all the big lies being swapped in sessions of hangar flying, is a favorite homebuilder's Sunday afternoon pastime, like going down to the railroad station to watch the trains come in. What trains?

In these days of Amtrak and international airlines, it's nice to know there's still someplace to go where you can get in a time machine and fly back to yesterday, a time machine with a pair of fabric wings held together with a birdcage maze of wires.

I found such a machine out at Flabob Airport, where I'd gone to fly Jim Osborne's *Acroduster One* and ran into Ed Marquart, who was chinning with another fellow in the airport café.

"I knew a feller had this old Hall-Scott airplane engine," the other fellow was saying to Ed.

"The darned thing would run forward or backward, either way. Well, he busted up his airplane and so he stuck this engine out in the barn and hooked it up to grind wheat. One day she started running

Detail of biplane wings of the *MA-5 Charger* glimpsed in flight.

Close-up view of *MA-5 Charger* with Ed Marquart at the controls.

backward, and before he could get her stopped she'd unground three bushels."

I listened awhile, then wandered with Ed over to his hangar, where he parks a very special homebuilt he designed—the *MA-5 Charger*. It was a beauty to behold, with 24-foot biplane wings, the top swept back to keep the center of pressure over the center of gravity when flown either solo or dual. Up front Ed installed a 125-horsepower Lycoming 0-290, enough for a cruise at 115 mph or to get around the sky in all sorts of aerobatics.

No back-of-the-envelope design, the *Charger* is a masterpiece of flowing lines and power, with elevators both statically and aerodynamically balanced, Friese-type slotted ailerons—everything for easy, graceful flight. *Charger* flies as beautifully as it looks, and plans are available.

Somewhere between the *Charger* and the *Baby Great Lakes* in size stands the popular little Smith *Miniplane,* of which some 300 versions are flying or being built around the country. The *Miniplane*'s top span is only 17 feet, its gross weight is 1,000 pounds. With a 65-horsepower engine it will cruise nicely at 100 mph.

The Smith *Miniplane.*

One quite special *Miniplane* was built by a well-known racing pilot, Don Janson, who has reengined his bipe a number of times, increasing the power from 85 to 125 horses. With the help of John Thorp, Janson designed a special landing gear of 4130 chrome-moly tubing bent into a U shape, nicely faired. He calls it the "bedstead" design. With that and other aerodynamic modifications, Janson has increased his speed to the point where he recently qualified in a sport biplane race at better than 156 mph.

Smaller than the *Miniplane* is a compact little biplane owned by an FAA medical examiner, Dr. Arthur M. Compher, who at 235 pounds weighs almost half as much as his flying machine, *Bitty Bipe.* Designed by a crop duster named Dick Bailey, *Bitty Bipe* weighs 550 pounds empty, has a span of only 16 feet, and carries a 125-horsepower Lycoming that gets it through most aerobatic maneuvers with consummate grace.

Harold G. Biddoulph, a Lockheed engineer, saw a lot of good things in a number of biplanes he studied and decided to put them all together in one wonderful machine. The result was a graceful, easy-flying bipe he calls the Biddoulph *P.T.A.*—for *Pepper Tree Airplane* —in honor of those unsung heroes of the barnstorming era who operated from the nearest shade tree.

Powered with a 125-horsepower Lycoming, it features a wide-tread landing gear for easy handling, staggered wings, and a sliding canopy cover that encloses a roomy cockpit built for two, with side-by-side seating. His total investment was about $2,500.

Cockpit of Dr. Arthur M. Compher's *Bitty Bipe.*

The *Bitty Bipe* in flight.

Another Lockheed engineer, Bob Hovey, went Biddoulph one better and designed his impish little biplane, *Whing-Ding,* to fly with a McCullough 101-A, two-cycle, go-kart engine that weighed only 11 pounds and put out 15 horsepower. Hovey went back to the Wright brothers and borrowed their idea of using wing warping instead of ailerons. The 17-foot wing spars are tiny fellows only 1.5 inches deep, the ribs consisting of three-eighth-inch aluminum tubing, all covered with doped polyester fabric.

Hovey designed the "fuselage" as a 6-inch-wide plywood box filled with urethane; it serves as a motor mount, a mast support for the wings, and a backrest for the intrepid low-and-slow pilot. A chain-driven propeller, 48 inches in diameter, winds up at 2,460 rpm while the engine whines along at 9,500 rpm.

To hold the gross weight under 300 pounds, Hovey used tail surfaces made from half-inch styrofoam art board, faced with high-strength kraft paper on both sides and reinforced with plywood gussets. The tail boom is simply an extruded aluminum pipe 3 inches in diameter, filled with isofoam.

Believe it or not, the *Whing-Ding* actually gets off the ground, though barely high enough to sail over barbed wire fences. Top speed is 50 mph.

One popular, fully aerobatic biplane of note is the Meyer Special *Little Toot,* which can be built with an all-metal fuselage or one fashioned from chrome-moly steel tubing. The wings are fabric covered, the whole ship beautifully streamlined for high performance, behind an engine of from 90 to 125 horsepower. Its top speed is 127 mph, yet its stall is down at 35 mph, making it an easy-to-fly weekender.

Little Toot grosses 1,230 pounds but weighs 914 pounds empty. One of the most beautiful models was a scarlet ship built by the late Dale Garot, an ex–Air Force pilot killed in a weather-related accident in 1973 while flying his *Little Toot* to the Merced, California, fly-in.

A novel, VW-powered biplane is *Scamp,* newest creation of designer Harris Woods of Holly Springs, North Carolina, famous for his little monoplane *Woody's Pusher. Scamp* comes as a prefab kit and is stressed for aerobatics from +6 to –3 Gs. Woods went to a tricycle gear, unusual for a biplane, because the majority of pilots today learned to fly with the tail wheel up front, he says. *Scamp* weighs 520 pounds empty, has a span of 17 feet 6 inches, and a wing area of 105 square feet. It cruises at 95 mph, stalls at 43 mph, with a 220-pound pilot and the 1,824-cc VW engine.

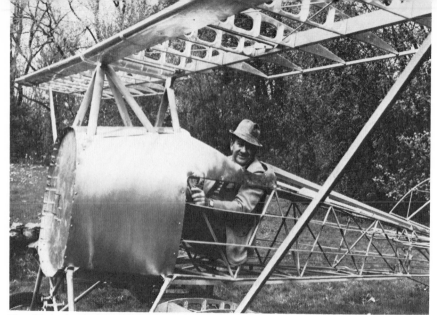

Don Dwiggins in *Foo Fighter*—early construction stage.

The bare bones of a *Foo Fighter.*

Don Dwiggins checking out a completed *Foo Fighter.*

Last but not least of the new crop of sports bipes is the delightful *Foo Fighter,* designed and built by two Allegheny Airlines pilots, Don Stewart and Tom Raybourn.

As I mentioned earlier, the *Foo Fighter* is a World War I fighter replica—and yet, in another sense, it isn't. Stewart and Raybourn simply wanted it to express all the good things they liked about that colorful era of combat flying, when pilots were as likely to throw bricks at each other as bullets.

Conceived in 1966 and first flown June 17, 1971, behind a Ford Falcon engine, *Foo Fighter* currently carries a Franklin Sport Four power plant and as I flew it at Oshkosh in the summer of 1973, it performed well on 130 horsepower. The flight was memorable, the sense of *déjà vu* so strong that suddenly I felt I was no longer at Wittman Field but taxiing over the grass at a secret forward base near the front lines, back in World War I.

I look around, noting the big Indian head painted on the side of my camouflaged fuselage. Here I am, a member of the Lafayette Escadrille, machine guns all checked out. Last night was wild, and the fragrance of perfume lingers on the white hankie given me as a to- ken of love by Mademoiselle Fifi of Armentières, France. I tie the hankie around my arm, roll onto the grass, and gun the big engine.

I steady my machine with a firm hand on the joy stick, singing "Over There!" at the top of my lungs. Up comes the tail, and I nail the horizon with my eagle eye as I swing into the deadly skies over Verdun. I bare my teeth, arm my guns, and remember what my squadron leader, Don Stewart, warned me:

"Always look behind you, that's where trouble comes from—the Red Baron *always* dives on your tail out of the sun!"

I glance over my shoulder. No Red Baron. I laugh derisively. What the hell—the Red Baron will be back in his barracks, telling the boys to look out for this mystery fighter over the western front. A sharp ship with the nose of a Pfalz, the fuselage of a Spad, the tail of a Bristol, the wings of an SE5.

I climb higher, to sneak up on the Flying Circus lurking behind that big black cloud. My airspeed reads 110. Full bore. Always climb fast, Squadron Leader Stewart had warned, "Always get above the enemy. Hide in the sun and come down with guns blazing!"

I'm clawing skyward at 1,500 feet per minute now, my ear tuned for trouble. "Come out and fight, Red Baron!" I yell into the wind. Nothing. I check my tach—the engine's winding up more than 2,500 revs, swinging the big Sensenich wooden prop, a 72/52.5 blade. The sun peeks out and for a moment I relax—a near-fatal mistake. I snap my head around. Here he comes!

I tense, expecting to meet a stream of tracers. But there are no tracers. Just an incredible framework whistling through the sky—a deadly *Breezy*! I'm astonished to see that the cowardly enemy is using lady pilots! In purple fighter suits yet! The shock is too much. Reality floods back.

Instead of the Red Baron over the western front, I'm being chased over Oshkosh by two homebuilt enthusiasts. I recognize them as Joan Moran and Ann Matthesius, who built their fantastic flying framework in their boudoir, or somewhere, and flew it to the EAA meet.

Well, that's what happens when you fly a real humdinger of a bipe like the *Foo Fighter*. And I guess that's the name of the game, what it's really all about—just good fun.

11
BUILD YOUR OWN
RACING PLANE!
How to Join the Homebuilt Hot Rods

Do you ever get the urge to slip on a pair of oval goggles, wrap a white silk scarf around your neck, pull on a pair of kid gloves, and overnight become a devil-may-care racing pilot? Escape from mundane drudgery to the excitement of the high sky, behind the scream of a hot engine, hell-bent for the next pylon?

If so, you're not alone, for a growing number of homebuilt enthusiasts are turning to the design, construction, and flying of competition racing planes, in a growing number of categories.

Whether or not they ever end up on the race circuit, homebuilt speedsters offer a challenge in themselves, for they represent the finest in workmanship, plus considerable originality in design. Two homebuilts may look exactly alike, but one may outfly the other because of minute detailing.

There are four classes of homebuilt racers in action today—the sport biplanes, the Formula Ones, the Formula Vees, and the unlimiteds—and every racing season new records are set, soon to be shattered. Some race pilots, like Don Beck of Tahoe Vista, California, own their own stable of racing planes. Others, like Dr. Sidney White of Sherman Oaks, California, fly exceptionally fine craft that are the end products of team design efforts.

Sid White's fantastic bipe, *Sundancer*, exploded on the scene at the Reno National Air Races in the fall of 1973 and emerged as best of the breed, after outclassing Don Beck's previously invincible biplane, the radical *Sorceress*. *Sundancer* was largely the inspiration of two top

Dr. Sid White standing beside his biplane, *Sundancer.*

Full front view of the *Sundancer.*

Don Beck in his radical, staggered-wing bipe racer, *Sorceress.*

aerodynamicists—Art Williams of Lockheed and Carl Conger of NASA's Ames Research Laboratory.

Art Williams already had a potential winner in the Formula One class—John Paul Jones's elliptical-winged *Stinger*, which was fast, but not fast enough in 1973 to whip Ray Cote's perennial winner, *Shoestring*. The Formula Ones go back to the Goodyear racers of a quarter-century ago—a time, incidentally, when another Williams homebuilt with elliptical wings—*Estrellita*—was the hottest thing in the sky. Those were the days when the homebuilt movement was just getting under way, in a revival movement following World War II, with such famous flying hot rods as Steve Wittman's *Bonzo* and the incredible Cosmic Wind monos.

Today Formula One racers must be built to strict specifications, including 100 horsepower engines, such as the Continental 0-200. A typical Formula One is roughly 16 feet long with a 15-foot wingspan and weighs close to the minimum allowable 500 pounds. While the rules prohibit prone-position cockpit designs, the pilot is permitted to lean back 20 degrees to cut down drag in the frontal area.

Standardization of the tiny monoplane racers for safety reasons goes back to 1939, when the Professional Race Pilots Association was incorporated by such noted race pilots as Tony LeVier, Art Chester, and Keith Rider, to save air racing from extinction. The trouble was that few pilots then could afford to build and fly racers able to compete with greats like Roscoe Turner and Earl Ortman. The Thompson Trophy Race had dwindled to only seven entries when PRPA was organized.

An entirely new concept of racers emerged from the early PRPA meetings and it was destined to change forever the old freewheeling, deadly game that had turned the Cleveland Nationals into a slaughterhouse on Labor Day weekends. A new class of small racers was introduced, with limited engine displacement and wing area, fixed landing gear, and rigid visibility rules for added safety. Variable-pitch propellers and hot-rodded engines were outlawed.

In the immediate postwar years, PRPA proposed another grouping of racers in the 190-cubic-inch class. Goodyear Tire and Rubber Company guaranteed it would sponsor a $25,000 trophy race for three years, and the result was a return of the homebuilts, which had been virtually forgotten with the appearance of war surplus flying gun platforms like the P-38 Lightning, the F-86 Sabrejet, and the P-51 Mustang.

Formula One racer *Shark* with elliptical wings.

Head-on view of Formula One Racer *Shark*.

Over the next two decades more than a hundred homebuilts were put together and flown in what became the Formula One class. Speeds climbed from 165 mph in the 1947 Goodyear Race to over 200 mph in the mid-1960s.

Emergence of VW-powered homebuilts made clear the need for still another class of racers, first proposed in 1965—the Formula Vees. What had started out as a simple, easygoing way to fly, low and slow, suddenly became a challenge to see who could fly the fastest in a careening "Kraut Kar," as some critics referred to these mighty midgets.

Steve Wittman's Formula Vee racer *Witt's Vee.*

Close-up view of tail assembly of *Witt's View.*

At the 1973 EAA convention in Oshkosh, seminars were held to decide which way to go with Formula Vees. A leader in these seminars was, naturally, Steve Wittman, who already was getting three miles a minute from his little green Formula Vee racer, *Witt's Vee.*

A major point that came up concerned the fact that if proposed rules limited Formula Vee racers to stock VW engines of 1,600-cc displacement or less, just what *is* a stock 1,600-cc VW engine?

Said EAA president Paul H. Poberezny: "The Volkswagen engine is a fine piece of machinery. However, without standardization of VW modifications, it has proven to be a problem in many amateur-built aircraft, and the cause of accidents. It is also being mismatched with some high-wing-loading aircraft that give minimum performance. This is not the best for the engine or its reputation."

Robert G. Huggins of Tulsa, Oklahoma, came to the rescue with an overhaul manual for VW aircraft conversions.

"The Volkswagen engine is precision-built throughout, and when properly converted should give excellent performance in the air," Huggins stated. "It fulfills all the fundamental requirements of an experimental aircraft engine."

A number of other Formula Vees were soon flying. One of the most promising was *Sonerai I,* a green streaker designed by John T. Monnett of Elgin, Illinois. *Sonerai I* is a combination sport plane and

Sonerai I Formula Vee racer with wings being folded back.

Formula Vee racer *Renegade.*

racer with aluminum mid-wings that fold back for trailing. The fuselage and tail are fabric-covered chrome-moly tubing, the cowling fiberglass. His VW conversion is a bolt-on affair.

Sonerai I, which weighs 440 pounds empty, is in the 170-mph speed class, and a two-place version, *Sonerai II,* with the bigger 1,700-cc VW engine, already has been clocked at 149 mph.

The bigger 1,700-cc VW engine is a standard dune buggy big-bore and bolt-together engine with 88-mm cylinders and a direct-drive propeller linkup. It is equipped with the unusual little Lake Injector carburetor, familiar to motorcycle buffs. *Sonerai II* is 225 pounds heavier than its little sister.

Down in Miami Lakes, Florida, Charlie Lasher, who sold racing plane kits designed by Tom Cassutt, has developed a Cassutt look-alike Formula Vee racer he calls *Renegade,* with a centerline thrust design to eliminate pitching forces. By placing it directly through the vertical center of gravity, he got away from any tendency for the nose to pitch up or down with throttle changes. Its wing loading is only 7.5 pounds per square foot, the same as an Aeronca *Champ. Renegade* weighs 330 pounds empty, has fiberglass wings, and at this writing carried a 1,300-cc VW engine for flight testing.

If you want to build something bigger, and perhaps faster, than a Formula Vee, there are homebuilt plans available for the hot little Formula One racers designed by George Owl, a North American Rockwell engineer, and designated *OR-71.* The first Owl Racer (OR) was *Pogo,* and others currently active include *Fang* and *Lil Quickie,* prototype for the *OR-71.*

Cutaway photo of VW-powered *Renegade.*

Pogo—the fast Owl Racer.

Another George Owl design—the Owl Formula One racer *Fang* with its annular air inlet for better cooling.

Lil Quickie has qualified at better than 223 mph and has a top speed of about 235 mph. A mid-wing design, it is lighter, more slender, and faster than the earlier *Owls*, with a wider wingspan (20 feet), improved airfoil and cowling. It uses an annular air inlet around the propeller hub, and a controllable cooling-air exhaust flap, to provide for maximum propeller efficiency and more efficient cooling during extended climbs.

As a combination racer and weekend sport plane, *OR-71* makes a nice flying package. George Owl and Vincent de Luca, the owner-builder of *Lil Quickie*, market plans from Vin-Del Aircraft in Miralesta, California.

Homebuilders can also purchase plans for a number of excellent biplanes—the Smith *Miniplane*, Knight *Twister*, *Starduster*, and Pitts *Special*—that can stay in a race with about everything except *Sundancer* and *Sorceress*. However, just as happened in the 1930s, a period remembered as the golden age of air racing, the most exciting breakthroughs in speed and performance are expected to come in the unlimited homebuilt category, a brand-new competition class. For the first time since World War II there's a chance for homebuilt enthusiasts to beat the records of the big surplus flying-cannon platforms that streak around the courses at better than 425 mph.

Right after PRPA president Lyle Shelton won the unlimited class event at Reno in 1973, at a record speed of 428.155 mph, flying a

Grumman F8F-2 Bearcat with a turbo-compound engine, PRPA stated its position on homebuilts:

"The time is drawing close when unlimited homebuilts will become a reality. Jim Wilson has a beautiful unlimited homebuilt well along down in Texas, with a great deal of aeronautical engineering experience and forethought put into it. There are several others in various stages of completion, one of which is being built by a PRPA associate member, Jim Carter, in Mill Valley, California."

Miller amplified on the PRPA statement: "By next year there should be two or three unlimited homebuilts ready for completion. In our case, even though this is a new airplane, we aren't going into air racing just for a ride—we expect to win. I hope the unlimited class rules are not changed with the appearance of these aircraft. The old World War II fighters *can be beaten*, and it is only a matter of time until that happens."

Carter's position was echoed by another top race pilot in Miami, Dave Garber: "There's no new unlimited class now, and we don't want one. We don't want to be outlawed, like Granatelli's turbine car at Indy."

In 1974 Garber had under construction the wings of a top-secret unlimited homebuilt to be powered with a unique rotary-V engine, developed in Graham, Texas, by an engineer named Frank Taylor. It is reported to be lighter than a standard reciprocating engine, with higher horsepower, more low-speed torque, more fuel economy, and fewer problems with moving parts, wear, and maintenance. Taylor is shooting for a power-to-weight ratio of one-half-pound engine weight per horsepower.

Garber's racer is designed to take two Turner engines mounted centerline fashion, one pulling and one pushing, like the Cessna 337 Skymaster, with each engine weighing about 215 pounds and delivering 300 horsepower. The design is basically a shoulder-wing monoplane with a 15-foot wingspan, 18-foot length, and a gross weight of 1,100 pounds, roughly the size of a Formula One but twice as heavy.

Jim Wilson's Texas wonder was reported to carry a V-12 Ranger engine, basically a pair of six-cylinder Rangers bolted together to produce more than 600 horsepower.

At Troutdale Airport near Portland, Oregon, Dennis N. Polen, a corporate pilot and EAA homebuilder, already has attained speeds above 400 mph with his *Polen II Special,* an all-metal, low-wing monoplane powered with a 200-horsepower Lycoming TSIO 360-A1A.

In Los Angeles, Ralph Wise, an ex-Marine fighter pilot who raced Formula One *Owls*, has designed a sleek little unlimited homebuilt he thinks will have a chance to beat the war birds.

"You get above 400 knots," says Wise, "your wing runs into the Mach numbers, and flying at high angles of attack required to take the pylons, there's an aerodynamic limit to how fast you can go."

To stay within this performance envelope is the big challenge to unlimited homebuilt designers, who don't believe a lot of weight and power is the answer. In their opinion, improved design will make a significant difference.

Wise's unlimited homebuilt will have a span of 18 feet, a length of 20 feet, and semitapered wings with an area of 70 square feet, the airfoil a laminar-flow curve of the NACA 6300 series, with squared tips. The pilot will sit in a semireclining position, and behind the cockpit the fuselage will largely resemble that of an Owl Racer. To withstand the high G forces of pylon racing at speeds above 400 mph, Wise is building his wing spars of 14 spruce planks joined into a single spar of super strength. A plastic-coated plywood wing skin should, he feels, be completely wrinkleproof.

"You have to consider more than simple power-to-weight ratios in designing an unlimited homebuilt," he says. "I consider parasitic drag elimination absolutely essential. You can't win races in this category by sticking tape over loose joints. Everything must be glassy smooth."

It's this kind of dedication that makes the new unlimited homebuilt category the most exciting thing in air racing's future. It will be like the golden age of air racing in the 1930s all over again, with the roar of the crowds pulling for their favorite do-it-yourselfer, in the tradition of Jimmy Doolittle, Jimmy Wedell, Art Chester, Benny Howard, and all the others who made air racing great.

12

THE WATER BIRDS
Amphibians and Seaplanes
Are More Fun

Back in 1911 Glenn Curtiss brought out the world's first practical seaplane by hanging a big float underneath the center section of his standard landplane and adding auxiliary wingtip floats for balance. Grover Loening, another pioneer of water flying, for years beat the drum for liquid instead of concrete runways, but today's thousands of "floatplane" and amphibian pilots figure there's plenty of water around, so why go to all the trouble of digging ditches?

The United States has thousands of miles of beautiful coastlines, rivers, and lakes to lure air-minded sportsmen off the beaten paths for happy weekend adventures fishing, swimming, or simply floating. Fortunately, thanks to the homebuilt aircraft movement, you don't have to be a millionaire to own your own private air yacht. You can make it yourself!

One of the simplest routes to go is to hang a pair of floats under a homebuilt like Peter Bowers's little *Fly Baby,* or imitate Lester Durden in Tallahassee, Florida—he and a buddy turned an empty airplane shed into a workshop and built themselves a little side-by-side, two-seat amphibian out of plywood, mounted an engine behind the wing as a pusher, and called it the *Catfish Special.*

At the other end of the line is the superb Spencer amphibian *Air Car,* a high-performance, four-place water bird that can operate in and out of lakes in mountain country with the greatest of ease.

The author seated in the cockpit of Lester Durden's (white T-shirt) two-seat amphibian, *Catfish Special.*

Powered with the Teledyne Continental Tiara engine, of 285 horsepower, the *Air Car* matches the performance of similar amphibians that sell for more than $60,000, yet the cost of materials and engine will run under $25,000. That isn't cheap but, on the other hand, if you can afford to build yourself a pretty air yacht, you shouldn't have to ask the price.

The *Air Car*, being custom-built, is not only a descendant of the Republic SeaBee, which it resembles, but also a much better performer, thanks to the inspiration of its designer, Percival H. Spencer, who also designed the popular Republic amphibian. Spencer has been involved in homebuilts since he was a young man; he inherited his genius for invention from his illustrious father, Christopher Spencer.

The elder Spencer, in fact, had a lot to do with the North's winning the Civil War. As a young man, he developed the amazing Spencer repeating rifle but couldn't get the Army interested in buying it. So he arranged an interview with President Abraham Lincoln, who took the rifle out behind the White House and plugged a bull's-eye in a pine board five times in a row. Satisfied, Lincoln ordered 100,000 Spencer repeaters for the Union Army.

Spencer and a partner, USAF Colonel Dale Anderson (Ret.), got the *Air Car* business rolling after Anderson pressed Spencer to finalize plans that had been lying around his office for several years, when he designed and built things like the amazing little "Wham-O" bird, a toy ornithopter that could flap its way right up into a cloud base.

Spence and Andy work at home in Sunland, California, making fiberglass parts for other *Air Car* builders, who are quite numerous.

143

Spencer *Air Car,* sporting a new three-blade prop, churns up a wake as it plows through the water.

Equipped with a new Tiara engine, the Spencer *Air Car*—its hull dripping—makes a steep climbout.

One similarity between the *Air Car* and the SeaBee is in the way the engine nacelle snuggles down close to the wing; it is high enough for the propeller blades to clear the spray pattern but low enough so that the thrust line of the engine doesn't produce undesirable pitching moments with power changes.

The *Air Car* rides evenly on the water, like a boat, and much of its success is due to sleek hull lines that throw the spray clear of engine and tail assembly. Initially the *Air Car* was powered with the 180-horsepower 0-360 Lycoming, but it has been uprated with the bigger Tiara, and a constant-speed three-blade Hartzell propeller.

Built of plywood instead of metal, this amphibian is not complicated to construct for anyone with basic woodworking skills. Its sleek fiberglass exterior is strong and waterproof, and the gross weight is a little over 3,000 pounds. Its climb at sea level is better than 1,000 feet per minute, and its cruise speed on 75 percent power is close to 140 mph.

Molt Taylor's two-place amphibian, the *Coot.*

Up in Longview, Washington, Molt Taylor markets plans for an interesting little water bird, the *Coot,* a two-place amphibian. Taylor's plans offer several options for materials—metal, fiberglass, or wood and fabric—and *Coots* are flying with engines rated anywhere from 125 to 160 horsepower. The wings carry a fair amount of dihedral, with the center section almost at waterline, eliminating the need for tip floats that add extra weight and drag. The first *Coot* was a single-tail seaplane, while later models have twin tail booms and hand-cranked retractable landing gear. One *Coot* builder, Joe Cook, fashioned his craft in 3,000 hours in a hangar near Los Angeles and installed a 160-horsepower Lycoming engine. It weighs 1,400 pounds empty and grosses 2,100 pounds, including novel extra fuel tanks made from 6-inch aluminum irrigation piping and located in the wing's leading edge. Cook's *Coot* is a single-tail variety and cruises at 110 mph on 65 percent power. Wings and horizontal tail surfaces fold back for trailing.

There is a certain kinship among homebuilders of water birds, who share an adventurous way of life foreign to the landplane pilot. They fly low and slow along distant waterways, raising flights of duck and geese, perhaps landing for a spot of bass fishing now and then.

With Lester Durden of Tallahassee, Florida, it's the call of the bayous. With George Periera of Sacramento, California, it's the lure of the Delta country, downstream from the confluence of the American and Sacramento rivers. The latter area is historic territory—the gateway to the gold diggings in '49, and today a wonderland of hidden waterways where holiday houseboat enthusiasts love to roam.

Periera wanted something special in which to explore the Delta country by air and, estimating that such an adventure was best carried out in solitude, he decided on a single-place flying boat, not an amphibian like Durden's *Catfish Special.* Who needs wheels, with all that water to play in? Periera designed his little flying boat, the *Osprey,* to be a whole new concept in sport flying. Using a special trailer, he hauls his machine out to a boat-launch ramp, folds out the wings, floats it off the trailer, and goes.

Construction of the *Osprey* is simple. The cantilevered wings are of constant chord (leading and trailing edges parallel), with full-span ailerons, so all the ribs are the same size and shape, and can thus be stack cut on a band saw. The spar is Z-shaped in cross section, easily formed of quarter-inch marine plywood placed between two fir cap

The little flying boat *Osprey* with cantilevered wings.

strips. A forward plywood D-section is rigid, and the whole wing is covered with glued-down dacron. Tip floats made from blocks of styrofoam shaped around a plywood silhouette are permanently attached under the wings.

Three main vertical tubes support the engine mount, atop a pedestal where a 90-horsepower Continental is pusher-mounted. Construction is mostly of marine plywood, the hull formed over V-shaped bottom bulkheads, and the whole thing is coated with fiberglass. Periera had his hull ready to cover in three days.

As it sits in the water, *Osprey* has a span of 23 feet, a length of 17 feet 3 inches, a wing area of 97 square feet, an empty weight of 600 pounds (900 pounds loaded). *Osprey* will taxi up to 70 mph on the water, or you can swing around in a tight step turn with a 60-yard radius at 50 mph, then straighten out and lift off at 55 mph.

Getting off the water in 7 seconds and barely 200 feet, *Osprey* has a startling climb rate of about 2,000 feet per minute and cruises along at 118 mph. When the day's flying is over, you simply land, taxi back to the boat ramp, fold up the wings, and trail *Osprey* back to the family garage.

Periera has continually uprated the *Osprey*'s plans, with input from a number of homebuilders. The prototype was sold to the Navy in July 1970, and after Periera demonstrated its capabilities off the American river, it was flown by the Navy from Warminster, Pennsylvania, on a flight test program as the *X-28A Air Skimmer.*

Eut Tileston, of Carmichael, California, who engineered the folding-wing mechanism and engine mount for the *Osprey*, has designed a new two-place amphibian, the *Drake*, with only the experience gained from work on the *Osprey* carried over. The *Drake* is being built in three versions, 27-foot and 32-foot fixed-wing designs and a 31-foot folding-wing model. A score were under construction in 1974 in the United States, Canada, and New Zealand.

Tileston describes the *Drake* as a "two-place, high-performance amphibian utilizing a modern STOL-type airfoil in conjunction with high-lift flaps and drooping ailerons." Tandem seating offers reduced frontal area and improved visibility. A tricycle landing gear is manually operated.

A novel innovation is a system for automatically lowering retractable wingtips for flotation stability when the water rudder is lowered. *Drake* weighs 973 pounds empty, grosses 1,600 pounds. With a 130-horsepower Franklin Sport Four engine, it climbs at 1,100 feet per minute and cruises at 120 mph. Total cost, excluding engine and avionics, should run under $2,000, Tileston says. The first completed *Drake*s were scheduled to fly in 1974.

More ambitious are plans of the Larkin Aircraft Corporation of Freedom, California, to mass produce a small, inexpensive, two-place amphibian kit sport plane with a unit price under $10,000. Dubbed the Larkin *Skylark*, it is the result of an effort that began in 1968 to

The Larkin *Skylark* converts easily from a landplane to a seaplane.

The Volmer *Sportsman VJ-22.*

provide the homebuilder with either do-it-yourself plans or a five-stage kit-purchase program.

Powered with a modified 1,600-cc VW engine uprated to 1,679 cc, the *Skylark* includes several interesting features, such as an unconventional airframe structure with all loads carried by a central L-shaped keel and mast of standard 4-inch aluminum tubing, to which all essential systems are mounted. Around this structure fits an easily removable, secondary fiberglass structure.

Another goodie is a patented interchangeable hydrofoil-ski assembly that can be quickly attached externally for normal operations from mud or snow, as well as land or water.

Skylark's initial flight tests proved out its cruise speed of 100 mph carrying a 450-pound payload. It reportedly stalls at 42 mph, weighs 814 pounds empty, has 113 square feet of wing area, wingspan of 26 feet 6 inches, and a length of 18 feet 2.5 inches. For water flying a fiberglass boat hull replaces the lower landcraft hull, with loads transferred to the keel through bulkheads. Sealed fiberglass wingtips droop for flotation use. It takes less than two hours to convert the *Skylark* from a landplane to a seaplane with amphibious capability.

Volmer Jensen has been designing homebuilts for a third of a century, ever since he built a Chanute-type hang glider back in 1940. I first met him at Van Nuys, California, Airport in 1946, where he let me fly his little *JF-1 Jaybird*, and again the following March when I flew his *VJ-21* high-wing pusher monoplane to an air show in Palm Springs. After twenty-seven years the *VJ-21* is still flying, having served well as a test bed for many ideas Volmer has now built into a fine little amphibian, the *Sportsman VJ-22.*

The *Sportsman*'s C-85 Continental engine is rear-mounted on a pylon, pusher-fashion, like the *VJ-21* installation, and the power is adequate for a comfortable cruising speed of 85 mph and a climb rate of 600 feet per minute. Volmer has flown his *Sportsman* more than 1,600 happy hours, and figures he has covered a distance equal to five trips around the world.

Hundreds of sets of plans for the *VJ-22* have been sold and close to 75 *Sportsmen* are currently airworthy and in action in many parts of the world. The *Sportsman*'s appeal is partly due to its stable and dependable design, with excellent visibility that is an improvement over the *VJ-21,* which was blind in a right turn. The propeller is mounted out of the way where nobody can walk into it.

Jensen has had his amphibian in many exciting waters, from the Frazier River in Canada to the Great Lakes, the Mississippi and Colorado rivers, and far down into Mexico, on skin-diving expeditions in the Sea of Cortez.

Construction is quite simple for the average homebuilder. The wings are wooden-spar Aeronca *Champ* or *Chief* wings, scrounged from a junkyard, or new ones—take your choice. The hull consists of aircraft-grade mahogany plywood and spruce, covered with fiberglass. In thirteen years of flying, says Volmer, his *Sportsman* has yet to spring a leak. It takes the average do-it-yourself builder about two years to construct a *Sportsman*, and the cost is under $2,000.

But if you're in a hurry and don't rate your homebuilding skills too highly, there's another way to go—by turning your *Sportsman* into a local school project. Read all about it in the next chapter!

13
PROJECT SCHOOLFLIGHT
Homebuilts Are a Young Person's Game

In the fall of 1967 a restless high school woodworking instructor named Allen V. Peterson began looking around for an advanced project—one that would offer his students an exciting new learning experience and be a departure from the ordinary run of tables and cabinets and chairs. He wanted something with more motivation, something imaginative, something that would help the boys in his class visualize creative ideas and then build them.

When a neighbor suggested building an airplane, Peterson was fascinated by the idea but hardly knew where to start. His neighbor told him about an article on the Volmer *Sportsman* amphibian, and a few days later, with encouragement from the school superintendent, Peterson mailed a request for a set of plans.

Lindbergh High School, in Minnetonka, Minnesota, is in the heart of the lake country. When word got out that Peterson's class was going to build an amphibian plane, enthusiasm immediately rose to a high pitch. But there were eight hard months ahead for Peterson, in planning, familiarizing himself with airplane construction methods, and scrounging materials.

He soon realized that it would take several thousand dollars to do the job right. Accordingly, he appeared before the school board, armed with slides he'd taken of similar airplanes being built by amateurs around the country. His research at the time indicated that

151

Woodworking instructor Allen V. Peterson seated in cockpit of the *Sportsman VJ-22*, built by students of Lindbergh High School in Minnetonka, Minnesota.

Lindbergh High School students working on wing rib for *Sportsman VJ-22*.

152

Lindbergh High School's *VJ-22* wing uncovered.

only thirteen schools had attempted to build airplanes, and only five ships had actually been completed. These rather disappointing facts did not deter him, however.

"After an hour's presentation, with plenty of questions to answer, I finally got the go-ahead," he says.

The school board took a gamble and agreed to underwrite the cost of the venture. The biggest expense was the engine, a rebuilt Continental C-90-12F that cost $1,850. As things turned out, it was a good investment.

Actual construction of Lindbergh High's homebuilt started in September 1968, with the entire class of twenty-four boys working on layouts and building component parts. There were more than 5,000 handmade items to fashion, and before the job was done the students had put in as many hours of labor. Peterson himself spent some 500 hours without pay to get the project rolling.

Interest soon began to lag, yet one month after the *Sportsman* project was started, Peterson and the boys set up the framework of the wings and fuselage on sawhorses and it really began to look like an airplane.

"We had thousands of people come through the shop that year," Peterson recalls. "Sometimes I had to lock the door to get any work done."

The wing as it looked covered.

From time to time FAA inspectors dropped by to make progress checks on the amphibian, long before the boys put on the fabric covering. More guidance and advice came from the Experimental Aircraft Association's national headquarters, located in a small nearby town called Hales Corners.

On June 13, 1969, Peterson hitched the *Sportsman* to the back of his car and towed it out to Flying Cloud Airport at nearby Eden Prairie. The whole class followed on bikes and in hot rods. They assembled the wings, and at sundown the plane sat in the golden rays, gassed and poised for flight.

The next day a friend, Captain Lloyd Franke of North Central Airlines, showed up, carefully looked the ship over, then hopped in and took off.

"I can't begin to express the excitement and the feeling of satisfaction of having completed a project of that magnitude and seeing it fly beautifully," Peterson recalls.

The amphibian had cost the school board $4,600, and what does a school do with a pretty new airplane? The only answer appeared to be to try to sell it.

"We advertised in all the local papers and invited everybody to come to an open house at our rented hangar," Peterson continues. "We noted also that we would receive sealed bids, starting with a base price of $4,600—our cost."

154

People came, admired, kicked the tires, and the experts admitted that the boys had done well. The ship had squared wingtips that gave 10 more square feet of wing area, and the boys had done such a good job that the ship was well under gross weight. It was the first *VJ-22* ever built with all-wooden wings.

Enter Dick Norby, an aviation-minded Minneapolis businessman who already had another homebuilt project going when he heard about the Lindbergh High ship. Norby dropped by, noted the excellent workmanship, saw and appreciated the 5,000 hours of tender, loving creativity that had gone into its construction. On an impulse he submitted a bid of $5,101, and subsequently he emerged the winner.

"I figured I'd stolen nine months of free labor," Norby grins. "It was a job that normally would have taken me four or five years, the fine way they did it!"

Norby's *Sportsman* was too good to be true. It flew 5 miles an hour faster than Volmer Jensen's original *VJ-22*, being lighter, and with extra long-range tanks in the baggage compartment he was all set for the fishing country. Since then Norby has flown his amphibian more than 200 hours, landing in relatively inaccessible northern Minnesota lakes, back in the Arrowhead country, where the fishing is unbelievable.

For Peterson this was only the beginning. In the fall semester of 1971 he got twenty students involved in a new project, building a Piel *Emeraude*. There was one minor delay while attorneys made sure that state liability laws would not compromise the school district. That cleared, the new project began to roll and everybody was happy. The school board had made a $501 profit on the *Sportsman*, the kids had had a fine time, and there was Dick Norby fishing his heart out.

In an effort to learn more about the makeup of a typical high school homebuilt aircraft program, Howard R. Schmidt gathered material for a doctoral disseration in industrial arts education at the University of North Colorado in 1970. Schmidt interviewed thirteen different high school program leaders who had been involved in such projects over the previous decade.

The typical shop teacher, he learned, was thirty-nine years old, a pilot, and a member of the EAA. Eight of the thirteen had never worked on a homebuilt project before. Among the students, girls were permitted to take classes in aircraft construction in ten of the thirteen schools, and the majority queried regarded the class as prevocational.

Financing school aircraft projects was handled in three ways—using school funds, using outside financing, and having the teacher

155

provide the materials. Under the first method the aircraft was sold to return money to the school. In the second situation, the aircraft was delivered to the party providing the funds. If the teacher paid the bills, he took title to the aircraft.

Schmidt pointed out the importance of understanding federal air regulations permitting aircraft construction in the experimental category for recreational and educational purposes, and to help fill this need the FAA on May 11, 1973, issued an advisory circular (AC 20-86). It provides information to high schools on available assistance, resources, methods, and opportunities for attaining basic educational goals by building an airplane.

"Many schools throughout the country," said the FAA, "have already completed their first amateur-built airplane and are now on their second. Student and teacher enthusiasm is running high. Student interest in schoolwork has taken an upward swing, and so have grades, performance, attendance, and general attitude."

The reason, the FAA pointed out, was simple—the schools were substituting aviation-related subject matter for previously unrelated, stodgy, dry classroom situations. They were teaching science concepts connected with aerodynamics of flight and flight surfaces by means of lectures, demonstrations, blackboard discussions, and shop projects, including construction of an airplane.

The advisory circular urged schools considering building an airplane to select a specific model; instead of assembling a "do-it-yourself kit," the students should be required to utilize their knowledge of mathematics, science, shop techniques, woodworking, and metal fabrication.

The government bulletin also advised consulting the Experimental Aircraft Association before selecting construction plans for any specific aircraft. One such aircraft is the EAA's own exciting biplane, the EAA *Acro Sport*, more than a dozen of which currently are under construction around the country as part of the EAA's Project School-flight.

Says EAA president Paul Poberezny: "The EAA *Acro Sport* was designed for several purposes, first, to retain the nostalgia of flying as it was in the helmet-and-goggle era, which has never left the aviation scene. Basically the *Acro Sport* was designed for use in high school industrial arts programs."

Of steel tube and spruce construction, this biplane was designed around a cockpit ample for a 6-foot, 5-inch pilot of 240 pounds—in other words, roomy. The prototype *Acro Sport* has a 20-gallon fuel tank, plus a 6-gallon smoke-oil tank behind the instrument panel, which can be used as an auxiliary fuel tank if desired.

Powered with a 180-horsepower engine, its top wingspan is 19 feet 7 inches, with a length of 17 feet 6 inches. Empty weight is 733 pounds and gross weight is 1,178 pounds. Highly maneuverable with four ailerons, its top speed is 180 mph, cruise speed 130 mph, stalling speed 50 mph. It will climb at 3,500 feet per minute. A complete kit of plans, parts, and materials, less engine and propeller, costs less than $3,000.

The Air Education Foundation has been established by the 72,000-member EAA at Box 229, Hales Corners, Wisconsin 53130, in a Milwaukee suburb. It maintains a fine aeronautical museum, and a library of thousands of aviation-related volumes. Around the world, the EAA has more than 415 local chapters, whose members can be of tremendous assistance in starting a school aircraft program.

A growing number of high schools now offer such programs, some with EAA assistance, others independently, but all FAA-monitored by local general aviation district offices and flight standards district offices. Advisory Circular 20-86 contains a list of such offices, and of other pertinent advisory circulars; it is available from the Superintendent of Documents, U.S. Government Printing Office, Washington D.C. 20590.

One FAA-recommended supplier of plans and kits for a school project biplane is La Mar Steen of Denver, Colorado, designer of the excellent Steen *Skybolt*. The first *Skybolt* was built by students at Denver's Manual High School and made its maiden flight on November 17, 1970, at Jefferson County Airport. Steen, the class teacher, was at the controls.

The *Skybolt,* like the *Acro Sport*, is a tandem two-place aerobatic bipe with a 180-horsepower Lycoming engine. Its wingspan is 24 feet, length 20 feet, empty weight 1,080 pounds, gross weight 1,650 pounds. Its top speed is 145 mph, and even at Denver's high airport it will climb at 1,100 feet a minute.

At Parkside High School in Jackson, Michigan, another homebuilt project made news in 1973 when students completed a fine model of an earlier EAA biplane, the *P-2 Eagle*. It took thirty-two students two years to complete, and during the process one sponsoring group produced a 16-mm color documentary, "The Wind Is Right," covering its construction and first flight on July 26, 1971.

A close-up of the Steen *Skybolt,* built by students at Denver, Colorado, Manual High School.

La Mar Steen and some of his students in the process of engine installation on their prototype *Skybolt. (Photo by Paul A. Wilkinson)*

158

Steen talking to a group of students using a scale model of *Skybolt* to illustrate construction practice. (*Photo by Paul A. Wilkinson*)

Two students holding up tail section of a *Skybolt* under construction. (*Photo by Paul A. Wilkinson*)

Anxious to broaden the scope of the aviation training, Parkside traded its *Eagle* one for one with Flightmatic, Inc., of Moonachie, New Jersey, for a professional ground trainer, the Vista Flight Simulator. The simulator is used for both instrument and primary flight training, and for implementing other aviation education programs at Parkside.

William H. Ghan, industrial arts instructor at Mansfield R-4 High School in Mansfield, Missouri, has been searching since 1966 for what he hopes will be the perfect school plane, but indicates he hasn't found it yet. Initially his class at Cabool High constructed a little Corben *Baby Ace* in one year, which pleased him, but the second effort was an original cabin biplane design they called the *K.G.*

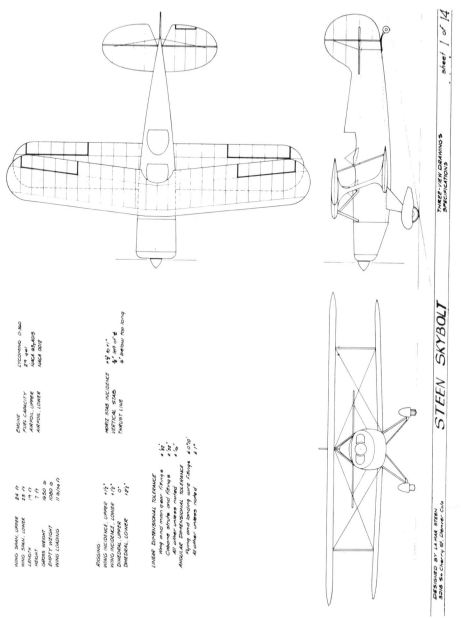

Detailed plans and specifications for Steen Skybolt. (*Courtesy of La Mar Steen*)

The *P-2 Eagle* built by students of the industrial arts aviation class at Parkside High School in Jackson, Michigan.

Special. It had a 150-horsepower engine and was fully instrumented, but it took two years to complete. The second class lost interest, he says, because it "just wasn't their plane." For this reason, Ghan doesn't favor biplane projects that take too much time to build.

In 1971 his class started a Bushby *Midget Mustang*, and the next year the boys started a Steen *Skybolt*, but before they could complete that one the owner-sponsor swapped it for a two-place factory job. Right now Ghan thinks he may have found the perfect school plane—John Monnett's *Sonerai I*, a VW-powered Formula Vee racing type. Since his early pioneering work in this area, Ghan has seen the total number of high school aircraft projects grow from two (his and one other) to more than a hundred.

From coast to coast planes are emerging from wood shops and metal shops, singly and in bunches. At Altavista, Virginia, High School, fourteen students and an industrial arts teacher in late 1973 undertook the construction of a modified Taylor monoplane with styrofoam wings, like those of Ken Rand's *KR-1*. The fuselage is plastic covered and the engine is a converted VW. Down in Clearwater, Florida, instructor Arnold Allen rented, at his own expense, a private garage where his students at Largo Senior High are building a *Jungster I*. They also have an Evans *Volksplane I* ready to fly, along with a modified Stits *Playboy SA3B*.

The fuselage side is built up in a jig and tack-welded. (Citizen Patriot *Photo by Steve McCourtie*)

An aircraft begins to develop. (Citizen Patriot *photo by Steve McCourtie*)

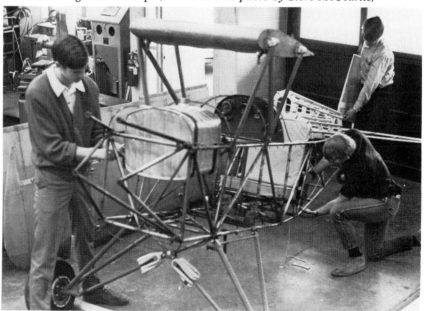

Jennifer L. Ayers of San Luis Obispo, California, has her hands full enlisting the aid of local EAA chapter members to help California State Polytechnic University students complete a whole squadron of personal homebuilts, including a *Baby Ace, Cassutt, KR-1, BD-5, Schweizer 1-26* sailplane, and three factory planes—a Cessna 140, an L-2, and a Model 415-C *Ercoupe,* her own.

Fred Ferdon, a drafting teacher at Cleveland High School in Reseda, California, spent money out of his own pocket to get a Thorp *T-18* metal homebuilt project under way, until the board of education finally backed him up. He talked a number of local firms into donating parts, scrounged a secondhand Lycoming ground power unit, and presto—a beautiful new tin bird took shape.

Don E. Roberts, aviation technology teacher at Noblesville, Indiana, High School, got the kids started on a 1932 Mead primary glider in 1968, then designed an original wooden ship the boys named the *Chinese Bandit.* Next came a three-quarter-scale replica of a Navy

Drafting teacher Fred Ferdon watches student Gary Weinrich working on engine of Thorp *T-18* at Cleveland High School in Reseda, California.

Sharon Young, Queen of Noblesville, Indiana, High School, reclining on wing of *Chinese Bandit* built by students at the school.

Instructor Don Roberts and students with their *Chinese Bandit.*

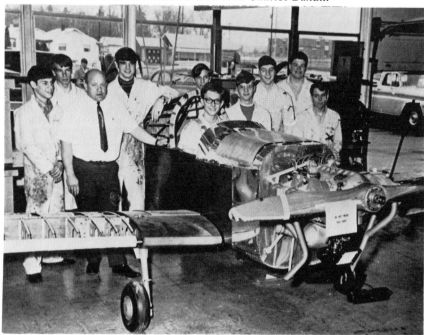

SBD-3 Dauntless dive bomber, powered with a 1963 Buick Special engine and a reduction gear.

In Thunder Bay, Ontario, Canada, David Carlson, instructor with the 85th Squadron, Royal Canadian Air Cadets at Hammarskjold High School, is busily scrounging parts to complete an Anderson *Kingfisher* amphibian. Construction began in September 1972, and the target completion date was June 1975, provided donors supply needed parts.

Down at the Green Bay Reformatory in Wisconsin, a group of inmates is busily engaged in building an *Acro Sport* from materials supplied by the EAA.

"It's no fantastic escape machine," shrugs Patrick Dorgan, one of the insiders most responsible for keeping the project moving along.

The project started when Dorgan and a pal, James Multaler, began writing letters to local flying clubs, seeking information on homebuilts. Dorgan admits to considerable surprise when Roger Davenport, president of local EAA Chapter 250, drove up with a truckload of parts.

With the blessings of the reformatory administrative staff, the inmates were making good progress late in 1974, and Dorgan says their only worry is that somebody may break in and swipe it. They hope to turn the completed *Acro Sport* back to the EAA as a finished product, one that gave them a lot of fun and direction.

"Even the guards help us when they can," Dorgan says.

14

RESTORATIONS
AND REPLICAS
*Wonderful Wings
from Yesteryear*

Bill Turner, a prominent California law school educator and 11,000-hour ex-Navy pilot, loves old airplanes. He first soloed at the age of twelve in an OX-5 Curtiss *Robin*, down in Texas, and as a teen-ager sneaked away to watch the Cleveland National Air Races, where he fell in love with a crimson streak called *Miss Los Angeles,* its paint job bright as fresh lipstick.

Miss Los Angeles wore the racing number 33 and was flown by hot pilots like Roy Minor and Marion McKeen and luckless Lee Williams, who was killed in number 33 the first time he raced her.

Today Bill Turner flies all over the country in *Miss Los Angeles*, a crimson replica of the original that even carries her old racing number, albeit a newer engine, an inverted Ranger 6-440C instead of the old C-6-S Menasco Buccaneer.

Originally designed by Larry Brown of Los Angeles, *Miss Los Angeles*, also known as the Brown *B-2 Special,* had vicious stall characteristics that Turner has attempted to reduce, with the help of Ed Marquart, a skilled aircraft restoration buff at Flabob Airport in Riverside, California.

Dwight Brooks, a West Coast corporate jet pilot, also likes old planes. He was especially attracted to a huge old World War II aircraft, largely forgotten over the years—the Westland *Lysander*. There was plenty of romance surrounding the *Lysander*. It was among the world's first STOL (short takeoff and landing) aircraft, and was used by the British Royal Air Force behind the lines for commando raids and to supply resistance forces in Fortress Europe.

The *Lysander* idea became an obsession with Brooks and, after considerable scrounging, he located two bare-boned hulks, one in Edmonton, Alberta, Canada, and the other at Camden, South Carolina. He had them both trucked to Van Nuys Airport in southern California, where a friend, Frank Nixon, ran an aircraft repair station.

The restoration project got under way with help from unexpected sources—the RAF museum, the Dunlop Tyre Company, and the Bristol Engine Division of Rolls Royce, Ltd. Somebody found a rusted old Lewis machine gun to stick in the rear gunner's position. The duke of Edinburgh sent his royal wishes for success with the project. It flew successfully in July 1974.

These two projects represent divergent approaches followed by a growing army of antique airplane buffs today—either find yourself a rare old bird and bring it back to life or start from scratch and build yourself an honest replica. Replica or restoration, they're all the same today, except in the eyes of the purists, and even they can't object to replacing rotted or rusted parts of an original with new and airworthy materials, unless it's to end up simply as a museum ship.

The antique aircraft fleet today is far from a collection of musty old museum ships. You'll find them flying thousands of miles for get-togethers with other antique buffs, at national and regional meets of both the Experimental and the Antique Aircraft Associations.

The EAA lists specific categories for old planes. Any aircraft built prior to January 1, 1942, is classified as an antique. World War II military combat craft and higher-powered trainers are called war birds. Then come the classics, built between January 1, 1945, and December 31, 1950. The classics fall into three subcategories: class I (under 100 horsepower), class II (100 to 165 horsepower), and class III (over 165 horsepower).

There's much bone-picking in the category of classics, for this covers an era when a lot of fine old airplane companies folded, during the depression of 1947–1948, a time when the predicted postwar boom in private flying got clobbered.

The Antique Aircraft Association, formed in 1953—the same year the EAA was born—now includes approximately 5,000 members who keep in touch via Post Office Box H, Ottumwa, Iowa 52501. AAA categorizes the oldies a little differently than EAA does: To the AAA, any bird built prior to 1935 is an antique. Aircraft from 1935 through the golden era of flying to World War II are looked upon as classics. AAA has a division for World War II war birds, and anything built after the war, from 1946 to 1950, is a neoclassic. AAA looks disdainfully upon more recent aircraft as simply transportation machines, to be used in the search for oldies to restore.

Call them what you will, there is undeniable nostalgia in old aircraft, regardless of their condition. To many, the worse they are, the better—meaning there will be more time to spend in restoration.

You never know just where you'll run across the remains of an antique or classic airplane—out behind a barn, buried in a mud flood, parked in a forgotten shed, or in somebody's attic. J-3 Cub wings have been found hinged to a farmer's fence to keep the cows out of the corn. The late movie stunt pilot Hank Coffin needed a pair of wheels and a landing gear to complete a replica of Lindbergh's *Spirit of St. Louis* for a film job. He knew precisely where to go—a fine pair was hanging in the branches of a tall pine at the edge of Monache Meadows, a U.S. Forest Service field at the 8,000-foot elevation in the High Sierra country.

Major A. P. de Jong, a Royal Netherlands Air Force officer, became obsessed with the possibility of recovering the wrecks of USAF planes in which 1,189 Yankee flyers had perished at the bottom of the Zuider Zee. Divers located the wrecks, and little by little sections of the shallow sea were diked off and drained. Many such combat ships have been recovered, the fate of their crews at long last a closed book instead of left open as "missing in action."

The thing in Walt Marple's garage in Chatsworth, California, is listed in the U.S. Civil Aircraft Register as an airplane, but nobody remembers when it last flew. It's bolted to the cement floor just to make it easier to work on, not because anybody would want to steal it.

When Marple hauled the pieces home in a junk wagon, it looked like a fugitive from a boneyard. Walt moved the family car out of the garage and dumped the pieces inside. It became his garage full of dreams, where he could go to drink beer and study the lines, the way some other guys sit around their garages studying the lines of a Marilyn Monroe calendar.

The object of Marple's attention and affection is a *Model G Dart*, a streamlined classic with full aerobatic capabilities, one that separated the men from the boys. Marple paid only $300 for the pile of junk, and considered it a bargain because it would provide a virtual lifetime of recreation getting it all together.

There is a wonderful little field out in California, in a lush valley where the Santa Clara River runs to the sea. There are orange groves and oil wells and other signs of prosperity, and right in the middle is Santa Paula Airport, a haven for antique airplanes, right out of yesterday.

In one hangar you'll find a retired FAA pilot named Jim Dewey working on his latest acquisition—a bare-bones *Monocoupe*, parked next to an old *Spartan Executive*. Up the line of hangars Ted Hohman, a retired airline pilot, is warming up the OX-5 engine in his restored *American Eagle*, a biplane from the 1920s once hailed as the "Master of the Skies"—it could do 99 mph, and still can.

At the other end of the field Clete Roberts, a television newsman, has a whole squadron of antiques in a hangar he calls his toy box—a Stinson *Voyager*, a Piper J-3 Cub, and a Buhl *Bull Pup*. I claim to be one of the few friends Clete ever permitted to fly the *Pup*, the brainchild of Etienne Dormoy, a noted French engineer who helped design the famous old Spad fighters of World War I.

The Buhl *Model LA-1 Pup* appeared in 1929, a time of depression, breadlines, poverty, and songs like "Brother, Can You Spare a Dime?" Dormoy had the idea that a low-cost, mid-wing, wire-braced monoplane that looked like an early Morane would help the nation forget its troubles. He installed a 45-horsepower, 3-cylinder Szekeley, but Clete couldn't find a Zeke for his *Pup*, so he stuck in a 65-horsepower Continental, which served as well.

Ted Hohman's restored *American Eagle.*

Bud Gurney's *Gipsy Moth.*

Flying a *Pup* out of Santa Paula Airport is an unforgettable thrill. There you are outdoors, the wind slapping at your cheeks, helmet, and goggles, and singing through the wires as you do chandelles and lazy eights and wild wingovers until Clete waves you down—it's his turn to show off.

Everywhere you look at Santa Paula, you find guys running around in puttees or greasy coveralls with big monkey wrenches and bigger grins, working on airplanes from the long-dead past. Take Hilda and Bud Gurney, trying to start their 1928 *Gipsy Moth,* perhaps the most graceful biplane ever designed.

Bud Gurney was a boyhood pal of Charles A. Lindbergh; the two of them learned to fly together back in Lincoln, Nebraska, in the front seat of Otto Timm's Standard. Now, whenever the Lone Eagle visits the West Coast, you'll find him up at Santa Paula, hangar flying with the gang or taking a turn around the field in Gurney's *Moth.* Ted Hohman has a big, red, heart-shaped patch sewn on the seat of a sofa in his hangar that says: Lindbergh Sat Here. They love him that much.

It's been said that the first step in restoring an antique airplane is getting it home safely—more than one tired old relic has flown off the back of a trailer and made its last crash landing by the side of the road. And once you get it home and start stripping off the rotted wood and fabric, you'll need to sandblast the bare metal bones to free them from rust and corrosion. The most likely person to have a portable sandblasting rig is your local tombstone dealer.

From there you're on your own, and your best bet is to join a local EAA chapter and secure the advice and help of willing members who can save you time, effort, and money in getting your wonderful old bird back into the sky. The FAA also should be consulted for the technical help it can offer.

Reworking old engines is an art in itself, and unless you're mechanically inclined you might be better off picking up a modern power plant you know is reliable. Ted Hohman stripped down an old OXX-6 engine that had been buried for years in a midwestern field, and virtually rebuilt every part. Today it runs perfectly.

Building up a replica, as Bill Turner and Ed Marquart did with *Miss Los Angeles*, is a different story, but one that is rooted in the same lore as a restoration project. There's tedious, time-consuming research to be done, poring through old magazines and manuals, to get the original specifications and dimensions of an aircraft that no longer exists. There are a number of fine libraries for this specialized research, such as the EAA museum in Hales Corners, Wisconsin, and the Northrop Institute of Technology's library of aeronautical history in Inglewood, California, run by a dedicated antique airplane buff, Dr. David Hatfield.

Not all aviation museums are full of stuffed birds that won't fly. Cole Palen turned beautiful Rhinebeck Airport in New York's Hudson Valley into a World War I-era flying field, complete with a grassy runway, old wooden hangars, and a flock of contemporary fighters that frequently are taken up for mock air-to-air combat routines.

Similarly, on the West Coast, movie stunt pilot Frank Tallman can be called on by movie moguls to produce and fly anything from a World War II Flying Fortress to a 1912 Curtiss *Pusher*.

Among the homebuilt people, replicas are a growing hobby. I've mentioned the exciting little *Foo Fighter*, a whimsical collection of ideas from World War I fighters, for which plans are available from its codesigner, Don Stewart. Other plans are available for more authentic, if not more satisfying, replicas, depending on your preferences.

Take Mike Murphy, of Oak Lawn, Illinois, who spotted a photograph of a 1912 *Bellanca*, virtually a two-dimensional wooden framework that supported a spread of wings and a 35-horsepower Anzani engine. Murphy and some friends, working from the

Mike Murphy's 1912 *Bellanca* replica.

snapshot, designed and built a replica with a Clark Y airfoil wing, wheels from a 1955 Harley-Davidson motorcycle, and a 1938 Continental A-50 engine. The amazing thing is that it flies, and not badly. It'll go 48 mph, and can land at 29 mph. Once, says Murphy, he was startled to see a flock of wild geese line up behind him in a V formation, giving him the lead position in the pecking order. "They finally passed me," he sighs.

Earl Adkisson, of Tuscola, Illinois, fell in love with a picture of a 1908 *Demoiselle*, designed and built by Alberto Santos-Dumont as the "world's smallest airplane." The *Demoiselle* was one of the first homebuilt projects for which plans were available—a set of seven blueprints for two dollars offered by *Popular Mechanics* in 1910 (see Chapter 2). Adkisson shuddered at the idea of a homebuilt made of bamboo poles, and substituted aluminum tubing in his *Demoiselle*, N6162, which is listed in the U.S. Civil Aircraft Register as a *Barndoor*. He also went to a higher-lift airfoil, the NACA 4412, and a modern power plant, for safety's sake.

A. H. (Bert) Lane's Bleriot *Model XI-2* monoplane.

The original *Demoiselle*, also called *Le Santos No. 20*, was the hit of the Paris Air Show in 1909 as the smallest ship that ever flew. Its total weight was only 240 pounds, its wingspan 20 feet. A 30-horsepower engine swung a propeller of 6 feet 6 inches, which forced air back over a maze of tubular radiator pipes.

There are differences of opinion about which is the oldest flying machine still active today, but evidence at hand would give the honors to A. H. (Bert) Lane's fine Bleriot *Model XI-2* monoplane, which he built in Santa Barbara, California. From the pieces of a Bleriot he found stored in a garage, Lane assembled a lovely flyable restoration of a monoplane built shortly after Louis Bleriot hopped the English Channel in his *Model XI* in 1909.

Lane spent more than $26,000 in time and materials, and hung a Continental C-85 engine in front until he could locate a vintage 80-horsepower LeRhone. Flying this antique was full of surprises for Lane, an experienced flight instructor. It had a habit of flying sort of sideways, with little directional stability—which is why, Lane observed, Bleriot used to make flat turns to avoid tipping over. It gets off the ground at 35 mph, cruises at 55, and lands "sort of like a parachute—there just isn't any stall, it just comes down," Lane explains.

You'll find a growing number of World War I replicas around the country nowadays, so many in fact that Dean Obrecht, of Rochester, New York, a cofounder of the World War I Club, once said: "Pretty soon we can fight the war all over again!" The WWI Club, affiliated with the AAA, serves as an information center for both restoration and replica projects of that period.

One excellent restoration is a 1916 *Spad VII*, complete with a 150-horsepower Hispano-Suiza A engine and an 11-mm Vickers machine gun, the workmanship of Rick Helicopters, Inc., of San Carlos, California.

Another fine World War I ship is a replica built by Walter Redfern of Athol, Idaho, of the Fokker DR1 triplane. "The German original could withstand 7.8 Gs and my ship is even stronger!" says Redfern, who now sells plans for replicas powered with a 145-horsepower Warner radial engine.

Like Don Stewart, Marshall White, of Anaheim, California, had in mind an offbeat WWI fighter when he designed *der Jager D.IX* in 1969 as a low-cost, easy-to-build-and-fly sport bipe with the look of a war eagle.

A restoration of a 1916 *Spad VII.*

White even formed a special Flying Eagle Squadron for homebuilders, and naturally they all wear white scarves and oval goggles and call themselves the Red Barons. This fun plane uses the M-6 airfoil for its good center of pressure travel in aerobatic flight. The upper span is 20 feet, the lower is 16 feet, and the wing area is 112 square feet. With a 160-horsepower Lycoming, White got a fantastic climb rate of 3,800 feet per minute, and a 143-mph cruise. *Der Jagers* weigh about 600 to 700 pounds, on the average, and more than 300 are now being constructed.

To many homebuilders, World War II fighters are even more exciting than those from World War I. Since there is a rapidly diminishing supply of *P-51*s, *P-38*s, *Hellcat*s, and similar planes around, the World War II replica business is booming. Scaled-down *Mustang*s are popular, and one intriguing new entry in the homebuilt field is a three-quarter-scale version being built by two brothers, Dr. Thayne Short, of Baton Rouge, Louisiana, and Thomas W. Short, an Arizonan who heads up a new firm called Avaiation AdVentures Unlimited, to market plans and kits.

Their prototype is named *Small Boy Here*, after a famous fighter of the 78th Fighter Group, 84th Fighter Squadron, 8th Air Force. What they were seeking was a smaller *P-51* with the feel and handling of a full-sized ship. The Shorts planned to offer a complete line of

Five-eighth-scale *Mustang.*

Five-eighth-scale RAF Hawker *Hurricane.*

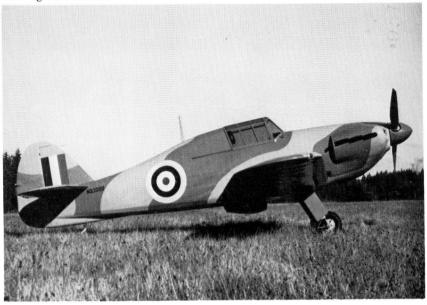

Mustang components, from a four-bladed propeller to a handcrafted fiberglass fuselage that fits over a rugged steel tube framework. For an engine, they favored a Ford V-8 conversion by Fred Geschwender, a fellow EAA member.

To Fred G. Sindlinger, of Puyallup, Washington, no World War II fighter was lovelier to look at than the RAF Hawker *Hurricane,* so he offers plans for a five-eighth-scale replica built entirely of wood, except for the engine mount and undercarriage. The power plant is an 0-320 Lycoming of 150 horsepower with a constant speed propeller. The *Hurricane* weighs 984 pounds empty and 1,375 pounds gross, has a 200 mph top speed, and cruises at 170 mph.

Recently an organization called Replica Fighters of America was formed to gather all information possible on ersatz World War II fighter homebuilts, including every model from Corsairs to FW-190s and Spitfires, all scaled down. RFA president Owen E. Stiegelmeier invites inquiries at Post Office Box 174, Berea, Ohio 44017.

Some of the most beautiful replicas flying today are the result of imaginative design work by Marcel Jurca, a French engineer with a flair for poetry in line. According to Kenneth W. Heit, of Mt. Morris,

Restored 1943 de Havilland *Tiger Moth DH 82A,* owned by screen actor Cliff Robertson.

Michigan, who represents Jurca in this country, he started off early in his career with a Jodel, adopting its basic design concept for his sleek, low-winged *Tempete* and *Sirocco* homebuilts. From this style of construction he graduated to scaled "minifighters."

So far this talented French designer has come up with nine different homebuilts, and he has a few more on the drawing boards, including a delta canard design reminiscent of Bert Rutan's *Vari-Viggen*.

At the bottom of the Jurca line are the single-seater *MJ-2 Tempete*, and the two-place *MJ-5 Sirocco*, while most of the others are scaled-down fighters, beginning with the 225-mph *MJ-7 Gnatsum* (Mustang spelled backward). The *MJ-8* is a baby Focke-Wulf *190* with retractable landing hear; the *MJ-9* a three-quarter-scale Messerschmitt ME-109; the *MJ-10* a similarly scaled Spitfire; the *MJ-12* a two seater *P-40*.

Marcel Jurca's replica plans are works of art in themselves, strictly off-the-cuff amateur drawings, full of funny cartoons but loaded with all the technical data you need to perform a sound construction job. Ken Heit foresees the day when Jurca minifighters will give Curtis Pitts a run for the money in aerobatic competition.

"When you sit up in a *Tempete*, it makes you feel like you're inside a Spit or a 107 or a Mustang," he says enthusiastically. "That's exactly the way Jurca's done it all up!"

15

SAILPLANES AND
GROUND-SKIMMERS
Riders of the Winds

High above many windy hills on a pleasant afternoon you can find a growing army of young men and women flying through the air with the greatest of ease, beneath odd-looking contraptions called hang gliders. These aerial adventurers are reviving an ancient sport that predates Kitty Hawk by many years. Many of them perform their antics hanging on to slender rails. Their support comes from billowing sheets of plastic cloth, like huge sails.

Despite the use of modern materials, hang gliding's heritage is a century old. In 1877 America's first hang glider was patented by a young Panther Springs, Tennessee, preacher, Melville M. Murrell, who reportedly soared across his father's apple orchard on his home-made wings. Back in the sixteenth century, Leonardo da Vinci experimented with flexible flapping wings and once described how birds soar along ridges supported by what he called reflex winds.

Today's sky surfers call these breezes slope winds. They blow particularly steady along California's coastal range, and often over the Alleghenies and the Blue Ridge Mountains of Virginia. Sweeping up grassy hillsides, slope winds can support hang gliders for hours at a time. One hang glider pilot soared for more than ten hours along a Hawaiian mountain slope, and only came down when he got hungry.

Hang gliders fall into two general categories—the flexible-wing type that intrigued da Vinci and the rigid-wing variety pioneered at the

Octave Chanute's Tri-Decker hang glider of 1896. (*National Air and Space Museum, Smithsonian Institution*)

W. H. Martin glider of the 1920s. It was towed by auto to become airborne. (*National Air and Space Museum, Smithsonian Institution*)

Jack Lambie's *Hang Loose* glider.

Jack's sixth-grade class pitches in to build the *Hang Loose*.

turn of the last century by the old bridge builder Octave Chanute and his disciples, Wilbur and Orville Wright.

The revival of hang gliding began in the United States in 1971 when a southern California schoolteacher, Jack Lambie, helped his sixth-grade class build a Chanute-type glider from $24.95 worth of wood scraps, wire, and plastic. The kids called it *Hang Loose* and were pleased when their teacher made a number of flights in it with no serious injury—just a scratch incurred during one bad landing.

Soon other biplane hang gliders appeared, like one graceful, swept-wing, tailless ship built by Taras Kiceniuk, Jr., the sixteen-year-old son of an engineer, who named his ship *Icarus II*. Lately Taras has gone ahead and designed a more advanced hang glider, *Icarus V*, a graceful swept-wing monoplane with movable wingtips that serve as combination ailerons and rudders by inducing a yaw that produces a roll into the desired bank, the way a bird flies.

Another popular type of hang glider was developed in 1958 by Francis M. Rogallo, a NASA engineer at Langley Research Center, for possible space and military applications. Rogallo "paragliders" were first used for sport gliding in Australia, where one devotee, Bill Bennett, adapted them for flight while water-skiing behind speed-boats.

Bennett's idea was imported to this country by Dave Kilbourne and Donnita Holland, of San Jose, California. Both set enviable endurance records riding the slope winds along Mission Peak, not far from the spot where another pioneer hang glider builder, John J. Montgomery, hired acrobats who rode his machines down the sky after being carried a mile aloft beneath hot-air balloons. Kilbourne repeated this stunt.

Old Montgomery would have been amazed at the performance of such modern hang gliders as *Seagull III*, an advanced Rogallo type with a curved leading edge wing spar that adds much safety through greater stability in flight. The curved leading edge provides the same aerodynamic function as "washout" in the rigid wing of modern air-craft—a geometric twist that makes the wingtip fly at a lower angle of attack than the wing root section, so that in stalling, the stall begins at the root and progresses outward. The wingtips of *Seagull III*, like ailerons on a washed-out wing, thus keep flying longer, and so offer better control for stall recovery.

In a Rogallo hang glider, it is desirable to have the center of pressure remain forward when a stall occurs, to provide the pilot with

Rogallo *Eipper Bird* hang glider ground-skimming.

Taras Kiceniuk's *Icarus V* hang glider.

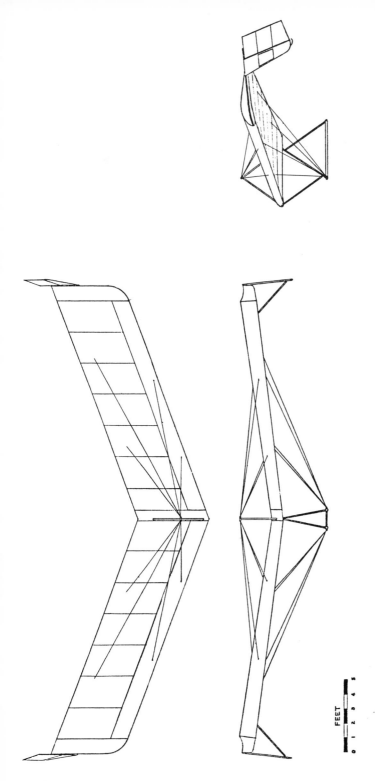

Three-view drawing of *Icarus V. (Copyright © 1974 by Taras Kiceniuk, Jr.)*

FEET
0 1 2 3 4 5

183

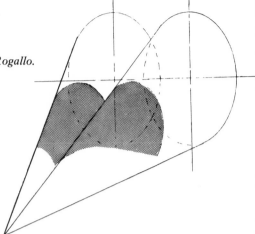

Seagull modification of the conical *Rogallo.*
(*Courtesy of Seagull Aircraft*)

sufficient control to pull out of a dive, should he pitch over too steeply
and cause his sail to "luff," in the manner of a sailboat pointed too
high into the wind. Rogallo sails are generally of two types—the
cylindrical and the conical. *Seagull III* is of the latter variety.

Aside from the few modern, high-performance hang gliders that are
now evolving, most in use today are homebuilt Rogallos used for
"ground-skimming"—slides down the sky only inches above the
ground. Sometimes a hang glider pilot accidentally lands in a treetop
or other obstruction, but the only fatalities that have occurred with
ground-skimmers have resulted from auto-towing the frail machines
or encountering dangerous downdrafts.

However, more daring Rogallo enthusiasts now launch themselves
from such high places as a 1,500-foot hill near Sylmar, California, for
long, thrilling rides down the sky to a tiny landing area at the base of
the hill. There have been a number of accidents at Sylmar, including
fatalities, resulting from gross carelessness, when overly enthusiastic
pilots attempted such foolhardy stunts as hanging by their heels
upside down on the control bar and lost control. Flown properly, such
kites are quite safe, but mistreated, they can become lethal.

Because of the rapid and widespread interest in this new do-it-yourself sport, a nationwide organization has been formed to coordinate all
activities, insofar as possible, and to act as an information center for
local groups. The organization is called the United States Hang
Gliding Association, Inc. Its address is Post Office Box 66306, Los
Angeles, California 90066, telephone (213) 390-3065.

The *Seagull III* hang glider being piloted over Torrance Beach, California, by co-designer Bob Keeler.

VJ-23 Swingwing hang glider.

President of USHGA is Lloyd Licher, a veteran soaring pilot and officer of the Soaring Society of America. Vice-president is Bill Allen, editor of *Ground Skimmer* magazine. So far USHGA has more than 10,000 members in virtually every state in the union.

Among the more popular hang gliders, besides *Icarus V* and such Rogallos as the *Wills Wing* and *Free-Flight,* are Volmer Jensen's *VJ-11* Chanute-type biplane, his monoplanes *VJ-23 Swingwing* and *VJ-24 Sunfun*; the tailed monoplane *Quicksilver B*; and the three-axis control tailed *Waterman Biplane.*

Others of recent interest include *Skysail,* a swept-wing monoplane designed by SSA's Ultralight Committee chairman Frank Culver; *Chandelle,* a one- or two-place Rogallo; and the Whitney Porta-Wing Rogallo, which folds down into a package the size of a golf bag.

The FAA has wisely given the new hang gliding movement a fairly free hand, to encourage a grass-roots interest in flying similar to that which rebuilt Germany's air power in the years between the two world wars, when powered flying was outlawed by the League of Nations.

So long as these kits remain away from busy air traffic control areas and stay below 500 feet, the FAA looks the other way.

On the other hand the FAA is keeping a watchful eye on the growth of the sport to make sure it is properly self-policed, for the safety of everybody concerned. One enthusiast who is helping the movement

186

The Jensen *VJ-11* hang glider under construction and in flight.

The Schweizer *1-26C* single-place sailplane.

grow in the right direction is Stan Hall, a Lockheed Sunnyvale space systems engineer, who is now working on his ninth sailplane, a two-place VW-powered motorglider, the *Oryx*. One of Hall's designs, the sailplane *Cherokee II,* is the world's most widely constructed experimental class homebuilt glider, with more than a hundred flying today.

"What these youngsters need," says Hall, "is a homebuilt sailplane that bridges the gap between ground-skimming and real soaring, without sinking them financially in the process."

High-performance sailplanes today cost anywhere from $10,000 to $20,000 and up, with avionics added, and Hall feels that soaring has too long been regarded as a rich man's game.

There are breakthroughs already, like Hall's *Cherokee II,* which costs under $500 to build and takes not more than 50 hours for an amateur builder to put together. Thus, he points out, a man and his high school-age son could build one in four to five months, working only on weekends.

There are a number of other sailplane homebuilt plans and kits on the market today, the most popular being the fine Schweizer *1-26C* single-place craft, which does not qualify as an amateur-built ship in the experimental category because all parts are cut and welded and ready to assemble. More than 560 *1-26* sailplanes have been produced, of which about 200 have been constructed from kits by their owners.

188

The *1-26* is a small sailplane with wingspan of 40 feet, wing area of 160 square feet, an empty weight of 370 pounds, and maximum gross weight of 600 pounds. It takes the average homebuilder from four to six months to put a *1-26* together in flight condition.

Another fine line of homebuilt sailplanes are those designed by Gus Briegleb, of Adelanto, California. One, the *BG-6*, was type certificated back in 1941 and became a popular wartime trainer. More advanced is the *BG-7*, designed primarily for cross-country soaring, with a span of 40 feet 3 inches—8 feet wider than the *BG-6*.

The *BG-12*, says Briegleb, is the only "you-build-it" sailplane with contest performance capability available at normal cost. It can be put together in a two-car garage with ordinary hand tools in less than 1,000 hours. It has graceful, slender wings of 50-foot span, a gross weight of 750 pounds, and a glide angle of 34:1.

Bryan Aircraft, Inc., of Bryan, Ohio, offers a line of homebuilt sailplanes that can be built more quickly, in approximately 500 hours— the *RS-15*, and the *HP-16, HP-17,* and *HP-18*. Except for 4-inch-spaced structural foam wing ribs, all-metal construction is employed throughout in the Bryans.

Every now and then, when you begin thinking that there can't be anything else new in the homebuilt field, something pops up. For example, there's Jim Marske's *Monarch*, a small, 125-pound ultralight soaring craft that, says the designer, was so named because "the

Briegleb's *BG-12* sailplane.

Monarch butterfly exemplifies the intimate relationship of a creature in flight with its environment."

Construction materials of the *Monarch* are, for the most part, plastic with a little wood and steel added for strength. Nose, fuselage, bucket seat, and instrument panel are all made of fiberglass. The leading edges of the wings are preshaped in molds for strength, and the aft section of wing and fin are dacron covered and doped.

With a wingspan of 36 feet, wing area of 155 square feet, and light wing loading of barely 2 pounds per square foot, *Monarch* can soar like a butterfly at very low altitudes, where thermal bubbles are just beginning to form. You can add a nose fairing—a streamlined pilot shield that cuts drag, offers crash protection, and looks nice.

You can tote a *Monarch* to a soaring slope in the back of a station wagon, with the wings cradled on top, and two small boys can set it up. With a glide angle of 16:1 at 40 mph, and a minimum sink rate of only 218 feet per second at 30 mph, it's quite a performer. Marske offers plans and both standard and deluxe kits.

There are a number of other homebuilt sailplanes on the market, such as the *Duster,* the *Tern,* the *SG-1,* and the *D-8,* so it looks as if American youths have ample opportunity to once again get into the

The Bensen gyrocopter *Scorpion.* (*Courtesy Bensen Aircraft Corp.*)

air in their own creations, as they did in the 1920s when the big craze was building and flying primary gliders. I know—I was one of them!

Lest we forget, there are still other unusual flying machines to be built at home. There are hundreds of rotorcraft fans flying experimental class whirlybirds, like the ubiquitous Bensen *B-8M* gyrocopter, the *Scorpion* "hover-lover" helicopter, and recently the little single-seat Jukka Tervamaki *JT-5 Autogyro* from Finland.

Bensen Aircraft Corporation of Raleigh, North Carolina, likes to call its gyrocopter the "world's most popular homebuilt aircraft," and it flies with wheels, floats, or snow skis. Its designer, Dr. Igor Bensen, established a number of world records for Class E-3A autogyros in his machine, which can be assembled in just a few weeks. It started out as a glider in 1953, to be auto-towed, but now can soar to 12,500 feet in free flight. With a free-swinging, 20-foot rotor, it's not a helicopter—it needs a run of some 600 feet to set it rotating for liftoff.

Unlike the Bensen gyrocopter, the *Scorpion,* with kits and plans offered by RotorWay Aircraft, Inc., Tempe, Arizona, is a full-fledged, albeit small, helicopter. Its builders like to call it a "hover-lover." Many are in use today for standard helicopter flight instruction. These machines have a service ceiling of 12,000 feet and weigh about 450 pounds. Their little 100-horsepower Vulcan V4 engines sound like mad hornets.

Suppose, in closing, you're tired of all that engine noise, can't afford a high-performance sailplane, but still would like to go out and goof around the sky, down under 150 feet altitude, where the FAA says officially you're a kite. That's what USAF Colonel Bill Skliar had in mind when he designed the funny little *Aqua Glider.*

Colonel Skliar is involved in flight test work at the Edwards AFB Flight Test Center, and now and then he likes to get away from the job. Sometimes he'll fire up an elliptical-winged homebuilt Formula One racer called *Shark* and chase other pilots around pylons.

At other times he ties his *Aqua Glider* to one end of a rope and a speedboat to the other. Then, at a hand signal, his *Aqua Glider* scoots over the water like a winged water-skier, and suddenly he's flying—up, up, and away! His little bird, with its 16-foot wingspan, drops free at around 250 feet, and Colonel Skliar is on his own, to go chase ducks. He lands at about 35 mph, hooks up the rope once more, and is off again. What a way to go!

After more that 1,000 flights the *Aqua Glider* still is his favorite flying machine. It was built by a Boy Scout Air Explorer Squadron in eight months. After a story appeared in *Popular Science,* requests for plans poured in. Today there are perhaps 30 *Aqua Gliders* flying happily over the waters of Brazil, Japan, and Bermuda, as well as the United States.

When Colonel Skliar shipped off to Vietnam for a tour of duty, he donated his prototype to the EAA museum for permanent display, where it now rests, among the other wonderful homebuilt machines that have made America one of the world's most air-minded countries.

To many pilots there's nothing like learning to fly in a glider or sailplane to understand and appreciate the secret of bird flight. Instead of sitting behind a noisy engine, you're flying freely, riding the winds, drawing on the power of the atmosphere and its boundless energy, making it work for you.

Rudimentary hang gliders and ground-skimmers are launching a whole new generation of youths into the sky at nominal cost and relative safety. However, a word of caution is necessary: Building your own aircraft and flying it are two distinctly different things.

Before you launch yourself on a pilot's career in a homebuilt, call the nearest FAA general aviation district office (see page 236) and ask advice on where to go for flight instruction. And while you can legally slide down the sky in a hang glider without a pilot's license, you should at least discuss the technique with someone experienced in the art before attempting it yourself.

There are specific safety precautions that must be observed; fatalities have occurred when such precautions were disregarded. Among the most dangerous kinds of hang gliding operations are those in which the device is towed behind a speeding auto for launch. There is more chance of structural failure during an auto-tow, and a bad maneuver can suddenly turn into a deadly plunge to earth.

Equally dangerous to hang gliders are unseen turbulent wind currents usually found near the ground, downwind from clumps of trees, buildings, and other obstructions. Avoid them at all cost, for they can cause a slow-flying hang glider to stall and crash.

There are many fine glider schools and power plane flight schools where dual instruction can be obtained at nominal cost, to properly qualify you to join the ranks of the three-quarters of a million rated pilots flying today. And even if you're already a rated pilot, be sure you're "current" before attempting a flight in a homebuilt.

Once you're sure of your own proficiency, and have the FAA's stamp of approval on your personal aircraft, go ahead and enjoy yourself—it's the greatest sport in the world!

HOMEBUILT AIRCRAFT DIRECTORY

Ninety-six homebuilt aircraft are listed in this directory. Each individual homebuilt is represented by a small photograph that matches the detailed specifications outlined in the twelve columns of the directory.

The first column provides the name of the particular aircraft. The second column gives the seating capacity and type of plane (high-wing, biplane, aeorbatic, high-wing cabin, parasol, etc.). The third column indicates construction materials. The fourth column deals with the type of power plant and horsepower generated. The fifth column covers span, length, and wing area. The sixth column gives information on gross weight and empty weight.

Column seven gives the stall, cruise, and maximum speed of the plane. Column eight tells the rate of climb speed in feet and minutes, plus the ceiling. In column nine the author indicates the amount of roll in feet on takeoff and landing. Column ten gives the plane's fuel capacity and its range in miles. Column eleven gives the price of information brochures on the plane as well as the price for construction plans and information on whether a kit is available and, if so, its price. (All prices quoted are, of course, current prices and subject to change.) Finally, the last column provides the name and address of the distributor of kits and plans for the particular plane. Note that NA in a column indicates that information is not available.

KEY TO COLUMN HEAD ABBREVIATIONS
USED IN HOMEBUILT AIRCRAFT DIRECTORY

Aircraft:	Aircraft	Climb:	Climb
		fpm:	Feet per minute
Seat. & Type:	Seating and Type	Ceiling:	Ceiling
Constr.	Construction	Roll (ft.):	Roll in feet
Power:	Power	T/O:	Takeoff
		Land.:	Landing
Span:	Span		
Length:	Length	Fuel:	Fuel
W. Area:	Wing Area	gals.:	Gallons
		Range:	Range
Wt.:	Weight	mi.:	Miles
Gross:	Gross		
Empty:	Empty	Info.:	Information brochure
		Plans:	Construction plans
Spd.:	Speed	Kit:	Construction kit
Stall:	Stall		
Cruise:	Cruise	Distributor:	Distributor
Max.:	Maximum		

Ace Scooter Model D

Acey Deucy

Aerosport Quail

Aerosport Scamp

Aircraft	Seat. & Type	Constr.	Power	Span Length W. Area	Wt. Gross Empty
Ace Scooter Model D	1 high- wing	wood/ fabric	VW 1,500 cc	21' 10" 15' 6" 115	625 390
Acey Deucy	2 parasol	tube/ wood/ fabric	Cotinental A-65	32' 6" 20' 9" 155	1,275 750
Aerosport Quail	1 high- wing	all metal	VW 1,600 cc	24' 15' 12" 84	750 466
Aerosport Scamp	1 biplane	all metal	VW 1,824 cc	17' 6" 14' 105	725 450
EAA Acro Sport	1 biplane, aerobatic	tube/ wood/ fabric	Lycoming 180 hp	19' 7" 17' 6" 120	1,200 733
Aristocraft II	4-6 monoplane	all metal	Franklin Sport Six 215 hp	37' 25' 190	3,500 1,700
Baby Ace, Model D	1 parasol	tube/ wood/ fabric	Continental A-65	26' 5" 17' 9" 112	950 575
Baby Great Lakes	1 biplane, aerobatic	tube/ wood/ fabric	80 hp	16' 8" 13' 9" 86	850 475

EAA Acro Sport

Aristocraft II

Baby Ace Model D

Baby Great Lakes

Spd. Stall Cruise Max.	Climb fpm Ceiling	Roll (ft.) T/O Land.	Fuel (gals.) Range (mi.)	Info. Plans Kit	Distributor
34 75 90	550 10,000	250 300	5 175	$2 $36.50 partial	Ace Aircraft Manufacturing Co. 106 Arthur Rd. Asheville, N.C. 28806
25 87 104	650 12,000	250 300	14 250	NA $20 NA	John C. Powell 4 Donald Dr. Middletown, R.I. 02840
40 120 130	500 12,000	300 300	8 260	$5 $22 $2,995	Aerosport, Inc. Holly Springs Airport Holly Springs, N.C. 27540
42 85 120	700 13,000	300 250	6 200	$5 $32 $2,395	Aerosport, Inc. Holly Springs Airport Holly Springs, N.C. 27540
50 130 180	3,000 20,000	150 800	20 350	$5 $60 NA	Experimental Aircraft Assoc. Box 229 Hales Corners, Wis. 53130
40 120 135	510 14,000	1,200 1,000	76 700	$3 $85 $3,898	O'Neill Airplane Co. 791 Livingston St. Carlyle, Ill. 62231
35 100 110	1,200 16,000	200 250	17 350	$2 $28.50 yes	Ace Aircraft Co. 106 Arthur Rd. Asheville, N.C. 28806
50 118 138	2,000 17,000	300 400	12 250	$3 $6 NA	Barney Oldfield Aircraft Co. P.O. Box 5974 Cleveland, Ohio 44101

Bantam W-3

BD-4

BD-5A

BD-5J

Aircraft	Seat. & Type	Constr.	Power	Span Length W. Area	Wt. Gross Empty
Bantam W-3	1 low-wing	all metal	Lycoming 0-145	18' 5" 13' 9" 75	790 535
BD-4	2-4 folding-wing	metal/ fiberglass	Lycoming 180 hp	25' 7" 21' 4" 102.4	2,000 1,080
BD-5A	1 pusher	all metal	Hirth 70 hp	14' 3" 13' 3" 32.2	640 335
BD-5J	1 jet	all metal	TRS-18 Jet, 220# thrust	17' 12' 5" 38	910 425
BD-6	1 high-wing	all metal	Hirth 55-70 hp	21' 5" 16' 9" 55.5	650 375
Breezy RLU-1	2 open/ parasol	tube/ wood/ fabric	Continental 90 hp	33' 22' 6" 165	1,200 700
Cavalier SA-102	2 low-wing	wood/ fabric	135 hp	26' 10" 18' 4" 118	1,500 900
Cook JC-1 Challenger	4 low-wing	all metal	Lycoming 150 hp	27' 22' 131	2,150 930

BD-6

Breezy RLU-1

Cavalier SA-102

Cook JC-1 Challenger

Spd. Stall Cruise Max.	Climb fpm Ceiling	Roll (ft.) T/O Land.	Fuel (gals.) Range (mi.)	Info. Plans Kit	Distributor
52 115 140	1,000 16,000	500 550	11.5 450	$2 $75 canopy	Bill Warwick 5726 Clearsite Torrance, Calif. 90505
63 174 183	1,400 10,000+	600 600	58 750	$4.50 $50 $3,975	Bede Aircraft Co., Inc. Newton Airport Newton, Kans. 67114
66 237 241	1,890 24,500	820 650	20 490	$5 NA $3,110	Bede Aircraft Co., Inc. Newton Airport Newton, Kans. 67114
71 325 332	2,400 30,000	1,100 800	50 520	$6.50 NA $24,900	Bede Aircraft Co., Inc. Newton Airport Newton, Kans. 67114
50 140 200	900 14,000	600 400	21 450	$4 NA $2,500	Bede Aircraft Co., Inc. Newton Airport Newton, Kans. 67114
25 75 105	500 15,000	450 300	18 250	$1.50 $25 NA	Breezy Aircraft 8748 S. 82nd Ct. Hickory Hills, Ill. 60457
50 155 200	1,500 16,000	600 800	34 850	$4 $125 NA	K & S Aircraft 4623 Fortune Rd. S.E. Calgary 23, Alberta, Canada
54 145 150	750 15,000	620 400	40 600	$5 $200 partial	Cook Aircraft P.O. Box 1013 Torrance, Calif. 90505

197

Daphne SD-1A

Davis DA-2A

Der Jager IX

Draggin' Fly

Aircraft	Seat. & Type	Constr.	Power	Span Length W. Area	Wt. Gross Empty
Daphne SD-1A	2 high- wing	tube/ wood/ fabric	Continental C-85	26' 3" 19' 7" 139	1,350 825
Davis DA-2A	2 V-tail	all metal	Continental A-65	19' 3" 17' 10" 82.5	1,125 610
Der Jager IX	1 WWI replica	tube/ wood/ fabric	Lycoming 160 hp	20' 17' NA	888 534
Draggin' Fly	1 open parasol	tube/ wood/ fabric	VW 1,600 cc	24' 5" 17' 5" 110	680 430
Druine Turbulent	1 low- wing	wood/ fabric	VW 1,200 cc	21' 7" 17' 10" 80	690 455
Dyke Delta	4 folding tips	tube/ fiberglass	Lycoming 150 hp	22' 19' 180	1,750 1,000
EOS/001	1 retractable	all metal	Hirth 70 hp	26' 16' 7" NA	750 420
Evans VP-2	2 low- wing	wood/ fabric	VW 1,600 cc	27' 19' 130	650 440

Druine Turbulent

Dyke Delta

EOS/001

Evans VP-2

Spd. Stall Cruise Max.	Climb fpm Ceiling	Roll (ft.) T/O Land.	Fuel (gals.) Range (mi.)	Info. Plans Kit	Distributor
45 130 149	800 10,000	400 300	21 360	$2 $80 NA	Art Szaraz 419 Center Rd. Bedford, Ohio 44145
62 115 120	400 10,000	800 700	20 450	$2 $110 NA	Leeon Davis 3501 Baumann Ave. Midland, Tex. 79701
54 133 145	2,000 NA	175 250	24 532	$2 $40 NA	Marshall White 5141 Warner Ave. Huntington Beach, Calif. 92647
30 63 70	350 10,000	200 200	8 200	$2 NA NA	Ron Wier 6406 Burgundy San Diego, Calif.
55 93 101	410 10,000	400 450	10.5 350	$3 $60 NA	Sturgeon Air Ltd. 36 Airport Rd. Edmonton, Alberta, Canada
none 170 190	2,000 14,000	700 1,500	41 700	$3 $125 NA	John W. Dyke 2840 Old Yellow Springs Rd. Fairborn, Ohio 45324
52 181 200	2,160 15,000	NA NA	20 NA	$5 NA NA	Airmotive Engineers Oakland Pontiac Airport 6330 Highland Rd. Pontiac, Mich. 48054
45 75 95	600 10,000	450 200	14 250	$3 $45 NA	Evans Aircraft Box 774 La Jolla, Calif. 92037

Fly Baby

Focke-Wulf 190

Fokker DR-1

Grasshopper

Aircraft	Seat. & Type	Constr.	Power	Span Length W. Area	Wt. Gross Empty
Fly Baby	1 low-wing	wood/ fabric	Continental C-85	28' 18' 10" 120	924 605
Focke-Wulf 190	1 WWII replica	wood/ fabric	VW 1,600 cc	20' 16' 7" 70	850 500
Fokker DR-1	1 WWI replica	tube/ wood/ fabric	Warner 145 hp	23' 7" 19' NA	1,378 948
Grasshopper	1 high-wing	tube/ wood	Continental A-65	30' 26' 120	900 580
Gypsy Hawk	1 low-wing	all metal	Continental A-65	18' 6" 16' 63	820 520
5/8 Hawker Hurricane	1 WWII replica	wood/ fabric	Lycoming 150 hp	25' 1" 19' 8" 102	1,375 984
Heath Parasol Model V	1 parasol	steel tube/ fabric	Continental 40 hp	25' 17' 3" 110	550 350
Hiperbipe	2 aerobatic bipe	tube/ wood	Lycoming 180 hp	22' 10" 20' 150	1,800 1,150

Gypsy Hawk

5/8 Hawker Hurricane

Heath Parasol Model V

Hiperbipe

Spd. Stall Cruise Max.	Climb fpm Ceiling	Roll (ft.) T/O Land.	Fuel (gals.) Range (mi.)	Info. Plans Kit	Distributor
45 110 120	1,100 15,000	200 200	16 300	$1 $25 NA	Peter M. Bowers 13826 Des Moines Way S. Seattle, Wash. 98168
55 135 150	1,000 12,000	650 650	10 400	$6 $125 NA	War Aircraft Replicas 348 Eighth St. Santa Paula, Calif. 93060
40 100 120	2,000 20,000	100 250	30 300	$2 $50 NA	W. W. Redfern Route 1 Athol, Idaho 83801
25 75 85	1,000 12,000	200 200	NA NA	NA NA NA	Robert E. Barrows R.D. 2, Box 78 Frankfort, N.Y. 13340
60 115 130	800 15,000	400 400	20 400	NA NA NA	Richard Jameson 124-C N. Stamford Ave. Fullerton, Calif. 92631
62 165 240	1,350 15,000	490 550	32 575	$5 $115 NA	Sindlinger Aircraft 5923 9th St. N.W. Puyallup, Wash. 98371
30 85 90	500 10,000	300 250	NA NA	NA $10 NA	Ace Aircraft Co. 106 Arthur Rd. Asheville, N.C. 28806
49 160 170	1,600 20,000	390 595	37 480	yes yes partial	Sorrell Aviation Rt. 1, Box 660 Tenino, Wash. 98589

Miller JM-2

Jungster II

Jungster I

Jurca MJ-7 Gnatsum

Aircraft	Seat. & Type	Constr.	Power	Span Length W. Area	Wt. Gross Empty
Miller JM-2	1 Formula One	metal, plastic	Continental 0-200 (100 hp)	15' 19' 66	1,000 630
Jungster I	1 biplane	wood/ fabric	Continental 85 hp	16' 8" 16' NA	1,000 605
Jungster II	1 parasol	wood/ fabric	Continental 85 hp	22' 4" 16' 11" NA	1,375 739
Jurca MJ-7 Gnatsum	1 Baby P-51	wood/ fabric	220-350 hp	25' 10" 22' 4" 110	2,000 1,175
Jurca MJ-5 Sirocco	2 retractable	wood/ fabric	85-150 hp	21' 6" 20' 6" 102	1,300 726
Jurca MJ-2 Tempete	1 low- wing	wood/ fabric	65-125 hp	19' 6" 18' 6" 82	880 680
Jurca MJ-8 F/W 190	1 3/4 scale replica	wood/ fiberglass	160-300 hp	25' 10" 21' 8" 151	2,000 1,450
Ken Rand KR-1	1 low-wing, retractable	wood/ styrofoam/ epoxy	VW 1,200 cc	17' 2" 12' 8" 62	600 340

Jurca MJ-5 Sirocco

Jurca MJ-2 Tempete

Jurca MJ-8 F/W 190

Ken Rand KR-1

Spd. Stall Cruise Max.	Climb fpm Ceiling	Roll (ft.) T/O Land.	Fuel (gals.) Range (mi.)	Info. Plans Kit	Distributor
74 190 235	1,600 18,000	1,500 1,000	12.5 350	$5 no $8,000	J. W. Miller Aviation, Inc. Horseshoe Bay Airport Route 3, Box 757 Marble Falls, Tex. 78654
52 150 200	2,500 16,000	300 800	16 300	$4 $75 NA	K & S Aircraft 4623 Fortune Rd. S.E. Calgary 23, Alberta, Canada
55 148 170	3,500 6,000	200 800	16 NA	$4 $75 NA	K & S Aircraft 4623 Fortune Rd. S.E. Calgary 23, Alberta, Canada
65 175 225	1,500 16,000	900 800	30 570	$2 $120 NA	Jurca Plans 581 Helen St. Mt. Morris, Mich. 48458
60 162 190	2,500 20,000	820 750	36 570	$3 $100 NA	Jurca Plans 581 Helen St. Mt. Morris, Mich. 48458
41 150 174	1,800 16,400	600 750	16 375	$3 $70 NA	Jurca Plans 581 Helen St. Mt. Morris, Mich. 48458
55 150 180	1,650 NA	380 800	32 575	$2 $120 NA	Jurca Plans 581 Helen St. Mt. Morris, Mich. 48458
42 140 160	700 12,000	300 600	7 500	free $25 parts	Rand-Robinson Engr., Inc. 6171 Cornell Drive Huntington Beach, Calif. 92647

Marquart MA-5 Charger

Meyer Little Toot

Midget Mustang

Mini-Ace CA-61

Aircraft	Seat. & Type	Constr.	Power	Span Length W. Area	Wt. Gross Empty
Marquart MA-5 Charger	2 open biplane	tube/ wood/ fabric	100-180 hp	24' 19' 6" 170	1,550 1,000
Meyer Little Toot	1 aerobatic bipe	tube/ wood/ fabric	90-200 hp	19' 16' 6" 123	1,230 914
Midget Mustang	1 scale P-51	all metal	Lycoming 165	24' 10" 19' 6" 97	1,500 900
Mini-Ace CA-61	1-2 low-wing	wood/ fabric	Continental A-65	27' 6" 18' 11" 126.5	950 606
Mini-Ace CA-65	2 retractable	wood/ fabric	Lycoming 125 hp	25' 19' 108	1,500 900
Mini-Coupe	1 low-wing	all metal	VW 1,600 cc	22' 4" 16' 4" 78.4	850 494
Moon Maid	1 low-wing	tube/ wood/ fabric	VW 1,523 cc	23' 6" 20' 85	682 448
Mooney Mite	1 retractable	tube/ wood/ fabric	Lycoming 145 hp	26' 10" 17' 8" 95	780 505

Mini-Ace CA-65

Mini-Coupe

Moon Maid

Mooney Mite

Spd. Stall Cruise Max.	Climb fpm Ceiling	Roll (ft.) T/O Land.	Fuel (gals.) Range (mi.)	Info. Plans Kit	Distributor
42 130 (at 160 hp) 140 (at 160 hp)	1,600 (at 160 hp) 15,000	600 800	26 400+	$3 $75 partial	Ed Marquart P.O. Box 3032 Riverside, Calif. 92509
55 110 127	1,000 16,500	500 500	18 300	$2 $75 NA	Meyer Aircraft 5706 Abby Dr. Corpus Christi, Tex. 78413
57 180 240	1,800 16,000	600 800	25 500	$2 $125 NA	Bushby Aircraft 848 Westwood Glenwood, Ill. 60425
47 118 120	1,200 15,000	200 300	17 425	$3 $50 NA	Anton Cvjetkovic Box 323 Newbury Park, Calif. 91320
55 135 160	1,000 15,000	450 600	28 500	$3 $110 NA	Anton Cvjetkovic Box 323 Newbury Park, Calif. 91320
48 90 105	750 12,500	400 500	14 300	free free to members $1,695	Chris Tena Aircraft Association P.O. Box 1 Hillsboro, Oreg. 97123
45 80 95	600 12,000	200 250	12 200	$2 no no	Richard Doyle 104 S. Albert St. Mount Prospect, Ill. 60056
43 130 143	1,000 21,000	300 275	17 600	$5 $69.95 $1,800	Mooney Mite Aircraft Corp. Charlottesville, Va. 22903

2/3 scale Mustang

Owl OR-71

Pazmany PL-2

Pazmany PL-4A

Aircraft	Seat. & Type	Constr.	Power	Span Length W. Area	Wt. Gross Empty
2/3 scale Mustang	2 WWII replica	tube/ fiberglass/ aluminum wings	Geschwender Ford V-8 330 hp	19' 3" 24' 103.75	2,400 1,930
Owl OR-71	1 Formula One racer	tube/ wood	Continental 0-200 (100 hp)	20' 16' 4" 67	850 553
Pazmany PL-2	2 low-wing	all metal	Lycoming 150 hp	28' 6" 19' 4" 116	1,900 1,450
Pazmany PL-4A	1 low-wing	all metal	VW 1,600 cc	26' 8" 16' 6" 89	850 578
Pitts S-1S	1 aerobatic bipe	tube/ wood/ fabric	Lycoming 180 hp	17' 4" 15' 6" 98.5	1,150 720
Renegade	1 Formula Vee, midwing monoplane	steel tube/ spruce/ fabric	VW 36-65 hp	16' 14' 6" 75	700 400
Smith Miniplane	1 aerobatic bipe	tube/ wood/ fabric	Lycoming 125 hp	17' 15' 1" 100	1,000 616
Sonerai I	1 Formula Vee	steel tube/ aluminum	VW 1,600 cc	16' 8" 16' 8" 75	750 450

Pitts S-1S

Renegade

Smith Miniplane

Sonerai I

Spd. / Stall / Cruise / Max.	Climb fpm / Ceiling	Roll (ft.) / T/O / Land.	Fuel (gals.) / Range (mi.)	Info. / Plans / Kit	Distributor
70 / 250 / 300	3,000 / NA	NA / NA	50 / 1,000	free / NA / NA	Aviation Adventures, Unlimited Inc. 435 W. Gleneagles Dr. Phoenix, Ariz. 85023
70 / 210 / 255	2,500 / 20,000	600 / 1,000	9 / 250	$5 / $150 / yes	Vin-Del Aircraft 29718 Knollview Dr. Miraleste, Calif. 90732
54 / 136 / 153	1,700 / 22,000	700 / 700	25 / 381	$3 / $150 / NA	Pazmany Aircraft Box 10051 San Diego, Calif. 92110
48 / 98 / 120	650 / 13,000	486 / 436	12 / 375	$3 / $150 / NA	Pazmany Aircraft Box 10051 San Diego, Calif. 92110
62 / 150 / 176	2,600 / 20,000	450 / 1,000	19 / 350	$3 / $150 / $9,725	Pitts Aviation Enterprises, Inc. Box 548 Homestead, Fla. 33030
49 / 130 (varies w/power) / 145 (varies w/power)	1,000 / NA	500 / 500	8 / 325	$1 / $35 / $1,500	Southern Aeronautical Corp. 14100 Lake Candlewood Court Miami Lakes, Fla. 33014
56 / 122 / 130	1,000 / 14,500	374 / 500	17 / 300	$1 / NA / NA	Dorothy Smith 1938 Jacaranda Fullerton; Calif. 92633
44 / 150 / 160+	1,200 / NA	600 / 500	10 / 300	$1 / $50 / components	Monnett Experimental Aircraft 410 Adams St. Elgin, Ill. 60120

Sonerai II

Sportaire

Stephens Akro

Stewart Foo Fighter

Aircraft	Seat. & Type	Constr.	Power	Span Length W. Area	Wt. Gross Empty
Sonerai II	2, tandem mid-wing	steel tube/ aluminum	VW 1,700 cc	18' 8" 18' 10.5" 84	925 506
Sportaire	2 low-wing	tube/ wood/ fabric	Lycoming 125 hp	26' 4" 20' 6" 107	1,600 984
Stephens Akro	1 aerobatic	tube/ wood	Lycoming 180 hp	24' 4" 19' 98	1,300 830
Stewart Foo Fighter	1 WWI type	tube/ wood/ fabric	Franklin Sport Four (S-4)	20' 8" 18' 9" 130	1,100 720
Stewart Headwind	1 C-3 type	tube/ wood/ fabric	VW 53 hp	28' 3" 17' 9" 111	700 433
Steen Skybolt	2 aerobatic bipe	tube/ wood/ fabric	Lycoming 180 hp	24' 19' 155	1,650 1,080
Acroduster One	1 aerobatic bipe	tube/metal/ wood/ fabric	Lycoming 200 hp	19' 15' 9" 105	1,190 740
Acroduster Too	2 aerobatic bipe	tube/ wood/ fabric	Lycoming 180 hp	21' 5" 18' 6" 130	1,630 1,000

Stewart Headwind

Steen Skybolt

Acroduster One

Acroduster Too

Spd. Stall Cruise Max.	Climb fpm Ceiling	Roll (ft.) T/O Land.	Fuel (gals.) Range (mi.)	Info. Plans Kit	Distributor
44 140 160	600 NA	900 600	10 NA	$1 $75 yes	Monnett Experimental Aircraft 410 Adams St. Elgin, Ill. 60120
63 132 145	1,000 15,000	750 500	22 400	$3 $60 $3,432	Rogers Aircraft 758 Libby Dr. Riverside, Calif. 92507
50 150 200	3,000 18,000	300 300	32 450	$2 $150 NA	Stephens Aircraft P.O. Box 3171 Rubidoux, Calif. 92509
48 115 145	1,200 20,000	450 550	19 345	$2 $20 NA	Stewart Aircraft 11420 Route 165 Salem, Ohio 44460
35 75 85	650 10,300	650 300	5 195	$2 $15 $1,895	Stewart Aircraft 11420 Route 165 Salem, Ohio 44460
50 130 145	1,100 10,500	350 500	29 400	$2 $50 NA	Steen Aero Lab 3218 S. Cherry Denver, Colo. 80222
70 165 180	3,000 20,000	150 300	25 NA	$2 $60 partial	Stolp Starduster Corp. 4301 Twining St. Riverside, Calif. 92509
55 155 170	2,300 20,000	165 300	45 600	$2 $60 partial	Stolp Starduster Corp. 4301 Twining St. Riverside, Calif. 92509

Starduster SA-100

Starduster Too

Starlet SA-500

Teenie Two

Aircraft	Seat. & Type	Constr.	Power	Span Length W. Area	Wt. Gross Empty
Starduster SA-100	1 aerobatic bipe	tube/ wood/ fabric	Lycoming 125 hp	19' 16' 6" 110	1,080 700
Starduster Too	2 aerobatic bipe	tube/ wood/ fabric	Lycoming 125 hp	24' 20' 162	1,800 1,000
Starlet SA-500	1 parasol	tube/ wood/ fabric	VW 1,500 cc	25' 17' 83	1,058 550
Teenie Two	1 low-wing	all metal	VW 1,600 cc	18' 12' 11" 60	585 310
Thorp T-18	2 low-wing	all metal	Lycoming 125 hp	20' 10" 18' 86	1,500 900
Turner T-40B	2 low-wing	wood/ fiberglass	Lycoming 125 hp	26' 8" 19' 5" 102.5	1,500 950
Van's RV-3	1 low-wing aerobatic	all metal	Lycoming 150 hp	19' 11" 19' 90	1,050 695
Vari Viggen	2 canard/ delta	wood/ metal/ fiberglass	Lycoming 150 hp	19' 20' 123	1,700 1,020

210

Thorp T-18

Turner T-40B

Van's RV-3

Vari Viggen

Spd. Stall Cruise Max.	Climb fpm Ceiling	Roll (ft.) T/O Land.	Fuel (gals.) Range (mi.)	Info. Plans Kit	Distributor
50 132 147	2,000 20,000	200 300	24 450	$2 $25 partial	Stolp Starduster Corp. 4301 Twining St. Riverside, Calif. 92509
50 145 160	2,200 18,000	200 300	54 750+	$2 $50 partial	Stolp Starduster Corp. 4301 Twining St. Riverside, Calif. 92509
56 125 150	1,600 18,000	200 500	22.5 300	$2 $35 partial	Stolp Starduster Corp. 4301 Twining St. Riverside, Calif. 92509
50 110 150	800 15,000	300 600	9 300	$5 $45 $275	Cal Parker Box 3163 Pensacola, Fla. 32506
65 175 200+	2,000 20,000	300 900	29 500	$2 $150 NA	Thorp Engineering Box 516 Sun Valley, Calif. 91352
56 150 170	1,000 12,000	865 760	20 520	$3 $100 NA	Turner Aircraft & Engineering 12219 S. Menlo Hawthorne, Calif. 90250
47 171 195	1,900 23,000	250 300	24 600	$2 $75 partial	Van's Aircraft Rt. 2, Box 187 Forest Grove, Oreg. 97116
48 150 165	1,200 14,900	800 300	23 300	$9 $27 NA	Burt Rutan Box 656 Mojave, Calif. 93501

Wendt Traveler

Wittman Tailwind

Witt's Vee

Whing Ding II

Aircraft	Seat. & Type	Constr.	Power	Span Length W. Area	Wt. Gross Empty
Wendt Traveler	2-tandem low-wing	tube/ wood/ fabric	Continental 75 hp	30' 19' 7" 118	1,400 900
Wittman Tailwind	2 high-wing	tube/ wood/ fabric	85-140 hp	22' 6" 19' 3" 90	1,400 700
Witt's Vee	1 Formula Vee	tube/ wood/ fabric	VW 1,600 cc	17' 6" 18' 2" 77	700 430
Whing Ding II	1 ultralight	wood/ plastic/ fabric	McCullough 101A 12 hp	17' 13' 10" 98	310 122
Woody's Pusher	2 parasol	tube/ wood/ fabric	65-85 hp	29' 20' 5" 130	1,150 630
Zenith	2 low-wing	all metal	Continental 0-200 (100 hp)	23' 20' 6" 106	1,600 900
Anderson Kingfisher	2 amphibian	wood/ fabric/ fiberglass	Lycoming 115 hp	36' 1" 24' 183	1,500 1,032
Taylor Coot	2 amphibian	wood/ fiberglass	Lycoming 125 hp	36' 21' 80	1,950 1,250

Woody's Pusher

Zenith

Anderson Kingfisher

Taylor Coot

Spd. Stall Cruise Max.	Climb fpm Ceiling	Roll (ft.) T/O Land.	Fuel (gals.) Range (mi.)	Info. Plans Kit	Distributor
65 123 131	1,000 16,000	800 700	22 500	$3 $55 NA	Wendt Aircraft Engineering 9900 Alto Dr. La Mesa, Calif. 92041
55 150 165	900 17,000	800 600	25 600	$1 $125 NA	S. J. Wittman P.O. Box 276 Oshkosh, Wis. 54901
48 150 170+	1,000 15,000	800 600	10 400	$1 $100 NA	S. J. Wittman P.O. Box 276 Oshkosh, Wis. 54901
25 50 50	100 3,000	150 150	1/2 10	$1 $11 NA	R. W. Hovey Box 1074 Saugus, Calif. 91350
45 90 105	600 12,000	300 400	12 190	$2 $40 NA	Aerosport Inc. Holly Springs Airport Holly Springs, N.C. 27540
53 127 145	1,300 12,000	800 800	20 600	$2 $150 NA	Chris Heintz 236 Richmond St. Richmond Holl, Ont., Canada
42 85 90	550 13,000	NA NA	20 275	$3 $150 NA	Anderson Aircraft 40 Sunnywide Rd. Mahwah, N.J. 07430
50 125 135	1,000 16,000	8 sec. water takeoff NA	30 500	$3 $150 NA	Molt Taylor Box 1171 Longview, Wash. 98632

Tileston Drake

Larkin Skylark

Osprey I

Spencer Air Car

Aircraft	Seat. & Type	Constr.	Power	Span Length W. Area	Wt. Gross Empty
Tileston Drake	2 amphibian	wood/ fabric	Franklin Sport Four (130 hp)	31' 22' 5" NA	1,600 973
Larkin Skylark	2 amphibian	metal/ fiberglass	VW 1,700 cc	26' 5" 19' 5" 114	1,246 790
Osprey I	1 seaplane	wood/ fiberglass	Continental 90 hp	23' 17' 3" 97	900 600
Spencer Air Car	4 amphibian	wood/ fiberglass/ steel	Tiara 285 hp	37' 26' 85	3,100 2,050
Volmer Sportsman	2 amphibian	wood/ fiberglass/ metal	Continental C-85	36' 6" 24' 185	1,500 1,000
Volmer VJ-23 Swingwing	1 hang glider	wood/ tube/ fabric	NA	32' 7" 17' 5" 179	300 100
Briegleb BG-12-16	1 sailplane	wood	NA	50' 21' 11" 141	750 500
Cherokee II	1 sailplane	wood/ fabric	NA	40' 21' 6" 125	540 340

Volmer Sportsman

Volmer VJ-23 Swingwing

Briegleb BG-12-16

Cherokee II

Spd. Stall Cruise Max.	Climb fpm Ceiling	Roll (ft.) T/O Land.	Fuel (gals.) Range (mi.)	Info. Plans Kit	Distributor
49 120 129	1,100 4,500	NA NA	36 600	$3 $150 NA	Jet Plans 1800 Carmelo Dr. Carmichael, Calif. 95608
42 100 ,115	550 12,000	600 500	15 400	NA $90 $6,820	Larkin Aircraft Corp. 230 Airport Blvd. Freedom, Calif. 95019
54 118 120	2,000 NA	250 250	16 250	$3 $65 NA	George Periera 3741 El Rincon Way Sacramento, Calif. 95825
48 135 150	1,000 15,000	15 sec. (water) 750' (land)	94 700	$4 $185 partial	P. H. Spencer 8726 Oland Ave. Sun Valley, Calif. 91352
45 85 95	600 13,000	NA NA	20 300	$2 $125 partial	Volmer Aircraft 103 E. Providencia Burbank, Calif. 91502
15 20 NA	-- --	-- --	-- --	$2 $50 NA	Volmer Aircraft 103 E. Providencia Burbank, Calif. 91502
42 38 NA	-- --	-- --	-- --	yes $137.50 $3,400	Sailplane Corp. of America El Mirage Field Adelanto, Calif. 92301
39 46 110	-- --	-- --	-- --	no no no	Stanley A. Hall 1530 Belleville Way Sunnyvale, Calif. 94087

Explorer Aqua-Glider

Duster

Monarch

Schweizer 1-26C

Aircraft	Seat. & Type	Constr.	Power	Span Length W. Area	Wt. Gross Empty
Explorer Aqua-Glider	1 kite glider, water	wood/ fabric	--	16' 13' 6" 95	400 180
Duster	1 sailplane	wood/ fabric	--	42' 6" 19' 10" 104	620 390
Monarch	1 ultralight glider	plastic/ wood/ steel	--	36' 11' 4" 155	345 125
Schweizer 1-26C	1 sailplane	all metal	--	40' 21' 3" 160	600 370
Icarus V	1 hang glider, swept mono.	al.-pol. sheet foam	NA	32' Chord:5' 160	ar:6.4 emp.wt. 65
Bensen B-8MW Hydro-Copter	1 water-gyro	tube	McCullough 72-90 hp	21' 12' 4" NA	550 307
Scorpion	1-2 helicopter	tube/ fiberglass	Vulcan V-4 85-115 hp	19' 6" 17' 4" NA	750 450
Jukka JT-5	1 autogyro	tube/ fiberglass	VW 1,700 cc	7 m. 3.5 m. NA	290 kg 167 kg

Icarus V

Bensen B-8MW Hydro-Copter

Scorpion

Jukka JT-5

Spd. Stall Cruise Max.	Climb fpm Ceiling	Roll (ft.) T/O Land.	Fuel (gals.) Range (mi.)	Info. Plans Kit	Distributor
35 50 65	-- --	-- --	-- --	free $20 NA	Explorer Aircraft 5315 Palo Verde Edwards, Calif. 93523
42 54 135	-- --	-- --	-- --	$1 $75 $1,595	Duster Sailplane Kits 12676 Pierce St. Pacoima, Calif. 91331
24 70 75	-- --	-- --	-- --	$2.50 $45 $1,460	Marske Aircraft Corp. 30 Crestwood Dr. Michigan City, Ind. 46360
33 77 104	-- -- .	-- --	-- --	yes NA $4,235	Schweizer Aircraft Corp. P.O. Box 147 Elmira, N.Y. 14902
16 NA 60+	-- --	-- --	-- --	NA $5 $750	Taras Kiceniuk, Jr. Palomar Mt., Calif. 92060
NA 55 80	900 NA	NA NA	6 100	$5 $40 yes	Bensen Aircraft RDU Airport P.O. Box 2746 Raleigh, N.C. 27602
NA 65 75	NA NA	NA NA	10 140	$3 $75 yes	RotorWay, Inc. 14805 S. Interstate Tempe, Ariz. 85281
40 k/h 140 k/h 160 k/h	3 m./sec. 4,000 m.	80 meters 5 meters	40 liters 250 km	yes $60 NA	Jukka Tervamäki Aidasmaentie 16-20 E 00650 Helsinki 65, Finland

DIRECTORY OF LARGER EAA CHAPTERS

(CURRENT CHAPTER PRESIDENTS ARE LISTED BY NAME AND ADDRESS.)

RIVERSIDE, CALIFORNIA
Harold Nemer
5101 Victoria Hill Dr.
Riverside, Calif. 92505

FORT WAYNE, INDIANA
Steve Landis
2633 Lynn Ave.
Ft. Wayne, Ind. 46802

LONG ISLAND, NEW YORK
George W. Chiodini
103 Gail Ct.
Eastnorthport, N.Y. 11731

WASHINGTON, D.C.
Eugene H. Brown
9028 Hickory Hill Ave.
Lanham, Md. 20801
Hyattsville, Md.

ATLANTA, GEORGIA
John T. Griffin, Sr.
P.O. Box 184
Mableton, Ga. 30059

FULLERTON, CALIFORNIA
Ted Brownell
5557 N. Gondar
Lakewood, Calif. 90713

GREENSBORO, NORTH CAROLINA
Ronald Mangum
P.O. Box 8244
Greensboro, N.C. 27410

CENTRAL ORIO
Jim Layne
2216 Fenton Ave.
Columbus, Ohio 43224

TULSA, OKLAHOMA
William F. Welsh
3543 S. Urbana
Tulsa, Okla. 74135

LOS ANGELES, CALIFORNIA
Dave Hendrex
8855 S. Wilton Pl.
Los Angeles, Calif. 90047

HOUSTON, TEXAS
Ken Martin
13411 Kings Ridge
Houston, Tex. 77024

DETROIT, MICHIGAN
Stan Doyle
1136 Elliott
Madison Heights, Mich. 48071

SAN DIEGO, CALIFORNIA
Harold Wendt
9900 Alto Dr.
La Mesa, Calif. 92041

CHICAGO, ILLINOIS
Richard Fry
8610 W. 92nd St.
Hickory Hills, Ill. 60457

KNOXVILLE, TENNESSEE
Gene Easterday
803 Heins Ct.
Knoxville, Tenn. 37912

MILWAUKEE, WISCONSIN
Thomas Teschendorf
2575 S. Calhoun Rd.
New Berlin, Wis. 53151

SAN FRANCISCO, CALIFORNIA
Joseph Price
30845 Carroll Ave.
Hayward, Calif. 94544

EVANSVILLE, INDIANA
Steve Fowler
R. R. 2, Fugway Rd.
Newburgh, Ind. 47630

ROCKFORD, ILLINOIS
Rosemary Geddes
10618 Pearl St.
Roscoe, Ill. 61073

SALT LAKE CITY, UTAH
Keith Powell
307 W. 1450 N.
Layton, Utah 84041

OKLAHOMA CITY, OKLAHOMA
Robert McDonald
2812 N. Peniel
Oklahoma City, Okla. 73127

SEATTLE, WASHINGTON
Robert Hammer
4723 110th Ave., N.E.
Kirkland, Wash. 98033

NEW HAVEN, CONNECTICUT
Albert W. Kasfeldt
Fawn Ridge Ln.
Southport, Conn. 06490

PHOENIX, ARIZONA
Joel Mayhall
2174 E. Palmcroft Dr.
Temple, Ariz. 85282

CHAMPAIGN/URBANA, ILLINOIS
Terry Ladage
R. R. 1
Champaign, Ill. 61820

EDMONTON, ALBERTA, CANADA
Byrnes Fleuty
11122 - 54A Ave.
Edmonton, Alberta, Canada

WESTERN OREGON
Marion P. Hays
Rt. 3, Box 333-C
Veneta, Oreg. 97487

ST. LOUIS, MISSOURI
Marvin Anderson
10348 Old Olive Street Rd.
Creve Coeur, Mo. 63141

CEDAR RAPIDS, IOWA
James Backer
513 41st St., N.E.
Cedar Rapids, Iowa 52402

DAL-WORTH (ARLINGTON),
TEXAS
E. L. (Ernie) Duenzl
1920 N. Kimball Ave.
Grapevine, Tex. 76051

SAN ANTONIO, TEXAS
Daniel A. Cerna
123 Stardust
San Antonio, Tex. 78228

MIAMI, FLORIDA
Carl Schlick
16541 S. W. 102 Ave.
Perrine, Fla. 33157

MACON, GEORGIA
James Dent
889 Richmond St.
Macon, Ga. 31206

TORONTO DISTRICT, ONT., CANADA
George A. Jones
246 Renforth Dr.
Etobicoke, Ont., Canada

DENVER, COLORADO
James R. Ernst
5142 Eaton St.
Denver, Colo. 80212

ROCHESTER, NEW YORK
Alvin H. Garlick
277 Hayward Ave.
Rochester, N. Y. 14609

GREATER PITTSBURGH,
PENNSYLVANIA
Judy Frankiewicz
800 Overhill Dr.
North Versailles, Pa. 15137

BUFFALO, NEW YORK
Wolfgang Buergel
416 Campus Dr.
Buffalo, N. Y. 14226

TAMPA BAY, FLORIDA
Lou Johnson
7472 40th Terrace No.
St. Petersburg, Fla. 33709

DAYTON, OHIO
John Dyke
2840 Old Yellow Springs Rd.
Fairborn, Ohio 45324

SACRAMENTO, CALIFORNIA
William Rundall
5340 Sampson Blvd.
Sacramento, Calif. 95820

SOUTH CENTRAL NEW YORK
Norm Dibble
R. D. No. 2
Windsor, N. Y. 13865

ST. PAUL, MINNESOTA
Jack Hickey
596 Van Buren
St. Paul, Minn. 55103

LANSING, MICHIGAN
Ivan Rowell
3874 Sandhill Rd.
Lansing, Mich. 48910

SUDBURY, ONTARIO, CANADA
George McEwan
P.O. Box 1052
Sudbury, Ont., Canada

OGDEN, UTAH
Michael L. Baxter
4781 So. 2400 W.
Roy, Utah 84067

WACO, TEXAS
Bob Brashear
Rt. 5, Box 1118
Waco, Tex. 76705

HEART OF NEW ENGLAND
Normand Paulhus
R.F.D.
Charleston, N. H. 03603

SANTA CLARA VALLEY, CALIFORNIA
Duane Petitclerc
1030 El Monte No. 26
Mt. View, Calif. 94040

WINNIPEG, MANITOBA, CANADA
Vern Glass
521 Coventry Rd.
Winnipeg, Manitoba, Canada R3R1B5

HAMILTON, ONTARIO, CANADA
Frank Zaunscherb
95 Cameron Ave.
Dundas, Ont., Canada L9H 1R2

FORT MYERS, FLORIDA
Don Deets
1384 Evalena Ln.
N. Ft. Myers, 33906

ROCKLAND COUNTY (SPRING VALLEY), NEW YORK
Dave Davenport
34 Mearns Ave.
Highland Falls, N. Y. 10928

ALLENTOWN-BETHLEHEM, PENNSYLVANIA
Joe Christ
R. D. 1, Forest Dr., Box 25
Coopersburg, Pa. 18036

BAKERSFIELD, CALIFORNIA
William Richardson
301 Countryside
Bakersfield, Calif. 93308

COLORADO SPRINGS, COLORADO
P. D. Gonzalez
1318 Server Dr.
Colorado Springs, Colo. 80910

ORLANDO, FLORIDA
Ronald N. Dahly
1320 Powers Dr.
Orlando, Fla. 32808

DAVENPORT, IOWA
Les Koberg
606 W. 15th St.
Davenport, Iowa 52803

**DELAWARE COUNTY,
PENNSYLVANIA**
Earl Levers
1322 Elson Rd.
Toby Farms
Brookhaven, Pa. 19015

FLINT, MICHIGAN
Wayne Noall
2568 Tyrone St.
Flint, Mich. 48504

PHILADELPHIA, PENNSYLVANIA
Nicholas E. D'Apuzzo
1029 Blue Rock Ln.
Blue Bell, Pa. 19422

SPOKANE, WASHINGTON
Ed Carlson
Rt. 1, Box 168
Spokane, Wash. 99204

OMAHA, NEBRASKA
Philip Groelz
4925 William St.
Omaha, Nebr. 68106

TUCSON, ARIZONA
C. Louis Kelley
P. O. Box 195
Sahuarita, Ariz. 85629

TERRE HAUTE, INDIANA
William (Bill) Bensyl
2115 Plum St.
Terre Haute, Ind. 47808

EVERETT, WASHINGTON
John Wiles
18626 16th N. E.
Seattle, Wash, 98155

VANCOUVER, B. C., CANADA
C. R. (Gogi) Goguillot
953 Kirkmond Cr.
Richmond, B. C., Canada V7E 1M7

AUGUSTA, MAINE
Gary McCormick
P. O. Box 334
Brunswick, Maine 04011

WICHITA, KANSAS
Hugh Beckham
1920 High
Wichita, Kans. 67203

KANSAS CITY, MISSOURI
Larry Denning
3604 Appletree Ln.
Kansas City, Mo. 64119

ORANGE COUNTY, CALIFORNIA
Joel Confair
9661 Rocky Mountain Dr.
Huntington Beach, Calif. 92646

MADISON, WISCONSIN
James H. Otterback
3730 Dawes St.
Madison, Wis. 53714

MASON CITY, IOWA
Paul Metzger
R.R. No. 2
Osage, Iowa 50461

JOLIET, ILLINOIS
B. G. Simunich
P. O. Box 219
West Chicago, Ill. 60185

TORRANCE, CALIFORNIA
Jim Stothers
7035 Willowtree Dr.
Palos Verdes, Calif. 90274

GAINESVILLE, FLORIDA
Bob Sheffield
Rt. 1, Box 137T
Archer, Fla. 32618

VERO BEACH, FLORIDA
William L. Monroe
1165 28 St.
Vero Beach, Fla. 32960

ROCHESTER, MINNESOTA
Steve Schmitt
1925 18th St., N. W.
Rochester, Minn. 55901

BOISE, IDAHO
Eric L. Pankey
1212 N. 6th St.
Boise, Idaho 83702

GARY, INDIANA
Frank Zalouck
1641 W. 54th Ave.
Merrillville, Ind. 46410

PORTLAND, OREGON
Larry White
2305 N. W. 8th Ct.
Gresham, Oreg. 97030

GREATER BOSTON,
   MASSACHUSETTS
Richard E. King
149 Elm St.
Wakefield, Mass. 01880

SYRACUSE, NEW YORK
Bradley A. Meech
216 Everingham Rd.
Syracuse, N. Y. 13205

LOUISVILLE, KENTUCKY
Paul W. Cox
6720 Oak Valley Dr.
Louisville, Ky. 40214

ST. THOMAS/LONDON, ONTARIO,
   CANADA
Dick Eaves
1326 Langmuir
London, Ont., Canada

WEST DETROIT, MICHIGAN
Bruce Panzl
31011 Grandon
Livonia, Mich. 48150

BRANTFORD, ONTARIO, CANADA
Jack Dennis
P. O. Box 383
Port Dover, Ont., Canada

YOUNGSTOWN, OHIO
Charles R. Griffin
2997 Youngstown-Kingsville Rd.
Cortland, Ohio 44410

PAINESVILLE, OHIO
Richard Orris
2335 Townline Rd.
Madison, Ohio 44057

HARRISBURG, PENNSYLVANIA
John L. Storch
1922 Princeton Ave.
Camp Hill, Pa. 17011

MIDLAND/ODESSA, TEXAS
Donald Conley
Rt. 3, 51 Santa Fe Trail
Midland, Tex. 79701

EL PASO, TEXAS
Ralph Navar, Jr.
7301 North Loop
El Paso, Tex. 79915

WESTSIDE CLEVELAND, OHIO
George Larson
5532 W. 220 St.
Fairview Park, Ohio 44126

BLOOMINGTON, ILLINOIS
James Sturges
Rt. 2
Washington, Ill. 61571

NORWALK, CONNECTICUT
Russ Kinne
North Wilton Rd.
New Canaan, Conn. 06840

FORT LAUDERDALE, FLORIDA
Charles Boos
319 N. E. 19th Ave.
Pompano Beach, Fla. 33060

DES MOINES, IOWA
Dr. G. Robert Loerke
4001 S. W. 31st St.
Des Moines, Iowa 50321

LAWRENCE, MASSACHUSETTS
Richard Morton
32 Verndale St.
Haverhill, Mass. 01830

SPRINGFIELD/JACKSONVILLE,
   ILLINOIS
Harley Dahler
R. R. 2
Nokomis, Ill. 62075

CHARLESTON, WEST VIRGINIA
Raymond Shamblen
225 Viking Rd.
Charleston, W. Va. 25302

PLATTSBURGH, NEW YORK
Gerrit J. Vanderziel
896 B. Nevada Oval
Plattsburgh AFB, N. Y. 12903

PORTLAND, MAINE
William T. Barnett
9 Woodland Rd.
Cape Elizabeth, Maine 04107

VICTORIA, B. C., CANADA
T. J. Begin
7257 Veyaness
Saanichton, B. C., Canada

BALTIMORE, MARYLAND
William S. Ahalt
6003 Black Friars Circle
Baltimore, Md. 21228

GRAND RAPIDS, MICHIGAN
Ron Fritz
1989 Wilson N. W.
Grand Rapids, Mich. 49504

ALBANY, NEW YORK
Richard T. Thomas
9 Twilight Terr.
Albany, N. Y 12211

AKRON, OHIO
Larry Hawk
2471 Tyro Ave.
Akron, Ohio 44305

ASHLAND/MANSFIELD, OHIO
Dale E. Wolford
RD 2, Box 154A
Ashland, Ohio 44805

TOLEDO, OHIO
George R. Hart
1003 Mambrino
Oregon, Ohio 43616

CHATTANOOGA, TENNESSEE
Clarence K. Andrews
204 Grayson Rd.
Signal Mountain, Tenn. 37377

BIRMINGHAM, ALABAMA
W. M. Caudle, Jr.
420 4th Ave. West
Birmingham, Ala, 35204

REGINA, SASKATCHEWAN, CANADA
Bob Hamilton
3915 Montague St.
Regina, Sask., Canada

NEWPORT NEWS, VIRGINIA
Chet Piekielniak
822 Lipton Dr.
Newport News, Va. 23602

ERIE, PENNSYLVANIA
LeRoy Sweatman
7016 Belle Rd.
Harborcreek, Pa. 16421

NASHVILLE, TENNESSEE
N. Frank Arb
215 Town Park Dr.
Nashville, Tenn. 37217

LAS VEGAS, NEVADA
Charles Bartolo
1901 Collins Ave.
Las Vegas, Nev. 89106

WATERLOO/WELLINGTON, ONTARIO, CANADA
W. W. Spring
128 Highman Ave.
Cambridge (Galt), Ont., Canada

GREATER HARTFORD, CONNECTICUT
Joseph J. E. Gauthier
9 Kowal Dr.
Cromwell, Conn. 06416

NAPA/SOLANO COUNTY, CALIFORNIA
Bob MacDonald
40 Creek Ln.
Sonoma, Calif. 95476

DALLAS, TEXAS
Keith M. Cobb
P.O. Box 458
Addison, Tex. 75001

LEXINGTON, KENTUCKY
John Peck
131 Ravenwood, Rt. 4
Versailles, Ky. 40383

SAN LUIS OBISPO, CALIF.
John P. Dagle
225 Cabrillo Ln.
San Luis Obispo, Calif. 93401

DOVER, DELAWARE
Morris T. Turner
199 South St.
Camden, Del. 19934

AUGUSTA, GEORGIA
Gordon Lewis
2721 Vernon Dr., North
Augusta, Ga. 30906

CINCINNATI, OHIO
J. David Hiller
10354 Birkemeyer Dr.
Cincinnati, Ohio 45242

TAMPA, FLORIDA
Gene Roberts
120 Windy Circle
Brandon, Fl. 33511

TRENTON, NEW JERSEY
Keith Caulton
110 Summit Ave.
West Trenton, N. J. 08628

ALBUQUERQUE, NEW MEXICO
William G. Barber
1610 Monroe, N. E.
Albuquerque, N. M., 87101

MEMPHIS, TENNESSEE
Bob Norville
808 N. Graham
Memphis, Tenn. 38122

HAWAIIAN ISLANDS
Frank Gomes
1535 Pensacola St.
Honolulu, Hawaii 96822

WINDSOR, ONTARIO, CANADA
Bob Daudlin
11 Rickway Dr.
Leamington, Ont., Canada

AUSTIN, TEXAS
James E. Newman
3618 Quiette Dr.
Austin, Tex. 78754

FITCHBURG, MASSACHUSETTS
David Knight
3 Beacon St.
Maynard, Mass. 01754

SCARBOROUGH, ONTARIO, CANADA
Herb Cunningham
16 Acre Heights Crescent
Scarborough, Ont., Canada

HUNTSVILLE, ALABAMA
Joe H. Leibacher
6203 Menifee Dr., N. W.
Huntsville, Ala. 35810

CORPUS CHRISTI, TEXAS
Maj. D. M. Bassett
466 Coral Pl.
Corpus Christi, Tex. 78411

JACKSONVILLE, FLORDIA
Bill Priester
Rt. 3, Box 32F
St. Augustine, Fla. 32084

PONTIAC, MICHIGAN
Richard Pearsall
56 Clayburn St.
Pontiac, Mich. 48054

CENTRAL MASSACHUSETTS
Robert Burke
3 Cassidy Ln.
Medway, Mass. 02053

SARNIA, ONTARIO, CANADA
Roger Van De Weghe
R.R. No. 2
Wyoming, Ont., Canada

EASTERN KANSAS
Al D. Jonas
8915 Suitzer Ave.
Overland Park, Kans. 66214

WEST PALM BEACH, FLORIDA
Lou Green
2608 Park Rd.
Lake Park, Fla 33403

CARMEL VALLEY, CALIFORNIA
William G. Gee
432 Clay St.
Monterey, California 93940

GODERICH, ONTARIO, CANADA
Denver Dickie
R. R. No. 5
Lucknow, Ont., Canada

YAKIMA, WASHINGTON
Don Clark
Rt. 2, Box 2134
Wapato, Wash. 98951

HOBBS, NEW MEXICO
Ronnie Mecklenburg
2430 Brazos
Hobbs, N. M. 88240

SOUTH NEW JERSEY
William J. Hibbs
Hurff Lane, R. D. No. 2
Turnersville,
Blackwood, N. J. 08012

KENOSHA, WISCONSIN
Gordon La Combe
2405 Lincoln Rd.
Kenosha, Wis. 53140

SPRINGFIELD, MISSOURI
Robert D. Hancik
Rt. 4, Box 520
Springfield, Mo. 65802

KALAMAZOO, MICHIGAN
Cornelius Baden
3711 Wolf Dr.
Kalamazoo, Mich. 49001

BEAUMONT, TEXAS
Burt Thibodeaux
3632 W. Lark
Orange, Tex. 77630

ALHAMBRA, CALIFORNIA
Jack Halbert
1823 N. Sierra Bonita
Pasadena, Calif. 91104

ANDERSON, INDIANA
Paul Schermerhorn
R. R. 8, Box 147
Muncie, Ind. 47302

WATERLOO, IOWA
William W. Asher
4316 Veralta Dr.
Cedar Falls, Iowa 50613

MESA/TEMPE/SCOTTSDALE,
ARIZONA
Dick Farrington
1449 W. 7th Dr.
Mesa, Ariz. 85201

RICHMOND, VIRGINIA
Ronald D. Sutton
8504 Colebrook Rd.
Richmond, Va. 23227

WABASH, INDIANA
Ron Freiberger
204 So. McCann
Kokomo, Ind. 46901

MORRISTOWN, NEW JERSEY
Jack H. Tarner
4 Forest Trail
Basking Ridge, N. J. 07920

DE KALB, ILLINOIS
Joe Kukura
202 W. Hill
Genoa, Ill. 60135

BATON ROUGE, LOUISIANA
Larry Bourg
3146 Crestaire Dr.
Baton Rouge, La. 70814

OTTAWA, ONTARIO, CANADA
Major R. (Red) Morris
261 Cooper St., Apt. 1010
Ottawa, Ont., Canada K2P 0G3

GUELPH, ONTARIO, CANADA
William Brubaker
Haines Ave.
Greensville, Ont., Canada

GREENVILLE, SOUTH CAROLINA
Kirby McKinney
7 Windemere Dr.
Greenville, S. C. 29607

MENOMONEE FALLS, WISCONSIN
Roger F. Davenport
1210 St. Hubert's Dr.
Hubertus, Wis. 53033

OSHKOSH, WISCONSIN
Ray Ellingsen
4840 Fairview Beach Rd.
Oshkosh, Wis. 54901

LAFAYETTE, INDIANA
Charles H. Armstrong
2400 Maumee Pl.
Lafayette, Ind. 47905

NEW ORLEANS, LOUISIANA
Don Gillam
2711 Bristol Pl.
New Orleans, La. 70114

BREVARD COUNTY, FLORIDA
William Scarboro
234 Micanopy Ct.
Indian Harbor Beach, Fla.

MINOT, NORTH DAKOTA
Kenneth J. Curle
412 12th Ave., N. E.
Minot, N. Dak.

AMARILLO, TEXAS
Joe Jordan
4006 Tulane Dr.
Amarillo, Tex. 79110

DULUTH, MINNESOTA
Lawrence Besser
3535 Getchell Rd.
Duluth, Minn. 55811

DECATUR, ILLINOIS
Dick Burge
R. R. No. 6, Box 41
Decatur, Ill. 62521

LOMPOC, CALIFORNIA
Lee Miller
537 Venus
Lompoc, Calif. 93436

JACKSON, MISSISSIPPI
James L. Burris
360 Queen Alexandria Ln.
Jackson, Miss. 39206

SOUTHEASTERN MASSACHUSETTS
Frank Brown
80 Nash Memorial Dr.
Abington, Mass. 02351

FORT WORTH, TEXAS
C. E. Calvert
2917 San Marcos Dr.
Fort Worth, Tex. 76116

CLEARWATER, FLORIDA
Charles E. Stasek
1357 Irving
Clearwater, Fla. 33516

DAYTONA BEACH, FLORIDA
Odbert H. Cornwell
907 E. Rich Ave.
DeLand, Fla. 32720

SIOUX FALLS, SOUTH DAKOTA
Robin Hermanson
R. R. No. 2
Garretson, S. Dak. 57030

UTICA, NEW YORK
Richard M. Thompson
5781 Morris Rd.
Marcy, N. Y. 13403

WILMINGTON, NORTH CAROLINA
John F. Combs
16G Cypress Grove
Wilmington, N. C. 28401

SOUTH DENVER, COLORADO
Kent Paser
5672 W. Chestnut Ave.
Littleton, Colo. 80123

SANTA PAULA, CALIFORNIA
Frank Cavanagh
1131 Devonshire
Oxnard, Calif. 93030

JACKSON, MICHIGAN
A. D. Ashley
1579 Winnebago Ln.
Jackson, Mich. 49201

DARTMOUTH, NOVA SCOTIA, CANADA
Ronald E. Gourley
P. O. Box 179
Stewiacke, Nova Scotia, Canada

LACROSSE, WISCONSIN
James A. Barney
P. O. Box 36
Gays Mills, Wis. 54631

CHARLOTTE, NORTH CAROLINA
H. L. Puckett
Rt. 7, Box 668-J
Charlotte, N. C. 28213

TOPEKA, KANSAS
Richard Johnson
4204 W. 28th
Topeka, Kans. 66614

FARGO, NORTH DAKOTA
James Bortnem
Rural Rt.
Hawley, Minn. 56549

CALGARY, ALBERTA, CANADA
Clark G. Seaborn
R.R. No. 8
Calgary, Alberta, Canada T2J 2T9

MEDFORD, OREGON
Jerry Wruck
919 E. Pine St.
Central Point, Oreg. 97501

READING, PENNSYLVANIA
Bruno Gennerella, Jr.
304 Wilson Ave.
Port Carbon, Pa. 17965

SHERMAN, TEXAS
Wayne Kyle
P. O. Box 296
Collinsville, Tex. 76233

CLEVELAND, OHIO
John W. Grega
355 Grand Blvd.
Bedford, Ohio 44146

TACOMA/PUYALLUP,
WASHINGTON
Hubert R. LeRoy
1619 25th Ave., N. E.
Puyallup, Wash. 98371

DUBUQUE, IOWA
Wayne Reicher
65 S. Algona
Dubuque, Iowa 52001

SAVANNAH, GEORGIA
Merle Miller
P. O. Box 8
Claxton-Evans Co. Airport
Claxton, Ga. 30417

NASHUA, NEW HAMPSHIRE
Anthony Wojcicki
268 Main St.
Nashua, N. H. 03060

SAULT STE. MARIE,
MICHIGAN/CANADA
Larry L. Black
Rt. No. 1, Box 314
Sault Ste. Marie, Mich. 49783

SAN JOSE, CALIFORNIA
Leo Howard
1060 Danbury Dr.
San Jose, Calif. 95129

NORFOLK, VIRGINIA
Henry S. Proescher, Jr.
5308 Ashby St.
Norfolk, Va. 23502

VICTORIA COUNTY, TEXAS
Gorman W. Prince
3004 E. Red River
Victoria, Tex. 77901

BARNESVILLE, OHIO
Chester E. Hartley, Jr.
Rt. No. 3
Barnesville, Ohio 43713

CHEYENNE/LARAMIE, WYOMING
Budd Chapman
1783 Newton Dr.
Cheyenne, Wyo. 82001

SHREVEPORT, LOUISIANA
James Norman
3809 Eddy Pt.
Shreveport, La. 71107

NORTHWEST HOUSTON, TEXAS
Ken Dwight
12231 Perry Rd.
Houston, Tex. 77070

MONMOUTH, ILLINOIS
Ed Schultheiss
109 W. Jackson
Abingdon, Ill. 61410

SOUTHEASTERN ALABAMA
Billy D. Daughtry
107 Magnolia Circle
Enterprise, Ala. 36330

PRINCE EDWARD ISLAND, CANADA
Capt. J. C. Hansen
Box 151, Slemon Park
Summerside, PEI, Canada

GLENS FALLS, NEW YORK
George T. Thurston
11 Meadowview Rd.
Glens Falls, N. Y. 12801

ALBANY, GEORGIA
Thomas A. Cook
1500 Fifth Ave.
Albany, Ga. 31707

KAPUSKASING, ONTARIO, CANADA
Julien Proulx
Experimental Farm
Kapuskasing, Ont., Canada

OSHAWA, ONTARIO, CANADA
Arthur Stevens
R. R. No. 1
Brooklin, Ont., Canada LOB 1CO

NORTH BAY, ONTARIO, CANADA
W. W. Quirt
314 Foster Ave.
North Bay, Ont., Canada

ABERDEEN, WASHINGTON
Richard E. Logston
326 E. Marion St.
Aberdeen, Wash. 98520

NORTHEASTERN IOWA
Wayne L. DeSotel
P. O. Box 31
367 W. Stoneman
Postville, Iowa 52162

SHERBROOKE, P. Q., CANADA
Lucien Beaulieu
650 Galt Ovest
Sherbrooke, P. Q., Canada J1G 2C9

PORTAGE, WISCONSIN
Gordon York
112 Ontario St.
Portage, Wis. 53901

RICHMOND, INDIANA
Marvin Stohler
199 N. Elm
Hagerstown, Ind. 47346

KINGS RIVER AREA, CALIFORNIA
Robert Lock
19342 E. South Ave.
Reedley, Calif. 93654

GARDEN CITY, KANSAS
Jim Burling
202 W. Thompson
Garden City, Kans. 67846

PIEDMONT, NORTH CAROLINA
Donald W. Sink
210 Hillcrest Circle
Boone, N. C. 28607

GRAND FORKS, NORTH DAKOTA
J. G. (Bud) Roller
R. R. No. 1
Grand Forks, N. Dak. 58201

RHODE ISLAND AREA
Robert A. Johnson
S. Meadow Rd., RFD No. 3
Plymouth, Mass. 02360

SPRINGFIELD, OHIO
Orin Z. Brenning
1925 Harshman Blvd.
Springfield, Ohio 45504

MANITOWOC, WISCONSIN
Richard E. Randolph
1130 N. 6th St.
Manitowoc, Wis. 54220

OAK HARBOR, WASHINGTON
Hal Seligmiller
1247 E. Silverlake Rd.
Oak Harbor, Washington 98277

CAROLINAS-VIRGINIA EAA-ANTIQUE
Jim Clevenger
P.O. Box 1044
Black Mountain, N. C. 28711

JACKSON, TENNESSEE
William Stoner
78 Sweet Bay Dr.
Jackson, Tenn. 38301

ALTOONA, PENNSYLVANIA
Robert K. Sell
R.D. No. 1
Woodbury, Pa. 16695

CARSON CITY, NEVADA
Werner Hohn
605 Jeanell Dr.
Carson City, Nev. 89701

BELLINGHAM, WASHINGTON
Derek Looker
635 Malloy Dr.
Ferndale, Wash. 98248

BREMERTON, WASHINGTON
Vernon Kennedy
2317 Holman
Bremerton, Wash. 98310

IDAHO FALLS, IDAHO
Jon A. Braithwaite
P. O. Box 917
Moore, Idaho 83255

SQUAMISH, B. C., CANADA
Nick Candy
Box 48
Brackendale, B. C., Canada

OTTUMWA, IOWA
Don Williams
1018 Glenwood
Ottumwa, Iowa 52501

ROCK FALLS, ILLINOIS
Hal Christianson
R.R. 1, 513 Thome Rd.
Rock Falls, Ill. 61071

KLAMATH FALLS, OREGON
Joseph Q. Fisher
P. O. Box 965
Klamath Falls, Oreg. 97601

LOGANSPORT, INDIANA
Dale K. Packard
R. R. No. 3, Box 159 DD
Logansport, Ind. 46947

WAUKEGAN, ILLINOIS
Frank Gattolin
426 Hull Ct.
Waukegan, Ill. 60085

LONGUEUIL, QUEBEC, CANADA
Michel L'Esperance
8261 Cure Clermont
Ville d'Anjou, Que., Canada

MURFREESBORO, TENNESSEE
Gene Sloan, Jr.
412 Lillard Rd.
Murfreesboro, Tenn. 37130

CASPER, WYOMING
Jack Thomas
3044 E. 2nd
Casper, Wyo. 82601

BELLEFONTAINE, OHIO
James A. Craft, Sr.
Rt. 1
East Liberty, Ohio 43319

WICHITA FALLS, TEXAS
Delmar W. Ebert
305 W. Third
Burkburnett, Tex. 76354

MADISON, INDIANA
Jim Green
Box 126
Butlerville, Ind. 47223

ZANESVILLE, OHIO
Robert L. Reeves
3280 Buena Vista Circle
Zanesville, Ohio 43701

CUMBERLAND, MARYLAND
Fidelis V. Miltenberger
531 Cumberland St.
Cumberland, Md. 21502

NEW LISKEARD, ONTARIO,
CANADA
D. E. (Bud) Green
100 John St., Box 1256
New Liskeard, Ont., Canada POJ 1PO

JEFFERSON CITY, MISSOURI
W. E. (Tony) Munzell
2009 Birch Dr.
Jefferson City, Mo. 65101

PORT ANGELES, WASHINGTON
Gary Walters
1420 E. Second St.
Port Angeles, Wash. 98362

CANON CITY, COLORADO
Richard D. Baker
1626 Sherman Ave.
Canon City, Colo. 81212

PENTICTON, B. C., CANADA
Harold Brown
29 Lee
Penticton, B. C., Canada

PLAINVIEW, TEXAS
Melvin Bozeman
2100 W. 16th St.
Plainview, Tex. 79072

MARQUETTE, MICHIGAN
James E. Lyle
141 Albatross
Sawyer AFB, Mich. 49843

DALLAS, TEXAS (SKYLINE HIGH SCHOOL JUNIOR CHAPTER)
William Mathews
8822 Daytonia
Dallas, Tex. 75218

KENT, WASHINGTON
Bernard L. Claus
3630 So. 243 Rd.
Kent, Wash, 98031

JOHNSON CITY, TENNESSEE
Davis Garrison
1318 Lynnwood Dr.
Johnson City, Tenn. 37601

COLUMBUS, OHIO
Billie L. Lamb
2378 Norton Rd.
Galloway, Ohio 43119

APPLETON, WISCONSIN
Richard W. Schmidt
1530 E. Edgewood Dr.
Appleton, Wis. 54911

TALLAHASSEE, FLORIDA
Robert Hayden
1207 Clarke St.
Tallahassee, Fla. 32301

LOCKPORT, ILLINOIS (ROTARY WING)
Russ Jansen
Ridott, Ill. 61067

POMONA VALLEY, CALIFORNIA
Will Storland
357 N. Trayer
Glendora, Calif. 91740

ALBERT LEA, MINNESOTA
Larry Olson
2153 Bridge
Albert Lea, Minn. 56007

MILLVILLE, NEW JERSEY
Howard Wilson
71 Porreca Dr.
Millville, N. J. 08332

BURLINGTON, NORTH CAROLINA
Warren H. Hall
1711 Pinecrest St.
Burlington, N. C. 27215

RENO, NEVADA
Warren C. Estes
1025 Meadow St.
Reno, Nev. 89502

LAKELAND, FLORIDA
Jack Bowling
723 Saratoga Ave.
Lakeland, Fla. 33801

DETROIT, MICHIGAN (SO. METRO AREA)
Larry C. Jones
10857 Melbourne Ave.
Allen Park, Mich. 48101

TULLAHOMA, TENNESSEE
Allen D. Henninger
939 McKellar Dr.
Tullahoma, Tenn. 37388

COLLEGE STATION, TEXAS
Jon Fisher
Box 7116
College Station, Tex. 77840

PLAINFIELD, ILLINOIS
Arthur E. Froehlich
4619 Schwartz Ave.
Lisle, Ill. 60532

NORTH READING,
  MASSACHUSETTS
Warren Cochrane
26 County Rd.
Reading, Mass. 01867

ATLANTA, GEORGIA (SO. METRO
  AREA)
James A. Hoak
Rt. 2, Box 479W
Stockbridge, Ga. 30281

NORTH ADAMS, MASSACHUSETTS
Albert Barbuto
6 B St.
North Adams, Mass. 01247

ABILENE, TEXAS
Bobby E. Nichols
2233 Barrow
Abilene, Tex. 79605

BUCKSPORT, MAINE
Warren Nickse
31 Spring St.
Newport, Maine 04953

CHARLESTON, SOUTH CAROLINA
Ralph Blackstock
22 Murray Hill Dr.
Charleston, S. C. 29407

GULFPORT, MISSISSIPPI
W. Gibson Berry
Box 1238
Gulfport, Miss. 39501

TRAVERSE CITY, MICHIGAN
  (NORTHWESTERN MICHIGAN
  COLLEGE)
John Gamble
807 Wayne St.
Traverse City, Mich. 49684

PORT CHARLOTTE, FLORIDA
Otis Sawn, Jr.
795 Mirado Lane
Port Charlotte, Fla. 33952

SAN ANDREAS, CALIFORNIA
Weston H. Ament
P. O. Box 194
Mokelumne Hill, Calif. 95249

PENSACOLA, FLORIDA
LCDR James E. Fausz
1803 Broyhill Ln.
Pensacola, Fla. 32506

SCHOOLFLIGHT TECHNICAL REPRESENTATIVES
(Operating under EAA's *Project Schoolflight*)

John Archibald 8160 NW 183 St. Miami, Fla. 33015	At large	Herman Linder Western Michigan Univ. Kalamazoo, Mich.	EAA 221
Paul Bannister 1042 Lauwanda Pl. Placentia, Calif. 92670	EAA 92	Don Simmons Box 242 Reading, Mich. 49274	EAA 403
John Zimmerman, Pres. 8111 W. 91 St. Hickory Hills, Ill. 60457	EAA 15	A. C. Cross 6000 Jefferson Blvd. Groves, Tex. 77619	EAA 223
James M. Hamm, Pres. 1230 N. Highland Ave. Jackson, Tenn. 38301	EAA 396	James Snyder Box 696 Heston, Kans. 67062	EAA 88
Jim Cox 2113 Bingle Rd. Houston, Tex. 77055	EAA 345	Les Elliott Elliott Flying Service Valley City, N. Dak. 58072	EAA 317
Cecil J. Clark, Secy. RFD 1, Box 74 Warren, Maine 04864	EAA 87	Harry Harnden, Secy./Treas. 58 Hickory Rd. Leominister, Mass. 01453	EAA 188
Frank D. Nixson Wilson Jr. H.S. P. O. Box 1088 Nederland, Tex. 77627		Robert N. Luther, Pres. 2115 Buckingham Dr. Huntsville, Ala. 35803	EAA 190
Bruce E. Graham 819 Red Apple Rd. Wenatchee, Wash. 98801	At large	Joel Keith Caulton, Pres. 110 Summit Ave. West Trenton, N.J. 08628	EAA 176
Charles W. Billings 3743 Croton Ave. Whittier, Calif. 90601	At large	Lawrence L. Dreyer, Pres. 5800 Melville Rd. Ft. Pierce, Fla. 33450	EAA 99
LeRoy Sweatman, Pres. 7016 Belle Rd. Harborcreek, Pa. 16421	EAA 160	William S. Radune 77 Mildrum Rd. Berlin, Conn. 06037	EAA 166

Kenneth Heidger 703 Jo Anne Ln. Roseville, Calif. 95678	EAA 52	Neil Brundidge 831 Ann Arbor Ventura, Calif. 93003	At large
Frank Taillon 2311 Hutchinson Rd. Duluth, Minn. 55811	EAA 272	Roger Davenport, Pres. 1210 St. Hubert's Dr. Hubertus, Wis. 53033	EAA 250
Antonio M. De Angelo 1670 Providence Ave. Schenectady, N.Y. 12309	EAA 146	S. E. (Ben) Owen P. O. Box 229 Hales Corners, Wis. 53130	
W. A. (Bill) McKenzie 6 Wolcott Terr. Winchester, Mass. 01890	EAA 106	Dave Jameson 4322 Bellhaven La. Oshkosh, Wis. 54901	EAA 252
Evert H. Young 12075 Medford Dr. Los Altos, Calif, 94022	At large	Don Lockhart 5901 Greenwood Rd. Louisville, Ky. 40258	EAA 110
Ed Schultheiss, Pres. 109 W. Jackson St. Abingdon, Ill. 61410	EAA 350	J. W. Knapp Rt. 3, Box 121 Edinburg, Tex. 78539	
Peter Beck, Pres. 1454 Todds Ln. A33 Hampton, Va. 23366	EAA 156	Dick Maulsby 31 Prospect Ave. Darien, Conn. 06820	
C. F. O'Neil Kick-Shaw, Inc. 3511 Hixson Pike Chattanooga, Tenn. 37415	EAA 150	Gary Carlson 3324 Second Ave. Council Bluffs, Iowa 51501	
Gerard L. Blake R.D. #3 Newark, Del. 19711	EAA 240	John M. Lee 4974 Highland Beaumont, Tex. 77705	EAA 223
Harold H. Brown, Pres. 29 Lee Ave. Penticton, B. C., Canada	EAA 433	Don Lockhart c/o E. J. Schickli, Jr. 100 E. Liberty St. Louisville, Ky. 40202	
Leo Kitchen 17353 W. Poe Rd. Bowling Green, Ohio	At large	Ernest Craven Rt. 6, Box 165 Asheboro, N.C. 27203	EAA 378
Bob Mick 401 E. Roberta Waukesha High School Waukesha, Wis. 53186	EAA 18	Larry Black Rt. 1, Box 314 Sault St. Marie, Mich. 49783	
C. L. (Bud) McHolland 1432 Big Horn Ave. Sheridan, Wyo. 82801		Doug Griffin, Pres. 1200 N. Kirkwood Rd. St. Louis, Mo. 63122	EAA 331

Lindy Mueller, Pres.   EAA 32
980 Paddock Dr.
Florissant, Mo. 63033

Ivan McLay
c/o Jo Mackey Elementary School
2726 England
North Las Vegas, Nev. 89030

Albert Kimball
10623 Lebanon St.
Baton Rouge, La. 70816

Vernon Kennedy   EAA 406
2317 Holman Rd.
Bremerton, Wash. 98310

FEDERAL AVIATION ADMINISTRATION

GENERAL AVIATION DISTRICT OFFICES

Alabama
Municipal Airport
6500 43rd Ave., North
Birmingham, Ala. 35206

Alaska
13th and Orca Sts.
Anchorage, Alaska 99501

Arkansas
Terminal Annex Bldg.
Adams Field
Little Rock, Ark. 72202

California
FAA Bldg., Suite 1-B
Fresno Air Terminal
Fresno, Calif. 93727

Suite 3, Municipal Airport
3200 Airport Ave.
Santa Monica, Calif. 90405

Administration Bldg. Annex
International Airport
Ontario, Calif. 91761

Sacramento Municipal Airport
Sacramento, Calif. 95822
1387 Airport Blvd.
San Jose, Calif. 95110

Colorado
FAA Bldg.
Jefferson County Airport
Broomfield, Colo. 80020

Florida
P. O. Box 38665
Jacksonville, Fla. 32202

Bldg. 121, Opa Locka Airport
P. O. Box 365
Opa Locka, Fla. 33054

St. Petersburg-Clearwater Airport
St. Petersburg, Fla. 33732

Georgia
FAA Bldg., Rm. 200
Fulton County Airport
3999 Gordon Rd., S.W.
Atlanta, Ga. 30336

Idaho
3113 Airport Way
Boise, Idaho 83705

Illinois
DuPage County Airport
P. O. Box H
West Chicago, Ill. 60185

Rm. 201, Facilities Bldg.
Capital Airport
Springfield, Ill. 67205

Indiana
St. Joseph County Airport
South Bend, Ind. 46628

Iowa
Municipal Airport
204 Administration Bldg.
Des Moines, Iowa 50321

Kansas
2nd Floor, Administration Bldg.
Fairfax Airport
Kansas City, Kans. 66115

Flight Standards Bldg.
Municipal Airport
Wichita, Kans.

Kentucky
Administration Bldg.
Bowman Field
Louisville, Ky. 40205

Louisiana
Rm. 227, Admin. Bldg.
New Orleans Lakefront Airport
New Orleans, La. 70126

Satellite Office:
Lafayette Airport
Lafayette, La. 70501

Rm. 202, Terminal Bldg.
Downtown Airport
Shreveport, La. 71107

Maine
1001 Westbrook St.
Portland, Maine 14102

Maryland
Friendship International Airport
Baltimore, Md. 21240

Massachusetts
Municipal Airport
Norwood, Mass. 02062

1st Floor, Terminal Bldg.
Barnes-Westfield Municipal Airport
P. O. Box 544
Westfield, Mass. 01085

Michigan
Kent County Airport
5500 44th St., S. E.
Grand Rapids, Mich. 49508

Minnesota
Wold-Chamberlain Airport
6301 34th Ave., So.
Minneapolis, Minn. 55450

Mississippi
P. O. Box 5855, Pearl Station
Jackson, Miss. 39208

Montana
Rm. 216, Admin. Bldg.
Billings-Logan Field
Billings, Mont. 59101

Rm. 3, FAA Bldg.
Helena Airport
P. O. Box 1167
Helena, Mont. 59601

Nebraska
General Aviation Bldg.
Lincoln Municipal Airport
Lincoln, Nebr. 68524

Nevada
2601 East Plumb Ln.
Reno, Nev. 89502
5100-C South Haven
Las Vegas, Nev. 89119

New Jersey
Teterboro Air Terminal
510 Industrial Ave.
Teterboro, N. J. 07608

New Mexico
Albuquerque Museum Bldg.
P. O. Box 9045, Sunport Station
Albuquerque, N. M. 87119

New York
Albany County Airport
Albany, N. Y. 12211
Bldg. 53, Republic Airport
Farmingdale, N. Y. 11735

Hangar 3, Rochester-Monroe Co. Airport
Rochester, N. Y. 14624

North Carolina
FAA Bldg., Municipal Airport
Charlotte, N. C. 28208

Rm. 204, Admin. Bldg.
Raleigh-Durham Airport
P. O. Box 1858
Raleigh, N. C. 27602

North Dakota
Rm. 216, Admin. Bldg.
Hector Field, P. O. Box 2128
Fargo, N. D. 58102

Ohio
Hangar 5, Lunken Airport
Cincinnati, Ohio 45226

Rm. 215, New Terminal Bldg.
Port Columbus Airport
4393 E. 17th Ave.
Columbus, Ohio 43219

Oklahoma
FAA Bldg., Wiley Post Airport
Bethany, Okla. 73008

General Aviation Terminal
Rm. 110, Tulsa International Airport
Tulsa, Okla. 74115

Oregon
3410 NE Marine Dr.
Portland, Oreg. 97218

Route 1, Box 717
Eugene, Oreg. 97402

Pennsylvania
Allentown-Bethlehem-Easton Airport
Allentown, Pa. 18103

Rm. 201, Admin. Bldg.
Capital City Airport
New Cumberland, Pa. 17070

Allegheny County Airport
West Mifflin, Pa. 15122

Administration Bldg.
North Philadelphia Airport
Philadelphia, Pa. 19114

South Carolina
Metropolitan Airport, Box 200
West Columbia, S. C. 29169

South Dakota
Municipal Airport, RFD 2, Box 633B
Rapid City, S. D. 57701

Tennessee
2488 Winchester
P. O. Box 30050
Memphis, Tenn. 38130

303 Doyle Terminal
Metropolitan Airport
Nashville, Tenn. 37217

Texas
Redbird Airport
Dallas, Tex. 75332

Rm. 202, FAA Bldg.
6795 Convair Rd.
El Paso, Tex. 79925

Rm. 201, Admin. Bldg.
Meacham Field
Fort Worth, Tex. 76106

P. O. Box 194Z
Executive Air Terminal
Lubbock, Tex. 79417

Satellite Office:
Rm. 213, Terminal Bldg.
Midland-Odessa Reg. Air Terminal
Midland, Tex. 79701

8345 Telephone Rd.
Houston, Tex. 77017

1115 Paul Wilkins Rd., Rm. 201
San Antonio, Tex. 78216

Satellite Office:
Rt. 2, Box 903
Bledsoe Hangar 3
Corpus Christi, Tex. 78408

Utah
116 North 23rd West, Rm. 100
Salt Lake City, Utah 84116

Virginia
Byrd Field
Sandston, Va. 23150

Washington
Rm. 104, FAA Bldg.
Boeing Field
Seattle, Wash. 98108

5629 E. Rutter Ave.
Spokane, Wash. 99206

West Virginia
Kanawha County Airport
Charleston, W. Va. 25311

Wisconsin
General Mitchell Field
Milwaukee, Wis. 53207

Wyoming
1187 Fuller St.
Casper Air Terminal
Casper, Wyo. 82601

(Available for consultation by homebuilders for further FAA approval of their projects)

Alaska
5640 Airport Way
Fairbanks, Alaska 99701

R. R. 5, Box 5115
Juneau, Alaska 99801

Arizona
2800 Sky Harbor Blvd.
Sky Harbor Airport, Rm. 112
Phoenix, Ariz. 85034

California
Municipal Airport
2815 E. Spring St.
Long Beach, Calif. 90806

Box 2397
Oakland International Airport
Oakland, Calif. 94614

3750 John J. Montgomery Dr.
San Diego, Calif. 93123
7120 Havenhurst Ave.
Van Nuys, Calif. 91406

District of Columbia
West Bldg.
Washington National Airport
Washington, D. C. 20001

Hawaii
Air Service Corp. Bldg.
218 Lagoon Dr.
Honolulu International Airport
Honolulu, Hawaii 96820

Indiana
FAA Bldg. 1, Municipal Airport
P. O. Box 41525
Indianapolis, Ind. 46241

Michigan
Flight Standards Bldg.
Willow Run Airport
Ypsilanti, Mich. 48197

Missouri
North Terminal Bldg.
Municipal Airport
Kansas City, Mo. 64116

Ohio
Cleveland-Hopkins International Airport
Cleveland, Ohio 44135

Puerto Rico
RFD 1, Box 29A
Loiza Station
San Juan, P. R. 00914

ENGINEERING AND MANUFACTURING DISTRICT OFFICES

(Available for consultation by homebuilders for engineering advice and inspection)

Alabama
P. O. Box 5196
Fulton Road Station
Mobile, Ala. 36615

California
5885 West Imperial Hwy.
P. O. Box 45018
Los Angeles, Calif. 90045

2815 East Spring St.
Long Beach, Calif. 90806

7200 N. Vineland Ave.
Sun Valley, Calif. 91352

Colorado
Park Hill Station
P. O. Box 7213
Denver, Colo. 80207

Connecticut
1209 John Finch Blvd., Rt. 5
South Windsor, Conn. 06074

Florida
P. O. Box 2014
Miami, Fla. 33159
P. O. Box 578
Vero Beach, Fla. 32960

Georgia
1568 Willingham Dr.
Suite C, Rm. 207
College Park, Ga. 30337

Box 13457
Oglethorpe Branch
Savannah, Ga. 31406

Illinois
2300 E. Devon Ave.
Des Plaines, Ill. 60018

Indiana
FAA Bldg. #1
Municipal Airport
Indianapolis, Ind. 46241

Kansas
Flight Standards Bldg.
Municipal Airport
Wichita, Kans. 67209

Administration Bldg.
Fairfax Airport
Kansas City, Kans. 66115

Michigan
Westgate Medical Tower
750 W. Sherman Blvd.
Muskegon, Mich. 49441

New Jersey
510 Industrial Ave.
Teterboro, N. J. 07608

New York
Melville Park Bldg.
435 Broad Hollow Rd.
Melville, N. Y. 11746

Ohio
5241 Wilson Mills Rd.
Suite 27
Richmond Heights, Ohio 44143

Room 214, Terminal Bldg.
Dayton Municipal Airport
Valdalia, Ohio 45377

Oklahoma
Room 112, General Aviation Terminal
Tulsa International Airport
Tulsa, Okla. 74115

Pennsylvania
Federal Bldg., Box 640
228 Walnut St.
Harrisburg, Pa. 17108

Texas
Room 219, Terminal Bldg.
P. O. Box 2531
Greater Southwest Airport Station
Fort Worth, Tex. 76125

Room 203, Executive Aircraft Terminal
1115 Paul Wilkens Rd.
International Airport
San Antonio, Tex. 78216

Washington
Room 210 (2nd Floor)
Terminal Bldg.
Boeing Field International
Seattle, Wash. 98108

GLOSSARY

Aerobatic aircraft An aircraft built to withstand limit-load factors of +6.0 to –3.0 times its gross weight.

Aerobatic flight Defined by FAR 91.71 as "an intentional maneuver involving an abrupt change in an aircraft's attitude, an abnormal attitude, or abnormal acceleration not necessary for normal flight."

Aileron A movable control surface attached to the wing to impart a roll.

Airfoil A body such as a wing or propeller blade designed to produce a desired reaction force when in motion relative to surrounding air.

Airframe The fuselage, booms, nacelles, cowlings, fairings, airfoil surfaces, and landing gear of an aircraft, and their accessories and controls.

Airplane An engine-driven, fixed-wing aircraft heavier than air, supported in flight by dynamic action of air against its wings.

Airworthy The status of being in condition for safe flight.

Amphibian An aircraft capable of operating from land or water.

Angle of attack The acute angle between the chord of an airfoil and the relative wind.

Aspect ratio Wingspan squared divided by wing area.

Attitude The inclination of an airplane's axis in relation to the earth's horizon.

Axis A theoretical line extending through the center of gravity of an airplane in each major plane—longitudinal, vertical, and lateral.

Ceiling An airplane's maximum altitude under standard conditions, either absolute or service (the altitude at which an aircraft can still climb 100 feet per minute).

Center of gravity The point within an aircraft through which, for balance purposes, the total force of gravity is considered to act.

Chord The width of a wing from leading edge to trailing edge.

Conical cambered wingtips Special devices attached to wingtips to improve slow-flight controllability through their effect on tip vertexes.

Control surfaces Hinged airfoils, exposed to the airflow, that control an aircraft's rotation about its three axes—in pitch, roll, and yaw.

Cruising speed A speed lower than maximum speed, used for maximum efficiency on extended flights.

Cylindrical Rogallo wing A hang glider design with a helical leading edge that produces a cylindrical airfoil shape.

Delta wing A triangular-shaped wing with sharply swept leading edges.

Dihedral   Upward angling of wings designed to create a condition of static stability.

Downwash   The downward thrust imparted to relative airflow by the wing, to create lift.

Drag   The combination of induced and parasitic forces opposing forward motion of the aircraft.

Dual ignition   The use of redundant magnetos and spark plugs, as in some VW engine conversions.

Elevator   A hinged, horizontal control surface used to vary the aircraft's pitch attitude.

Elliptical wing   A wing planform whose leading and trailing edges roughly form an ellipse.

Empennage   A French term for an airplane's "tail feathers," or fixed and movable rudder and elevator surfaces (from Fr. *empennage,* to feather an arrow).

Empty weight   The weight of an aircraft including fixed ballast, unusable fuel, undrainable oil, engine coolant, and hydraulic fluid.

Engine cowling   A cowling around the engine to direct and control the flow of cooling air, for streamlining and protection.

Fixed-pitch propeller   A propeller whose blades cannot be adjusted in flight.

Flap   A hinged, pivoted, or sliding airfoil, normally at the rear of a wing, extended to increase camber for lowering stall speed, especially during takeoff and landing.

Flat spin   A spin in which pitch attitude is less than normal and centrifugal force holds the aircraft away from the spin axis.

Flutter   A vibration or oscillation of definite period set up in a wing, aileron, or other surface by aerodynamic forces.

Formula One   An air racing category, for midget planes of 100 horsepower and restricted size.

Formula Vee   An air racing category, for aircraft powered with converted Volkswagen automotive engines.

Fowler flap   A type of flap that increases both camber and wing area when extended.

Fuselage   The body of an aircraft, to which wings, landing gear, and empennage are attached.

G   A force equal to the acceleration of a falling body in the earth's gravitational field, 32 feet per second per second.

Geometric twist   The twist of an airfoil having different geometric angles of attack at different spanwise stations, as in a propeller blade.

Glider   A heavier-than-air craft supported in flight by dynamic reaction of the air against its lifting surfaces.

Glide ratio   The ratio of horizontal distance traveled to the vertical distance descended in a glide.

Gross weight   Empty weight plus crew, passengers, fuel, baggage, ballast, and cargo.

Ground effect   The effect of the ground in turning the downwash, or induced flow from the wings, thus reducing induced drag and increasing lift.

Ground skimmer   A type of hang glider designed to fly in ground effect.

Gyrodyne   A type of rotorcraft whose rotors are normally engine-driven for takeoff, hovering, and landing, and for forward flight through part of its speed range, and whose means of propulsion (usually conventional propellers) is independent of the rotor system.

242

Gyroplane A rotorcraft whose rotors are not engine-driven except for initial start-up, but are made to rotate by the action of relative air. Normal propellers operate independently of the rotor system.

Hang glider An aircraft of the glider type in which the operator is freely suspended below a wing sail, from a trapeze bar or other device.

Helicopter A rotorcraft that, for its horizontal motion, depends principally on engine-driven rotor blades.

Induced drag The part of drag caused by lift, i.e., induced by downwash.

Infinite span wing In theory, a wing of endless span having no tip vertexes and no induced drag.

Kite According to Federal Air Regulations, Part 1, a covered framework intended to be flown at the end of a rope or cable, supported only by the wind moving past its surfaces.

Laminar flow A smooth airflow in which no cross flow of fluid particles occurs, conceived as made up of layers.

Landing speed The speed at which an aircraft touches down on a runway, frequently the same as its stalling speed.

L/D The ratio of lift to drag, largely influenced by aspect ratio.

Lift The supporting force induced by dynamic action of relative airflow over a wing.

Lift coefficient A specific coefficient representing the lift of a given airfoil or other body.

Limit load The calculated maximum load that an aircraft member or part will experience in normal service.

Load factor The sum of the loads on a structure, including static and dynamic loads, expressed in units of G.

Longeron The principal longitudinal structural member of a fuselage.

Longitudinal stability The stability of an aircraft in respect to pitching moments.

MAC The mean aerodynamic chord of an imaginary rectangular airfoil that would have pitching moments throughout the flight range the same as those of an actual airfoil under consideration.

Maneuvering speed The maximum speed at which flight controls can be fully deflected without damage to aircraft structure.

Minimum flying speed The lowest steady speed at which an aircraft can maintain altitude out of ground effect.

Monocoque A type of fuselage construction in which stresses are carried by the skin.

Negative dihedral A downward inclination of a wing.

Negative G The opposite of positive G force, as experienced in an outside loop.

Oleo A shock-absorbing strut in which spring action is dampened by oil.

Parasitic drag The drag of all parts of an aircraft not contributing to lift.

Parasol wing A wing placed above the fuselage.

Pitching moment A change in attitude about the lateral axis.

Planform The profile of a wing as seen from above.

Power loading Gross weight divided by engine horsepower.

Propeller efficiency The ratio of power delivered to power supplied.

Propeller pitch The distance forward a propeller moves during one revolution.

Range The maximum distance an aircraft can travel with onboard fuel (usually given with 45-minute fuel reserve).

Rate of climb The rate at which an aircraft gains altitude, usually given in feet per minute.

Redline speed The certificated, calibrated airspeed (CAS) of an aircraft, marked on the airspeed indicator with a red line. Also called V_{ne} (never-exceed velocity).

Replica An exact copy of another aircraft, usually one no longer in existence.

Restoration An aircraft restored from damaged or aged condition to original airworthiness.

Roadable aircraft A craft that can be driven or towed along a road, as from airport to home, usually with folding wings.

Rogallo sail A type of hang glider of delta shape, invented by a NASA engineer, Francis Rogallo.

Roll The movement of an aircraft about its longitudinal axis.

Root stall A flight condition in which the stall begins initially at the wing root (near the fuselage) and progresses outward.

Rudder A vertical control surface, used primarily to produce a smooth turn entry by offsetting aileron drag.

Sailplane A high-performance glider whose sink rate is less than the ascending rate of a thermal bubble.

Seaplane An aircraft with flotation hull or pontoons, designed to operate from water.

Shrouded propeller A propeller surrounded by a circular airfoil to reduce tip loss; a ducted fan.

Sink rate The velocity in feet per minute at which an aircraft, such as a glider or sailplane, loses altitude in dead air.

Slope wind A movement of air deflected upward mechanically by a hill or mountain, usually smooth on the upwind side and turbulent on the lee side.

Span The dimension of an airfoil from wingtip to wingtip, or from root to wingtip.

Spar The principal longitudinal member in an airfoil structure.

Stagger The relative position of the upper and lower wings of a biplane, positive if upper wing is forward, negative if lower wing is forward.

Stall An abrupt loss of lift occuring when relative airflow velocity decreases to the minimum that will support an aircraft at its existing wing loading.

Sweepback Backward slant of a wing from root to tip.

Symmetrical airfoil An airfoil with common curvature top and bottom, suitable for inverted flight.

Taildragger Vernacular for a tail-wheel aircraft.

Thrust The forward force acting on an aircraft in flight from engine-propeller train or from a jet exhaust.

Thrust line The longitudinal axis along which thrust force acts.

Tip stall A stall that begins at the wingtip; the opposite of a root stall.

Tricycle gear An aircraft undercarriage with a nosewheel instead of a tail-wheel.

Vortex Roll-up of airflow behind the wingtips, generated by high pressure under the wing flowing toward low-pressure area on top, producing lift. The strength of the vortex is governed by the weight of the aircraft, speed, and wing shape.

Weight and balance Distribution of fuel, cargo, and personnel within an aircraft to keep its center of gravity within prescribed limits.

Wing loading An aircraft's gross weight divided by its wing area.

X planes   Experimental certificates are granted by the FAA to approved amateur-built aircraft, provided the major portion of the aircraft has been fabricated and assembled "by persons who undertook the construction project solely for their own education or recreation."

BIBLIOGRAPHY

Adleson, Joe and Bill Williams. *Hang Flight.* Eco-Nautics, P. O. Box 1154, Redlands, Calif. 92373.

Airtex Products. *Modern Aircraft Recovering.* Box 177, Morrisville, Pa. 19067.

Bowers, Peter M. *Guide to Homebuilts.* New York: Sports Car Press, 1962.

———. *Bowers Fly Baby Builders Manual.* 13826 Des Moines Way, Seattle, Wash. 98168.

Experimental Aircraft Association publications. Hales Corners, Wis.:

    File Number 1: *Wood.*

    File Number 2: *Welding.*

    File Number 3: *Design,* 2 vols.

    File Number 4: *Dope & Fabric.*

    File Number 5: *Engines,* 2 vols.

    File Number 6: *Aircraft Homebuilding Tips.*

    Data Book for the Aircraft Homebuilder.

    EAA Aircraft Builders Handbook.

    Engineering for the Amateur (by Raoul J. Hoffman).

    Aircraft Builder.

    Aircraft Powerplant Handbook, TM 107.

    Flying Manuals 1929–1933.

Federal Aviation Administration publications. Superintendent of Documents, Government Printing Office, Washington, D. C. 20402.

    Aircraft Inspection and Repair. AC 43.13-1 (1965).

    Aircraft Alterations. AC 43.13-2 (1965).

Huggins, R. G. *Volkswagen Experimental Aircraft Engine Overhaul Manual.* 4915 S. Detroit, Tulsa, Okla. 74105.

Pazmany, Ladislao. *Light Airplane Design.* Box 10051S, San Diego, Calif. 92110.

Poynter, Dan. *Hang Gliding.* 48 Walter, Suite 135, N. Quincy, Mass. 02171.

Sherwin, Keith. *Man Powered Flight.* London: Argus Press, 1971.

Teichmann, Frederick K. *Airplane Design Manual.* New York: Pitman Publishing Co., 1950.

Wood, K. D. *Aircraft Design.* Johnson Publishing Co., Department S.A., Box 990, Boulder, Colo. 80302.

INDEX

Ace, 13
Ace Aircraft Company, 17, 88
Ace Scooter, 88–89, 194–195
Acey Ducey, 88, 194–195
Ackerman, C. A., 64
Acro Sport, 122, 156–157, 165, 194–195
Acroduster One, 118, 120, 121–122, 123, 208–209
Acroduster Too, 118, 208–209
Acroduster Too SA750, 121
Adkisson, Earl, 172
Aerial Experiment Association (AEA), 40
Aerodrome Number 5, 10
Aeronca *C-2 Bathtub,* 82
Aeronca *Champ,* 137, 150
Aerosport *Quail,* 88, 194–195
Aerosport *Rail,* 88
Ailerons, 40–41; flight testing, 73
Air Campers, 17–20, 60
Air Car, 62, 74, 142–145, 214–215
Air Commerce Act of 1926, 15
Air-cooled radial engines, 59–60
Air Education Foundation, 157
Aircraft Engineering Corporation, 13
Airfoils, 37, 38–39
Airmotive Engineers, 93, 96
Allen, Arnold, 161
Allen, Bill, 186
Allenbaugh, Ed, 100
Altavista High School, 161
Aluminum structural surfaces, 48
American Eagle, 169
Ames Research Laboratory, 133
Amphibians and seaplanes, 142–150
Anderson, Dale, 74, 143
Anderson *Kingfisher,* 165, 212–213
Angle of incidence, 39–40

Antique Aircraft Association (AAA), 167–168, 173
Antoinette engine, 58
Anzani, Alessandro, 58
Anzani engine, 171
Aqua Gliders, 191–192, 216–217
Aristocraft II, 102–104, 194–195
Aspect ratio, 28
Automobile engines, converting to aircraft use, 60–66
Aviation, 15
Aviation AdVentures Unlimited, 174
Ayers, Jennifer L., 163

Baby Ace, 17, 18, 77, 88, 159, 163, 194–195
Baby Bullet, 16
Baby Great Lakes, 122–123, 124, 194–195
Baby Mustang, 6
Bailey, Dick, 125
Bantam W-3, 90, 196–197
Barker, Ted, 64, 65, 71, 84
Barndoor, 172
Barnstorm flyers of 1920s, 15
Barrows, Robert, 4, 5, 87–88
Becar, Noel, 38–39
Beck, Don, 131, 132
Bede, Jim, 49, 62, 91–93
Bede *BD-1,* 91
Bede, *BD-2,* 92, 93
Bede *BD-4,* 93, 196–197
Bede *BD-5,* 62, 96, 163
Bede *BD-5A,* 196–197
Bede BD-5J, 7, 62, 91, 93, 196–197
Bede *BD-5 Micro,* 49, 73
Bede *BD-6,* 92, 93, 196–197
Bede Aircraft, 111

Beech *Model 17 Staggerwing*, 44
Bell, Alexander Graham, 40
Bellanca, 171–172
Bennett, Bill, 181
Bensen, Dr. Igor, 191
Bensen Aircraft Corporation, 191
Bensen *B-8M*, 191
Bensen *B-8MW Hydro-Copter*, 216–217
Bensen *Scorpion*, 190–191, 216–217
Biddoulph, Harold G., 125, 127
Biddoulph *P.T.A.*, 125
Big Dipper, 97
Biplanes, 115–130, 139
Birkigt, Marc, 59
Bitty Bipe, 125–126
Blackstrom, A. A., 39
Bleriot, Louis, 6, 58, 76, 173
Bleriot *Model XI*, 6, 58, 76, 173
Bleriot *Model XI-2*, 172
Bonzo, 36, 97, 133
Bowers, Peter M., 55–56, 77, 142
Boy Scout Air Explorer Squadron, 191
Breezy RLU-1, 196–197
Briegleb, Gus, 189
Briegleb *BG-6*, 189
Briegleb *BG-7*, 189
Briegleb *BG-12*, 189
Briegleb *BG-12-16*, 214–215
Bris, Jean-Marie le, 10
Bristol Cherub engine, 16
Bristol Engine Division, 167
Brooks, Dwight, 71, 166–167
Brown, Larry, 166
Brown *B-2 Special*, 166
Bryan, Dewey, 6–7
Bryan Aircraft, 189
Bryan III Roadable Aircraft, 6–7
Bucker Jungmeisters, 44
Buhl *Bull Pup*, 169
Buhl *Model LA-1 Pup*, 169
Bureau of Air Commerce, 26
Bushby, Bob, 99

Cabool High School, 159
California State Polytechnic University, 163
Cantilever Aero Company, 13
Carlson, David, 165
Carter, Jim, 140
Cassutt, Tom, 137
Cassutt, 163

Catfish Special, 4, 5, 142, 143, 146
Cavalier SA-102, 196–197
Certification and Operation of Amateur-Built Aircraft (FAA Advisory Circular AC 20-27A), 22
Cessna Aircraft Company, 97
Cessna 140, 163
Cessna 170, 37
Cessna 337 Skymaster, 140
Cessna UC-78 "Bamboo Bomber," 54
Challenger, 104, 196–197
Champ, 137, 150
Chandelle, 186
Chanute, Octave, 10, 76, 179, 181
Chanute-type biplanes, 10–12
Charger, 123–124, 204–205
Cherokee II, 188, 214–215
Chester, Art, 133, 141
Chevrolet engine, 60
Chiang Kai-shek, 50
Chief, 150
Chinese Air Force, 50
Chinese Bandit, 163, 164
Christmas, William, 13
Christmas Bullet, 13
Chummy Flyabout, 13
Clark, Virginius E., 39
Clement–Bayard engine, 58
Cleveland High School, 163
Cleveland National Air Races, 133, 166
Coffin, Hank, 168
Collier Trophy, 58
Compher, Arthur M., 125, 126
Conger, Carl, 133
Construction tips, 42–56; basic considerations, 48; riveting, 52; use of metal, 48–52; use of wood, 52–56
Continental engine, 107, 147
Continental A40 engine, 62
Continental A-50 engine, 172
Continental A-65 engine, 18, 88, 90, 105, 107, 123
Continental A65-8 engine, 89
Continental C-85 engine, 150, 173
Continental C-90-12F engine, 153
Continental 0-200 engine, 133
Continental 0-200A engine, 107
Continental 0-200B engine, 96
Cook, Joe, 146
Cook Aircraft, 104
Cook *JC-1 Challenger*, 104, 196–197

Cook's *Coot*, 145–146
Corrosion, metal, 48
Cosmic Wind, 72, 133
Cote, Ray, 133
C.P. 60 Daimant, 114
C.P. 80 Cougar, 114
C.P. 328 Super-Emeraude, 114
C.P. 750 Beryl, 114
Culver, Frank, 186
Curtiss, Glenn, 58–59, 142
Curtiss Exhibition Company, 11
Curtiss OX-5 engine, 58, 59, 115, 169
Curtis Pitts *Specials*, 116–118, 121, 139
Curtiss *Pusher*, 4, 171
Cvjetkovic, Anton, 104–105
Cvjetkovic *CA-61*, 104
Cvjetkovic *CA-65*, 104
Czechoslovakian Zlin, 117

Da Vinci, Leonardo, 9, 178
Daphne SD-1A, 101–102, 103, 198–199
Davenport, Roger, 165
Davis, Leon D., 105–107
Davis *DA-2A*, 104, 105–107, 198–199
De Havilland Mosquito bomber, 53–54
De Havilland *Tiger Moth DH 82A*, 176
D-8 sailplane, 190
Delta, 111, 112, 198–199
Demoiselle, 12–13, 76, 172, 173
Depression of 1947–1948, 167
Der Jager D-IX, 173, 198–199
Derringer, 97
Dewey, Jim, 169
Dihedral, wing, 39
Distance-measuring equipment (DME), 4
Doolittle, James, 59, 91, 141
Dorgan, Patrick, 165
Dormoy, Etienne, 169
Doyle, Richard, 28–29
Drag, 38; varieties of, 34
Draggin' Fly, 5, 29, 30, 68, 79, 198–199
Drake, 148, 214–215
Druine, Roger, 113
Druine *Turbulent*, 63, 113–114, 198–199
D-12 racer, 36
D-2 twin-engined fighter, 54
Dual ignition, 65
Dunlop Tyre Company, 167
Duramold, 54
Durden, Lester, 4, 5, 142, 143, 146

Duster, 190, 216–217
Duthiel–Chalmers engine, 58
Dwiggins, Don, 68, 128, 129
Dyke, John, 111, 112
Dyke *Delta*, 111, 198–199
Dyke *JD-2 Delta*, 111, 112

Eaves, Leonard, 29
Edwards Air Force Base, 111, 191
Eiffel 36 aerofoil, 20
8th Air Force, 174
86-horsepower engine, 56
Emeraude, 155
EMG Engineering Company, 62
Encoding altimeters, 4
Engineering Standard Committee, 48
Engines: air-cooled radial, 59–60; controversy over, 60; conversions, 60–66; dual ignition, 65; rotary, 62–63; selecting right one, 57–66; water-cooled, 58–60
Englehardt, Dean, 100
E.N.V. engine, 58
EOS/001, 96, 198–199
Ercoupe, 89, 163
Estrellita, 133
Evans, Bud, 78
Evans *Volksplane I*, 78–79, 161
Evans *VP-2*, 78, 79, 198–199
Experimental Aircraft Association (EAA), ix–x, 8, 38, 41, 56, 122, 136, 154, 156, 171; categories for old planes, 167; directory of (larger) chapters, 219–232; members of, ix, 1
EAA *Acro Sport*, 122, 156–157, 165, 194–195
EAA Air Museum, 2–4, 15, 171, 192
EAA Fly-In (1973), ix, 1–2, 3, 6–7, 29, 46, 129, 130, 136
Explorer Aqua-Glider, 216–217

Fairchild PT-19, 54
Fang, 137, 139
Farrand, Lowell, 48
Fausz, James E., 82
FAA Advisory Circular AC 20-27A, 22–24
FAA Advisory Circular AC 20-86, 156
Federal Aviation Administration (FAA), 8, 67–68, 75, 104, 154, 157, 171,

186, 191, 192; engineering and manufacturing district offices, 239–240; flight standards district offices, 239; general district offices, 236–237

Ferdon, Fred, 163

5/8 Hawker Hurricane, 200–201

5/8 Mustang, 175

F-86 Sabrejet, 133

Flaglor, Ken, 88–89

Flightmatic, Inc., 159

Flutter: avoiding (in the ailerons), 41; flight testing, 72–74

Fly Babys, 55-56, 77–78, 142, 200–201; performance, 78; preliminary woodwork in, 53; unfinished fuselage and tail assembly, 54; wing hinge, 77

Flying Bathtub, 5, 20, 29, 79

Flying Eagle Squadron, 174

Flying Flea, 20

Flying Mercury, 20

Focke–Wulf *190,* 176, 177, 200–201

Fokker *DR-1,* 173, 200–201

Foo Fighter (or the *JD-1*), 6, 7, 128–129, 130, 171, 208–209

Ford Falcon engine, 129

Ford Model A engine, 18, 60

Ford Model B. engine, 60

Ford V-8 engine, 58, 60, 176

Formula Ones, 131, 133–135, 137–140; standardization of, 133

Formula Vees, 2, 131, 135–137, 161; *Renegade* racer, 25, 137, 138, 206–207

Franke, Lloyd, 154

Franklin engine, 18, 107, 111, 148

Free-Flight, 186

Gallatin, Harold, 62

Gallaudet Aircraft Corporation, 13

Garber, Dave, 140

Gee Bee, 59

Geschwender, Fred, 176

Ghan, William H., 159–161

Gilmore, Lyman, 10

Gipsy Moth, 170

Gliders, in the 1890s, 10

Goodyear Race (1947), 135

Goupil, Alexander, 40

Granatelli, Andy, 140

Grasshopper, 4, 5, 87–88, 200–201

Great Lakes 2T-1, 122

Green Bay Reformatory, 165

Gross weight, estimating, 27

Ground effect, 36–37

Ground Skimmer, 186

Ground-skimmers, 178–186

Grumman American Trainer, 91

Grumman F8F-2 Bearcat, 140

Gs (forces of gravity), 26

Gulhareff G8-2 jet engine, 62

Gunderson, Tom, 14–15

Gurney, Hilda and Bud, 170

Gypsy Hawk, 90, 200–201

Gyrodynamic Systems, 64

Hall, Jim, 44

Hall, Stan, 188

Hammarskjold High School, 165

Hang gliding, 5–6, 178–186; categories of, 178–181; dangerous kinds of, 192; first U.S. patent, 178; schools for, 192; for water-skiing, 181

Hang Loose, 180, 181

Harlequin Longster, 20

Hatfield, David, 171

Hawker *Hurricane,* 175, 176, 200–201

Headwind, 63, 79–82, 208–209

Headwind B, 82

Heath, Edward B., 16–17

Heath *Parasol Model V,* 16, 17, 200–201

Heintz, Christophe, 113

Heintz *Zenith,* 113, 212–213

Heit, Kenneth W., 176–177

Hellcats, 174

Henderson motorcycle engine, 16

Henson, William, 76

Hines, Bud, 117

HiperBipe, 46, 47, 200–201

Hirth engine, 62, 93

Hispano–Suiza engine, 58, 59, 173

HK-1 flying boat, 54

H-1 racer, 54

Hoerner, Sighard F., 34, 35–36

Hohman, Ted, 59, 169, 170

Holland, Donnita, 181

Homebuilt aircraft: advisory circular on, 22–24; amphibians and seaplanes, 142–150; aspect ratio, 28;

beginning of, 9–20; best building method, 31; biplanes, 115–130; choices to consider (for the novice), 21–31; engines, 57–66; "eyeball" designs, 28–31; first popularized set of plans, 12; improving performance, 91–114; landing gear, 25; monoplanes, 76–90; performance, 24–25; racers, 131–141; reason for, 1–8; restorations and replicas, 166–177; safety factor, 21, 31; sailplanes and ground-skimmers, 178–192; structure, 25; test flights, 67–75; "three-view" sketch, 27–28; tips on construction, 42–56; weight limit, 26–27; wing design, 32–41; wing loadings, 26; See also Project Schoolflight

Homebuilt Aircraft Directory, 21, 193–218; key to abbreviations, 193
Hovey, Bob, 62, 88, 127
Howard, Benny, 91, 141
HP-16 sailplane, 189
HP-17 sailplane, 189
HP-18 sailplane, 189
Huff, LeRoy, 29
Huggins, Robert G., 64–65, 136
Hughes, Howard, 54
Hurricane, 175, 176, 200–201

Icarus II, 181
Icarus V, 181, 182, 186, 216–217; three-view drawing of, 183
Irwin Meteorplane, 20
Ison, Wayne, 47–48

Jacobs radial engine, 102
Jameson, Richard, 90
Janson, Don, 125
JC-1 Challenger, 104, 106–197
Jeanie's Teenie, 82–84
Jensen, Volmer, 149, 155, 186
JF-1 Jaybird, 149
JLO German snowmobile engine, 47
JN4D, 13
JN4D Jenny, 115
Jodels, 63
Johnson, Bill, 89
Jonathan Livingston Seagull, 44

Jong, A. P. de, 168
JT-2, 84
Jukka JT-5, 191, 216–217
Jungster I, 43, 44, 45, 161, 202–203
Jungster II, 43, 44, 202–203
Jungster III, 44, 45
Jungster IV, 44, 46
Jungster V, 44
Jurca, Marcel, 176–177
Jurca MJ-2 Tempete, 177, 202–203
Jurca MJ-5 Sirocco, 177, 202–203
Jurca MJ-7 Gnatsum, 202–203
Jurca MJ-8 F/W 190, 202–203

K.G. Special, 159–161
K & S Aircraft Supply, 107
Kaminskas, Rimbydas, 42–44
Keeler, Bob, 185
Ken Rand KR-1, 66, 82, 83, 84–86, 161, 163, 202–203
Kiceniuk, Taras, Jr., 181, 182
Kilbourne, Dave, 181
Kilmer, Joyce, 52
Kingfisher, 165, 212–213
Kitty Hawk, 11, 13, 40, 76
Knight Twister, 139
Knode, Doug and Maryann, 18–20
Kyrk, Dennie, 29

Lafayette Escadrille, 15, 129
Laird, Matty, 91
Lambie, Jack, 180, 181
Landing gear, 25; location for, 28
Lane A. H., 172, 173
Lane, Dick, 123
Langley, Samuel P., 9–10
Largo Senior High School, 161
Larkin Aircraft Corporation, 148
Larkin Skylark, 148–149, 214–215
Lasher, Charlie, 137
Lawrance, Charles L., 57–58, 60
L/D (ratio of lift to drag), 35–36, 38
Le Santos No. 20, 12, 173
League of Nations, 186
LeRhone engine, 173
LeVier, Tony, 133
Liberty engines, 13, 58, 59
Licher, Lloyd, 186
Lift distribution, 36
Lift, wing, 34–35
Lilienthal, Otto, 10

Lincoln, Abraham, 143
Lindbergh, Charles A., 4, 15, 16, 57, 168, 170
Lindbergh High School, 151–155
Liposky, Bob, 87
Little Dipper, 97
Little Toot, 127, 204–205
Littner, E., 114
Load factors, 26–27
Lockheed *Big Dipper,* 97
Lockheed *Little Dipper,* 97
Loening, Grover, 142
Long, Dave, 99
L-2, 163
Luca, Vincent de, 139
Lycoming engine, 98, 100, 107, 111, 118, 125, 146, 163
Lycoming O-145 engine, 18
Lycoming O-235 engine, 44
Lycoming O-290-G engine, 29, 86–87
Lycoming O-320 engine, 99, 104
Lycoming O-360 engine, 44, 120, 121, 145
Lycoming IO-360 engine, 62
Lycoming TSIO 360-A1A engine, 141
Lysander, 71, 166–167

M (airfoil) series, 39
McCullough engine, 62, 88, 127
Mace, Harvey, 36
McKeen, Marion, 166
McLeod, Stan, 107
MA-5 Charger, 123–124, 204–205
Magnesium structural surfaces, 48
Mansfield R-4 High School, 159–161
Manual High School, 157, 158, 159
Marple, Walt, 168
Marquart, Ed, 123–124, 166, 171
Marquart *MA-5 Charger,* 123–124, 204–205
Marske, Jim, 189–190
Marske *Monarch,* 189–190, 216–217
Martin, W. H., 179
Martin glider, 179
Matthesius, Ann, 130
Maule M-5, 104
Maximizer engine, 63, 64
Mead primary glider, 163
Mean aerodynamic chord (MAC), 28
Menasco Buccaneer C-6-5 engine, 166
Menley, Charles, 10

Messerschmitt ME-109, 177
Metal construction, tips on, 48–52
Metal corrosion, treating, 48
Meyer *Little Toot,* 127, 204–205
M-5 Maule Rocket, 101
Microturbo TRS-18 engine, 93
Midget Mustang, 99, 161, 204–205
Miller, J. M., 96
Miller, *JM-2,* 93, 94–96, 202–203
Miller Aviation, Inc., 93
Mini-Ace CA-61, 104, 204–205
Mini-Ace CA-65, 204–205
Mini-Coupe, 89, 204–205
Mini-Mustang, 6
Miniplane, 124–125, 139, 206–207
Minnow, 72
Minor, Roy, 166
Miss Los Angeles, 166, 171
Miss San Bernardino, 100
Mississippi State College, 39
Mister Mulligan, 91
Mites, 89–90
MJ-2 Tempete, 177, 202–203
MJ-5 Sirocco, 177, 202–203
MJ-7 Gnatsum, 177, 202–203
MJ-8 (baby *Focke–Wulf 190*), 177
MJ-9 (¾-scale Messerschmitt 109), 177
MJ-10 (¾-scale spitfire), 177
MJ-12 (two-seater *P-40*), 177
Model G Dart, 168
Model J-5 Wright Whirlwind, 57–58
Model T Ford engine, 17
Model W Winner, 102
Modern Mechanix, 18
Moisant International Flyers, 11
Monarch, 189–190, 216–217
Monnett, John T., 2, 64, 136–137, 161
Monocoupe, 169
Monoplanes, 13, 76–90; steam-powered, 9–10
Montgomery, John J., 181
Moon Maid, 28–29, 204–205
Mooney Mite, 204–205
Mooney Mite Aircraft Company, 89
Moran, Joan, 130
Motorcycle engines, 14
Multaler, James, 165
Munk, Max M., 39
Murphy, Mike, 171–172
Murrell, Melville M., 10, 178

Mustang, 6, 174–176; scale, 6, 175, 206–207
Mustang II, 99, 100

N (airfoil) series, 39
National Advisory Committee for Aeronautics (NACA), 38, 39, 52, 141
NACA Technical Reports, 93, 124, 183, 244, 315
NACA 2301 airfoil, 100
NACA 64-412 airfoil, 29, 99
National Aeronautic Association, 58
National Aeronautics and Space Administration (NASA), 38, 98, 133
National Air Races (1927), 16
National Air Races (1928), 16
Nilson, Ed, 100
Nixson, Frank D., 167
Noblesville High School, 163, 164
Norby, Dick, 155
North American *P-51,* 6, 99, 174
Northrop Institute of Technology, 171

Obrecht, Dean, 173
Oldfield, Barney, 122
O'Neill, Terrence, 102–104
Ortman, Earl, 133
Oryx, 188
Osborne, Jim, 118, 120, 121, 123
Osprey I, 146–147, 148, 214–215
Owl, George, 137, 139
Owl Racer *OR-71,* 22, 137, 139, 206–207
Owl Racers (OR), 22, 137, 138, 139, 141, 206–207
OX-5 Curtiss *Robin,* 166
OX-5 engine, 58, 59, 115, 169
OXX-6 engine, 59, 171

PA-14, 36
Palen, Cole, 171
Parasol, 16, 17, 77, 200–201
Paris Air Show of 1909, 173
Parker, Cal, 69, 70–71, 82
Parkside High School, 157–159, 161
PA-22 Tri-Pacer, 104
Payne, Earl, 69
Paynter, A. Lloyd, 65
Pazmany, Ladislao, 50–52, 65, 86
Pazmany *PL-1,* 50–52
Pazmany *PL-1B,* 52
Pazmany *PL-2,* 52, 206–207

Pazmany *PL-4A,* 49, 50, 65, 206–207
PDQ-2, 47–48
Pearson, Lloyd, 29
Penguin, 14–15
Pepper Tree Airplane, 125
Performance, 24–25; improving, 91–114
Periera, George, 146, 147
Peterson, Allen V., 151–155
Petersen, Roger F., 46, 47
P-51 Mustang, 133
P-40, 177
Philip (prince), 167
Piel *Emeraude,* 155
Pietenpol, Ben M., 17
Pietenpol *Air Camper,* 17–20, 60
Pietenpol *B.4A Air Camper,* 17
Pietenpol *Parasol,* 16, 17, 77, 200–201
Pilot's career, 192
Piper Aircraft Company, 99
Piper Cherokee, 97, 98
Piper J-3 Cub, 169
Piper *PA-12 Super Cruiser,* 87
Piper *PA-14 Family Cruiser,* 32–34
Pitts, Curtis H., 116
Pitts *Special,* 116–118, 121, 139
Pitts *S-1 Special,* 116, 118
Pitts *S-1C,* 118
Pitts *S-1S,* 206–207
Pitts *S-2A,* 117
Plymouth engine, 60
Poberezny, Paul H., 2, 136, 156
Pogo, 137, 138
Polen, Dennis N., 140–141
Polen II Special, 140–141
Pop rivets, 52
Popular Mechanics, 12, 13, 14, 82, 172
Popular Science, 191
Powell, John C., 88
Professional Race Pilots Association (PRPA), 133, 139, 140
Project Schoolflight, 8, 151–165; FAA circular on, 156; financing, 155–156; Lindbergh High's homebuilt, 151–155; technical representatives, 233–235
Propwash, 35
P-38 Lightning, 54, 133, 174
P-2 Eagle, 157–159, 161
Pups, 169–170
Pusher, 4, 88, 127, 171, 212–213
Pylon (engine mount), 28

Quail, 88, 194–195
Quicksilver B, 186

Racers, 131–141; biplane, 139; classes of, 131; Formula One, 133–135, 137–140; Formula Vees, 135–137; unlimited homebuilts, 140–141
Radial engines, 59–60
RAF Museum, 167
Rail, 88
Ramsey *Flying Bathtub,* 5, 20, 29, 79
Rand, Ken, 66, 82, 84–86, 161
Rand *KR-1,* 66, 82, 83, 84–86, 161, 163, 202–203
Ranger 6-440C engine, 166
Raybourn, Tom, 6, 129
R.D. 012 Edelweiss, 114
R.D. 013 Edelweiss, 114
Red Baron (Manfred von Richtofen), 130
Red Barons, 174
Red Brick, 90
Redfern, Walter, 173
Renegade Formula Vee racer, 25, 137, 138, 206–207
Reno National Air Races, 131
R.E.P. engine, 58
Replica Fighters of America, 176
Republic SeaBee, 143
Restorations and replicas, 166–177; EAA categories and classifications, 167; oldest active craft, 173; World War I, 173–174; World War II, 174–176
Revmaster Company, 65
Rick Helicopters, 173
Rider, Keith 133
Rivets and riveting, 52
RLU-1 Breezy, 87
Roberts, Clete, 169
Roberts, Don E., 163, 164
Robertson, Cliff, 176
Rockne, Knute, 49
Rogallo, Francis M., 181
Rogallo *Eipper Bird,* 182
Rogallo hang glider, 181–184, 186
Rogers, David M., 111
Rollason Aircraft, 113
Rolls Royce, Ltd., 167
Roloff, Charley, 87

Root stall, effect of, 40
Rotary engines, 62–63, 140
RotorWay Aircraft, 191
Rourke, Roger, 119, 121
Royal Air Force, 167
Royal Canadian Air Cadets, 165
Royal Netherlands Air Force, 168
RS-15 sailplane, 189
Russian Yak, 117
Rutan, Bert, 111–113, 177
Rutan *Vari-Viggen,* 111–113, 177, 210–211
RV-3, 41, 84, 85, 86–87, 89, 210–211
Ryan M-1 long-range conversion, 57
Ryan monoplane, 15

Sailplanes, 186–192
Salmon, Herman, 71–72
Santos-Dumont, Alberto, 12–13, 76, 172
SBD-3 Dauntless dive bomber, 163–165
Scamp, 127
Schmidt, Howard R., 155
Scholl, Art, 100, 117–118
Schrack, Morgan, 121
Schweizer 1-26, 163, 188–189
Schweizer *1-26C,* 188, 216–217
Scooters, 88–89
Scorpion, 190–191, 216–217
Seagull III, 181, 184, 185
Seaplanes, *see* Amphibians and seaplanes
SG-1 sailplane, 190
Shark, 36, 134, 191
Shelton, Lyle, 139–140
Shoestring, 133
Short, Thayne, 174–176
Short, Thomas W., 174–176
Sindlinger, Fred G., 176
Sirocco, 177, 202–203
Skeeter, 29, 30
Skelton, Betty, 117
Skliar, Bill, 191, 192
Sky Skooter, 97–98, 99
Skybolt, 157, 158, 159, 161, 208–209
Skyhopper, 111
Skylark, 148–149, 214–215
Skysail, 186
Small Boy Here, 174
Smith *Miniplane,* 124–125, 139, 206–207

Soaring Society of America, 186
Sonerai I, 2, 3, 136–137, 161, 206–207
Sonerai II, 2, 3, 137, 208–209
Sorceress, 131, 139
Sorrell brothers, 44–46, 47
Spad VII, 173, 174
Spanish–American War, 10
Spartan Executive, 169
Spencer, Christopher, 143
Spencer, P. H. 74
Spencer *Air Car,* 62, 74, 142–145, 214–215
Spencer engine, 62
Spilker, Herb, 107
Spirit of St. Louis, 4, 15, 16, 57, 168
Spitfire, 177
Spokane *Super Parasol,* 16
Sportaire, 110–111, 208–209
Sportsman, 149, 150, 151, 214–215
Sportsman VJ-22, 149, 152
Standard VOR (Very High Frequency Omnidirectional Radio Range), 4
Stearman PT-17A, 115–116, 121
Steel structural surfaces, 48
Steen, La Mar, 157, 158, 159
Steen *Skybolt,* 157, 158, 159, 161, 208–209
Stephens Akro, 100, 101, 208–209
Stewart, Don, 6, 7, 63–64, 79–82, 129, 130, 171, 173
Stewart, Elizabeth, 79
Stewart *Foo Fighter,* 6, 7, 128–129, 130, 171, 208–209
Stewart *Headwind,* 63, 79–82, 208–209
Stiegelmeier, Owen E., 176
Stimson, Dick and Dona, 80–81
Stimson, Richard, Jr., 84
Stinger, 33, 36, 133
Stinson *Voyager,* 169
Stits *Playboy SA3B,* 161
STOL (short takeoff and landing), 34, 166–167
Stolp, Lou, 118
Stolp Starduster Corporation, 118
Stolp *Starduster SA-100,* 118–120, 210–211
Stolp *Starduster Too,* 33, 118–121, 139, 210–211
Stolp *Starduster Too N2MR,* 121
Stolp Starduster Too N2MW, 121
Stolp *Starduster Too SA-300,* 118–121

Stolp *Starlet,* 22, 120
Stolp *Starlet SA-500,* 210–211
Storms Flying Flivver, 20
Stout, Bob, 29
Stringfellow, John, 76
Structure, 25
Sturgeon Air Ltd., 114
Summers, Rod, 96
Sundancer, 131–133, 139
Super Chipmunk, 118
Super-Daimant, 114
Super Solution, 91
Swingwing, 186, 214–215
Szaraz, Art, 101
Szekeley engine, 169

Tailwind, 2, 66, 96, 97, 101, 212–213
Tallman, Frank, 171
Taylor, Frank, 140
Taylor, Molt, 145, 146
Taylor *Coot,* 212–213
Teenie Two, 69, 70–71, 80–81, 82–84, 210–211
Teledyne Continental engine, 62, 142
Tempete, 177, 202–203
Tern sailplane, 190
Test flights, 67–75; airspeed calibrations, 74; FAA approval, 67–68; on final approach, 75; flutter, 72–74; paper work for, 68–70; prior to landing, 74–75; prior to takeoff, 71–72
Thompson Trophy Race, 133
Thorp, John, 31, 32–34, 52, 72, 73, 97–99, 125
Thorp *T-18,* 31, 32, 49, 52, 97, 98–99, 100, 163, 210–211
Tiger Moth DH 82A, 176
Tileston *Drake,* 148, 214–215
Timm, Otto, 170
Traveler, 104, 106, 107–109, 212–213
Trefethen, Al, 110–111
Tri-Decker hang glider, 179
TRS Turbine, 62
True airspeed (TAS), 29
Turbulent, 63, 113–114, 198–199
Turner, Bill, 166, 171
Turner, Eugene, 107, 110
Turner, Frank, 63
Turner, Roscoe, 133
Turner engines, 140

Turner *T-40,* 110
Turner *T-40A,* 110
Turner *T-40B,* 107, 110, 210–211
12-horsepower engine, 9, 58
24 horsepower engine, 58
2-cylinder engines, 12–13
2/3-scale Mustang, 206–207

Unger, Carl, 87
U.S. Aerobatic Team, 117
U.S. Civil Aircraft Register, 168, 172
United States Hang Gliding Association (USHGA), 184–186

VanGrunsven, Richard, 41, 86
Vari-Viggen, 111–113, 177, 210–211
Vin-Del Aircraft, 139
Vista Flight Simulator, 159
Visual flight rules (VFR), 23
Volkswagen engine, 2, 4–5, 29, 71, 78, 79, 82, 84, 89, 123, 149, 161, 188; converting to aircraft use, 63–65; dual ignition, 65; of 1,600-cc displacement, 136; propeller characteristics, 63
Volmer *VJ-11,* 186, 187
Volmer *VJ-21,* 149
Volmer *VJ-22 Sportsman,* 149, 150, 151, 214–215
Volmer *VJ-23 Swingwing,* 186, 214–215
Volmer *VJ-24 Sunfun,* 186
Vortexes, 34–35
Voyager, 169
V-Star SA-900, 120
V-12 Ranger engine, 140
Vulcan V4 engines, 191
V_y (best rate of climb velocity), 34

Waco *Model W Aristocraft,* 102
Wankel, Felix, 62
Wankel engine, 62
Ward, Mahlon, 121
Warwick, Bill, 31, 90, 98
Water-cooled engines, 58–60
Waterman Biplane, 186

Wedell, Jimmy, 141
W-8, 97
Weight and load limit, 26–27
Weinrich, Gary, 163
Weishaar, Larry, 113–114
Wendt, Harold, 106, 107
Wendt *Traveler,* 104, 106, 107–109, 212–213
Westland *Lysander,* 71, 166–167
Whing-Ding, 61–62, 88, 127
Whing Ding II, 212–213
White, George D., 14
White, Marshall, 173
White, Sidney, 131, 132
White Monoplane, 14
White Wing, 40
Whitney Porta-Wing Rogallo, 186
Wier, Ron, 4–5, 29, 30, 79
Williams, Art, 36, 133
Williams, Lee, 166
Wills Wing, 186
Wilson, Jim, 140
"Wind is Right, The," 157
Wing loadings, 26
Wings, 32–41; airfoil and platform, 37, 38–39; angle of incidence, 39–40; design considerations, 32–41; dihedral, 39; drag, 34, 38; elliptical shapes, 33, 36, 38; 40 ratio, 35–36, 38; ground effect, 36–37; lift, 34–35; lift distribution, 36; roadability design, 41; "root stall" effect, 40; span, 36, 38; squared-off arrangement, 36; types of, 32; vortexes, 34–35
Wise, Ralph, 141
Wittman, Steve, 2, 36, 66, 96–97, 101, 133, 135
Wittman *Tailwind,* 2, 66, 96, 97, 101, 212–213
Witt's Vee, 2, 135, 212–213
Witt's View, 135, 136
Wood construction, tips on, 52–56
Woods, Harris L., 88, 127
Woody's Pusher, 4, 88, 127, 171, 212–213
World War I, 16, 26, 48, 129–130, 169, 171; number of U.S. pilots, 13;

restorations and replicas, 173–174; surplus aircraft, 14, 58

World War I Club, 173

World War II, 15, 32, 53, 99, 115, 116, 140; restorations and replicas, 174–176

Wright brothers, 9, 10–11, 13, 40, 58, 60, 63, 76, 181

Wright Exhibition Company, 11

Wright-Martin Company, 59

"X" license, 22–23

X-28A Air Skimmer, 147

Y.C. 12 Tourbillon, 114

Young, Sharon, 164

Zenith, 113, 212–213